COPING WITH SEPARATION AND LOSS
AS A YOUNG ADULT

COPING WITH SEPARATION AND LOSS
AS A YOUNG ADULT

THEORETICAL AND PRACTICAL REALITIES

By

LOUIS E. LAGRAND, Ph.D.

Potsdam College
of the
State University of New York

With a Foreword by
Dan Leviton, Ph.D.

CHARLES C THOMAS · PUBLISHER
Springfield • Illinois • U.S.A.

Published and Distributed Throughout the World by

CHARLES C THOMAS • PUBLISHER
2600 South First Street
Springfield, Illinois 62717

© *1986 by* CHARLES C THOMAS • PUBLISHER

ISBN 0-398-05214-X
Library of Congress Catalog Card Number: 85-30268

With THOMAS BOOKS *careful attention is given to all details of manufacturing and
design. It is the Publisher's desire to present books that are satisfactory as to their physical
qualities and artistic possibilities and appropriate for their particular use.* THOMAS
BOOKS *will be true to those laws of quality that assure a good name and good will.*

Printed in the United States of America
SC-R-3

Library of Congress Cataloging-in-Publication Data

LaGrand, Louis E.
    Coping with separation and loss as a young adult.

    Bibliography: p.
    Includes index.
        1. Youth and death.   2. Death—Psychological aspects.
    3. Loss (Psychology)   4. Bereavement—Psychological
    aspects.   I. Title.
    BF724.3.D43L34   1986   155.9'37   85-30268
    ISBN 0-398-05218-2

The deeper that sorrow carves into your being,
the more joy you can contain.

Is not the cup that holds your wine the very
cup that was burned over the potter's oven?

And is not the lute that soothes your spirit,
the very wood that was hollowed with knives?

When you are joyous, look deep into your heart
and you shall find it is only that which has given
you sorrow that is giving you joy.

When you are sorrowful, look again in your
heart, and you shall see that in truth you are
weeping for that which has been your delight.

Some of you say, "Joy is greater than sorrow,"
and others say, "Nay, sorrow is the greater."

But I say unto you, they are inseparable.
Together they come, and when one sits alone with
you at your board, remember that the other is
asleep upon your bed.

KAHLIL GIBRAN

(Reprinted from THE PROPHET, by Kahlil Gibran, by permission of Alfred A. Knopf, Inc. Copyright 1923 by Kahlil Gibran and renewed 1951 by Administrators C.T.A. of the Kahlil Gibran Estate, and Mary G. Gibran.)

FOREWORD

The contemporary study of death, dying, grief and bereavement, and other death-related phenomena is relatively recent. In my opinion it began in 1969 with the publication of Dr. Herman Feifel's edited work, *The Meaning of Death*. Dr. Feifel did for death what Freud did for sexuality. Feifel theorized that the meaning we give to death strongly affects our personality, functioning, and state of health and well-being. The fact of death and our limited mortality gives meaning to our sense of futurity. Think how your entire philosophy and world view might change if you were guaranteed eternal life on earth as you exist today. It is this fact of guaranteed death that evokes individual and social anxiety. Except for suicide we know not how and when we will die. Consequently all societies have had to provide an answer to death.

The meaning given to death, dying, and loss affects individual and social health and well-being. Therefore, anything which could add to our knowledge of how the young grieve and the effects of suffering the death or loss of beloved persons, pets, or objects would be of importance in improving health and well-being. Once knowledge is gained then appropriate preventive, interventive, and postventive strategies can be planned so that the outcome for individual and society is constructive and healthy rather than destructive and unhealthy. This volume is a step in that direction. In particular, Dr. LaGrand has provided insight into how a specific population, a large group of non-randomly selected young adults, cope with these losses.

Why is such knowledge helpful? For two reasons. First, research on the effects of grief and bereavement indicate that the vulnerability to premature death and morbidity are increased under certain conditions. We also know that the death of a beloved can have a long lasting effect on one's personality and view of the world. If college students provide a disproportionate share of national if not world leaders then it would be of value to predict and control the outcomes of grief so that one will become sensitive to and act to improve the human condition rather than suffer illness or premature death.

Suffering the death of a beloved is coming to be recognized as a health risk. Recently the Institute of Medicine appointed a prestigious committee to review the literature on grief. Its conclusions and recommendations were published under the title, *Bereavement: Reactions, Consequences, and Care* (Osterweis, Solomon, and Green, 1984). One recommendation concerned the need for research among all age groups. Let me add that little research exists on the bereavement patterns, process, and outcomes of young adults. Thus, Dr. LaGrand's research is pioneering in that it provides some insights into a very specific population's reactions to life's great stressors.

Eisenstadt (1978), Frankl (1963), and others have indicated that suffering the death of a beloved is related to psychological growth, learning, and sensitivity as well as despair, depression, suicide, cancer, and coronary heart disease. What factors determine whether one learns and gains wisdom as opposed to dying prematurely or becoming ill? Suffering death and other forms of loss may serve as a teacher or it may kill. In order to harness the after effects of death and loss events we must understand the complex and rich meanings given to them and their effect on behavior at every level of psychological functioning. Research is a prerequisite to this end.

This is a valuable volume. Dr. LaGrand has integrated his own research on young adults with an insight that comes from years of experience as a teacher of Death Education. Thus, his interest, like mine, is to seek from the study of death that knowledge which will improve the quality of individual and social health and well-being. His research has been most fruitful.

DAN LEVITON, PH.D.
Department of Health Education
University of Maryland

RECOLLECTIONS

In the Spring of 1980, a young man unexpectedly knocked on my office door and asked if he could speak to me. I invited him in and I realized that he was enrolled in two courses I was teaching: "Alcohol Studies" and "Dying and Death." Because he had missed numerous lectures, he proceeded to explain his absences: "I've been having trouble attending class," he said. "It's because of some of the content being discussed." He began to cry. And the story came tumbling out. His father had died of a heart attack; months later an uncle and a cousin were killed in an automobile accident caused by a drunken driver. His mother could not discuss the deaths with him, and so many of his questions had gone unanswered. He had carried his personal tragedy deep within himself— for seven long years. He needed to accept the consequences of these losses, but their resolution had been denied to him.

What 21-year-old Mark experienced is suggestive of the millions of "separations" experienced annually by young adults, separations which are accompanied by a grief response so overpowering that many of these young people suffer unnecessarily. There probably is not a therapist in the country who has not had a similar experience with a frightened and bewildered young person—a person who desperately cries for understanding and support. Young adults, very much like Mark, are always victims of a culture which refuses to recognize the magnitude of their losses, suffering, and the emotional pain which accompanies these tragic experiences. They are the hidden mourners of an affluent society. Grief, in all its fury, is inescapable in their lives.

Who will help these hidden mourners? This is a question without a simple answer because people within our culture have differing views of how young adults are supposed to deal with loss: pain is not supposed to be associated with youth; the role of young people, as perceived by society, is for them to be perpetually happy, to *live* life to its fullest. In reality, the young are frequently unhappy, searching for someone who will help them by sharing experiences and assisting their return to a more manageable life, free from domination or preoccupation with the past. In the search for people who may help, they turn to professionals, paraprofessionals—and most frequently—to their untrained peers.

Seven years ago I began a systematic study of loss in the lives of young adults; I was stunned at the pervasiveness of loss and the impact it had on the emotions and general health of this age group. And as a result, my perspective underwent an abrupt and radical change. I could no longer look upon loss experiences as just "growing pains"; rather, I began to see them as monumental traumas, confrontations with an unexpected and unknown adversary. And the plight of grieving young adults was often hidden from the public.

This private burden—harsh, often brutal—is associated with grief and loss in contemporary America; it is as much a part of the lifestyles of the young as is the stigma which still pervades the families of suicide victims. However, this blemish, this mark of Cain, need not continue to cause a retreat into seclusion. Any major loss tends to isolate an individual. And those not presently dealing with loss often unwittingly contribute to the griever's isolation by their own need to have uncomfortable feelings put out of mind when they are around those in mourning. The result of this felt uneasiness is a host of verbal and nonverbal signals which shape the grief experience into psychological suppression instead of intended expression. Therefore, the bereaved often graciously hide their suffering from others and simply endure it. In a culture uncomfortable with pain, grief and grievers have become invisible. They choose to remain invisible so as not to add to their burdens, but in doing so, actually increase the pain they experience.

My own interpretation of the grief response is in part the result of working with young adults who were willing to risk sharing a part of themselves in a counseling relationship, and of my work with terminally ill people who tell us so much about how to live and grieve. While I will protect their privacy, I will share the essential elements of their experiences. Also, my daughter Karen, whose death in her crib was such a devastating blow to my wife Barbara and me, has been my silent mentor through the years. I will never forget that day and those that followed: the desperate call of my wife who found her, my frantic efforts to give mouth to mouth resuscitation, and the ever-efficient firemen who rushed the three of us to the hospital. Afterwards, the oppressive heat of summer went unnoticed as we returned home without our daughter. It is often difficult, if not impossible, to find meaning in the death of a child.

But my daughter's death taught me more about differences in the way men and women grieve than any book, lecture, or person ever could. Through the years she is responsible for unlocking the hearts and minds of others suffering loss and allowing me to counsel with them in an empathetic way.

As college professor and bereavement counselor, having studied the issue of loss in the lives of youth, it is apparent to me that in our society there is a genuine negation of the reality of loss and its intensity. Not only is the campus community in general (with the exception of counseling personnel) shielded from the loss experiences of students, but typically students themselves are totally unaware of the real trauma of loss—until it strikes them in a very personal way. In support of this argument, one finds the literature on loss and bereavement to be replete with studies of widows and adults of various age groups, whereas the paucity of research on the grieving young adult is striking.

There is also a tendency for people within some families, as well as the general public, to lump all grievers into one undifferentiated mass, as though they feel all grievers share the same emotional attachments to the object of loss. Sweeping statements regarding how one should be expected to grieve, as well as how to facilitate the grief process, are all too familiar. Such blanket behavioral prescriptions for a very personal and individual event are unrealistic at best. Even though they can underscore the commonalities, it is equally important to emphasize that the needs, the emotions, and the perceptions of loss vary immensely, and that each person's pain and loss is uniquely his or her own. Thus, it becomes the task of friends, family, and counselors to understand the individual meaning of loss, and give careful support based on that meaning.

The same quality support and understanding are needed when one recognizes that some young people have recurring grief experiences based on unresolved grief from losses which occurred before their entrance into college or the work force. The breakup of love relationships, parental divorce, separations from loved ones, and the deaths of loved ones are examples of losses which weigh heavily on the minds of many young people and strongly influence behavior. Unresolved anger or guilt, common emotions resulting from such loss experiences, oftentimes affect young people for years when such experiences have not been adequately dealt with early in the grief process.

For these and many other reasons, this book attempts to give the young a recognition that seems to have been denied them in the rush of thanatological literature which has mushroomed during the last decade. *I have chosen to illustrate this book with examples of various loss experiences provided by young adults in order to emphasize the fact that youth can help themselves and help each other with dynamic change, including relationship loss, that will be a continuous part of life, until the final change—death.* Because young adults are the best authorities on how they feel and act in the face of their crises, I will let them speak for themselves on many occasions. In order to do this, I will draw on the information on loss experiences collected from more than 3,500 young adults in 16 colleges and universities. This work has resulted in over 50,000 observations on how young people have individually experienced loss and grief. In addition to my many personal interviews, I have obtained another 5,000 handwritten responses on how young grievers have coped with loss and whether they feel they could or could not have been better prepared for emotional upheaval. This task has been a long, often disquieting process, but it has been also an enlightening one.

WHO THIS BOOK IS FOR

This is a book about loss and grief as integral parts of life, not as experiences separate from it. It is designed for young adults to help them find meaning in loss, assist their grieving peers, and manage their own grief, for in the final analysis individuals must make their own decisions about how loss will be resolved. Along the path to the resolution of loss, much support from peers and family is frequently needed. You may know someone right now who is grieving from a major loss and has turned to you for understanding and counseling. It may be your roommate, a long-time childhood friend, or someone you know at work. You have drawn a blank about what to say or do. This volume presents a practical approach to assist the development of your caring relationship. We are all called upon throughout life to help heal the wounds brought on by radical change. You *can* be a caregiver, a healer, as difficult as that may seem.

Perhaps you are a young person entangled in the problems of your own personal loss: a recent death, the breakup of a love relationship, or the divorce of your parents. You may be grieving the loss of your home, a cherished possession, or a rejection from graduate school, and you feel the need for help in beginning the journey of readjustment. This book will not magically remove pain; nothing I know of can do that. But it *can* help you gain control of the process of recovery and prevent additional burdens from complicating your future.

Although this is a book for young adults, grievers, and support persons, it will be helpful to anyone who must give nurturance to young people struggling to establish an identity and rebuild their shattered worlds. Whether you are young or old, as a part of their support system, you will come face-to-face with what they say helps or hurts the progress of recovery. You will come to see that grief has a purpose, just as it is a force in each person's emotional growth.

Part I of this book emphasizes the need for us to understand that *loss is a condition of existence*, regardless of how difficult it is to confront. Progressively, differences are examined in reactions to loss among youth on three levels: the emotional, the physical, and the behavioral. Coping techniques are studied in order to provide both an awareness of the individuality of one's response and the understanding that there is no "best" way to grieve.

In Part II, I suggest that one must be able to help oneself first before assisting others. Effective therapeutic intervention is grounded in the truism that self-help is the basis for adaptation to any loss. Therefore, analyzing the grief process and determining how one can manage his or her own grief sets the stage for deciding how to assist others in need. This is the topic of Part III where I suggest the importance of confidentiality and that caregivers must recognize the many antagonists and impediments to support. Discussion of the seven intense adapting experiences for coping with massive life change is augmented by specific recommendations for helping others in Chapters 8 and 9.

In an effort to dissent from the customary use of the personal pronouns "he" and "his," most personal pronouns in *Coping With Separation And Loss As A Young Adult* will be "she" and "her" unless otherwise stated. I hope this change will be a pleasant one and in no way alter the intent or meaning of content for the reader.

ACKNOWLEDGMENTS

The task of writing is not a singular experience; one receives many assists in the preparation of a manuscript. Therefore, I am deeply indebted to many people. First and foremost, I wish to acknowledge the untiring efforts of Professor Lawrence Rust, Department of Psychology, Potsdam College, who spent endless hours in editing and making suggestions. His insight and commitment were inspiring and his invaluable service will be long remembered.

I am also indebted to Dr. Catherine Sanders, Clinical Psychologist, Charlotte, North Carolina and Professor Charles Corr, Department of Philosophical Studies, Southern Illinois University at Edwardsville, who willingly read and offered suggestions for the final draft of the book. Also, Professor Norm Licht's generosity of time and counsel will not be forgotten.

Most important, I wish to thank the many, many young adults whose openness and honesty have educated me about their crises and provided much insight and understanding about their world of loss.

Louis E. LaGrand

CONTENTS

COPING WITH SEPARATION AND LOSS
AS A YOUNG ADULT

Part I

THE IMPACT OF LOSS

The artful denial of a problem will not produce conviction; on the contrary, a wider and higher consciousness is required to give us the certainty and clarity we need.

C.G. JUNG

Throughout the whole of life one must continue to learn to live, and what will amaze you even more, throughout life one must learn to die.

SENECA

Chapter One

WHAT IS LOSS?

L oss and its resolution is a life-span developmental task. Havighurst (1952) defines a developmental task as a task which arises during a specific period of one's life, "successful completion of which leads to his happiness and to success with later tasks, while failure leads to unhappiness in the individual, disapproval by society, and difficulty with later tasks." Completion of the ongoing confrontations with loss will lead to "success" with the increasing number of major losses to which everyone is subjected, or unhappiness and difficulty with later tasks. As a young adult, the incorporation of the concept of *loss* into your belief system as a lifelong "developmental task" will influence the management of loss events in your life.

> On New Year's eve of that year, she told me that she wanted to break up. I couldn't believe my ears. She didn't and wouldn't give me a definite explanation of why. I was devastated. The tears just started flowing uncontrollably. I became really angry with her. I tried to deny it by telling her she was wrong, that things were okay, and I kept trying to get her to change her mind. It was all no use. I felt intense frustration and helplessness.
>
> I left the party we were at as I was too upset to stay there any longer. I hopped in my car and just started driving. But I was too upset and felt a total emptiness. I felt like I was the only one left in the world. I had to talk to someone. I stopped at a pay phone and called Bill since he was my best friend, and I felt he was the only one that I could talk to. I ended up blaming him for what had happened. I never thought that I could ever get so out of control emotionally.
>
> I didn't know what to do. I felt extremely alone and started to get depressed. I drove around for about another four hours and finally went home. The next day was just filled with an emptiness. I couldn't eat, but I was able to sleep even better than normal. I would spend all of my time sleeping when I wasn't at work. I wouldn't talk to anyone in my family. I wouldn't talk to anyone at work either. I seemed to be withdrawing from everything. I even withdrew from college.
>
> Mike, a college senior

Loss is a condition of existence. Once we begin to understand and accept this universal truth, we can confront our losses with intelligence and wisdom. Nobody escapes the ravages of loss; everybody tries. It is everyone's companion from birth to the final change—death. Loss sails under the flag of disguise and distortion to appear as bad luck, utter surprise, punishment, misfortune, or a how-could-this-happen-to-me event. "What did I do to deserve this?" is the classic statement which has but a single answer: nothing. Loss is inevitable in life; it exists universally.

When Mike's girlfriend ended their relationship, it became one of many painful separations that always seemed to occur at the wrong time, in the wrong place, and to the wrong person. This breakup was an example of a major life change that takes place with death-like implications ("Why me?," as the title of a popular song goes). This kind of loss leaves one temporarily helpless, in desperate need to find anyone to share the pain. This is a loss which is part of the montage of abrupt changes in direction which everyone experiences.

An outlook which views loss as inhuman and un-American is in dire need of revision if we are to avoid the self-delusion which engulfs those of us facing crises. As Swift said, "There is nothing in the world constant but inconstancy."

We do much to shield ourselves from realizing that the severing of deeply felt attachments is a normal part of life. In the process, more often than not, we only increase the emotional pain we are trying to avoid. Loss wears many masks. For most, it becomes a mighty weight, lowering self-esteem, demoralizing the strongest. For others, it initiates a learning process. Many young people say: "I have grown from this death or that breakup, having found out much about life and my relationships with others." We learn most about ourselves when our character is formed during the struggle of adaptation. This struggle of readjustment to the changed relationship with the deceased, to the new environment, and to relationships that must be formed is referred to as *grief work* (Lindemann, 1944).

Be assured that, despite the ravages of loss, it is entirely normal to feel uneasy and uncomfortable (as most of us do, even the so-called experts) when reading or talking about loss. It is all right at times to feel that strange sensation in the pit of your stomach, to want to get away from all reminders and escape. That feeling is a natural product of your present relationship to and beliefs about loss, especially death.

Where can one begin? Perhaps it is best if we begin by becoming aware of the fact that magical thinking (psychiatrists would call it irrational or fantasy thinking) runs rampant when major loss occurs, whether it is the death of a loved one, a divorce, or the breakup of a love relationship. There is nothing abnormal in this, given the layers of insulation that have been placed between loss events and ourselves, and the fear that grips all. The insulation is, in part, necessary, but as we have grown in our rugged individualism, we have been forced to distance ourselves more and more from any perceived threat to our sense of personal power and control. We have been as consistent in these attempts to bury fear induced by loss as the Victorians were in burying sex. But the results have not been commensurate with the efforts; we have only succeeded in magnifying the fear of loss through our own self-deception.

Although loss seems to make life a paradoxical venture, it also reflects *continuous change* and can engender acceptance or even relief. Some young adults experience a sigh of relief when they have finally decided to end a relationship from which they have grown away. Others find relief from the grief and emotional pain of the anticipated death of a loved one when the final moment occurs. There is nothing to feel guilty about in this, yet many do. Still others feel guilt when they are relieved of the burden of caring for the loved one. Loss, then, is much more than a social event. Because it occurs when anything valued is removed from our lives, when we are deprived of a prized object or person, it holds deep developmental and psychological implications, *laying the groundwork to influence future behavior.* Loss is an endless chain of big and small life-events, often giving meaning to existence, and testing inner resources while uncovering knowledge which helps us understand ourselves better. The big questions remain: "Can we benefit from this ages-old source of knowledge?" "Can we conceptualize loss differently?" "Can we live with loss?"

LIVING WITH LOSS

The two things that helped me the most were (1) the love and support of my mother and (2) the caring and kindness of a friend who went out of his way to cheer me up yet did not press me into talking when I didn't really want to.... If you realize that you are no less a person as a result of the loss, and accept that it is the nature of the world to have these losses, it might be easier to deal with the fact that you've lost something or someone.

Anne, a college freshman

Loss heavily influences future behavior. And like all human behavior, the care with which we manage loss is a critical factor in how we live through it. As Anne indicated, there is no substitute for loving, caring support which is both sensitive to and aware of specific individual needs of grievers. Those who provide such support contribute to the integration of loss into life. Anne's insight, "that it is the nature of the world to have these losses," speaks eloquently of the need for this integration. She also calls our attention to the significance of realizing that because we experience loss we are not suddenly less important. On the contrary, experiencing loss makes us part of the vast majority. Nevertheless, major loss challenges our integrity, our wholeness—and our self-esteem.

Difficulties following loss are only to be expected when education about loss is not a priority and society treats it as irrelevant or incomprehensible, at best. Moreover, contemporary attitudes about loss heavily influence individual responses. People act in stereotyped ways when their beliefs (fashioned by past experience) are translated into action. Thus, we observe individuals who react with much guilt and blame to certain losses because they *believe* what has happened is a result of their action or their inaction, when in fact responsibility lies in conditions beyond human control (Kushner, 1981). Others react by withdrawing from all relationships, as Mike did through sleep and refusing to talk. At that time they may conclude that no one can be trusted or that they are unable to live normally without the "significant other." This type of behavior, based on early childhood learning, often permeates the loss experience. Consequently, the grief response is muted in its expression by those who refuse to acknowledge it as a normal reaction to our resistance to change (Parkes, 1972).

A central theme absent in such thinking is the understanding that losses of various kinds cycle throughout a lifetime. Life has never been problem-free. There has always been, and there will continue to be, pain and joy. But sensationalized journalism, coupled with exposure to unrealistic grief models in the visual media (sometimes even within the family) contrasts sharply with the reality of loss. Profound loss is glibly glossed over; one is told to get on with living, leaving the impression that the loss is hardly significant or demanding. The expectations for loss are categorized as nonemotional and sterile experiences, sometimes forgotten, but usually denied, avoided, or attacked, if possible, and invariably always unreal. Consequently, the responses which surface are unexpected, and their attendant effects devastating.

Nobody escapes. Parents, brothers, sisters, aunts and uncles—all have experienced and will continue to experience minor and major losses throughout their lives. *Accepting the fact that losses are ongoing is the beginning of a sound basis for emotional growth.* Such acceptance is the foundation for a new view of reality and for meeting the demands of life. However, society is not structured to allow this to occur, as witnessed by the glut of advertisements and television coverage which focuses on the here-and-now-instant-success, all attained with little waiting or long-term hard work. These popular distortions are in sharp contrast to the very real pain and anxiety which is part of everyone's lot.

What limits the awareness of loss for society in general and for young adults in particular? There are many answers to this question: a refusal by young people to be skeptical about what they are taught, or to question role models; a lack of self-discipline; their fears; and the natural inclination to avoid painful experiences at all costs. Negative stereotyping also plays a part. For example, the words "cancer," "old," "death," and "dying" carry specific images which are frequently based on fiction and fantasy. Using labels to pigeonhole people and their responses adds to the limitation of awareness. By labeling people, one forms specific expectations of them based on the meaning attached to the label. By accepting such labels uncritically, one distorts one's own self-concept. Therefore, labeling limits and ultimately distorts communication.

The orientation of society towards youth, beauty, and immediate gratification imposes another limit upon our awareness (Kavanaugh, 1974). Later, we will explore this question more thoroughly in terms of awareness of personal death. But for now, it should be apparent that living in a society which treats loss as a cruel affliction causes added burdens when it occurs. For young persons, this orientation is a tragedy of major proportions because it places emphasis on avoidance instead of accommodation.

There is also an intellectual elitism that pervades the college campus, as well as many American communities. This elitism fosters the belief that to examine loss as part of human experience, particularly dying and death, is ephemeral, lacking in substance, an unnecessary academic frill. Responding to personal loss is gauche. This is contrary to the experience of thousands of young adults each semester whose inquiries into the social and psychological implications of loss bring new insight into the "hows" and "whys" of their own behavior. They question their values, feelings, and beliefs through the lens of their confrontational experiences.

"I have learned so much about myself" or "I've learned so much about people, their emotions, and expectations" are typical responses of those who have the courage to risk the scorn of the "elite." Aristotelian logic does apply.

Many young adults also find that loss never occurs just in one's psyche; it engulfs the entire physical person as well. Perhaps this is one of the positive results of loss experiences. One learns that it is the total organism, not just the emotional self, that responds to major crises. This fact has far-reaching implications for interpersonal relationships, lifework, and general health. The mind-body coalition suggests a total response to all of life's experience, and we can learn that the relationship is two-way: thoughts have a profound effect on the body, and the body, if allowed to do so, will greatly influence how one thinks. We must be careful about what controls what. Thoughts and beliefs can reign and channel energies into coping with life's low points as well as its highs; however, thoughts and beliefs can be turned inward to accentuate depression and hopelessness as they feed on self-pity.

Specifically, anger often occurs with loss. I am reminded of a student who spoke to me about ... "why I have so much anger about this." His loss of a body part years before still caused him great tension and anger which he did not comprehend. Since his loss, the freedom to speak about it with his parents through the years was limited only to visits with them when a check-up with a physician was scheduled. At other times, it was not spoken about. However, there was a need for him to discuss and share his feelings with his parents which was never encouraged due to their guilt. His anger was intimately related to the physical loss, its social impact on relationships with others, and his inability to find outlets through which to vent anger and hurt. *We can learn to live with loss if we can learn to find someone to share its impact.* That is an important tool in dealing with suffering. But the advent of a single loss experience is not the only cause of suffering. It may also be linked to that which follows: the unsteady support network; very little freedom to speak, to cry, to seek redress. When these factors converge to form a blockade to the search for meaning, pain and suffering are prolonged. Also, so-called "little losses" frequently combine to precipitate what appears to be a major grief experience. Each individual has limits, and a series of losses, large and small, can cause a response which seems all out of proportion to the last loss which was the trigger releasing the full-blown stress response. When this occurs, one is often thought to be overreacting. Such a line of interpretation fails to appreciate one's reaction as being the result of all that preceded the immediate cause.

Managing a loss experience is more than demanding; it is painful and confusing. For example, the parents of a young woman who came to see me had attempted to escape the pain of separation from their daughter, and in doing so, had unknowingly inflicted great pain on her. She had originally enrolled at an out-of-state college, and immensely enjoyed her new environment. She did not return home to visit as frequently as the parents thought she should, and they decided to transfer her to a school much closer to home. By not giving her desires priority over their pain of separation, they had created a major grief experience for their daughter, who was forced to sever relationships with many new friends and the college she had grown to love and cherish. She was not given time even to say her good-byes. Her parents had found it too difficult to let go, to cope with separation. The result of this forced transfer was a confused young woman, having to establish herself in a new environment while mourning the loss of her relationships to the old one.

The natural tendency for someone dealing with loss is to circumvent the anguish and malaise it creates. Most start in this direction because the pain accompanying change, an experience which shakes the foundations of our security, is a natural result of progression and growth. But the more one hides from loss, the worse it eventually becomes. Efforts toward avoiding the consequences of loss also remove opportunities for (1) emotional growth, (2) self-understanding, and (3) developing skills needed to cope with future losses. Changes brought on by loss can be spiritual, emotional, social, occupational, and physical, affecting lives in ways most people refuse to recognize or are willing to admit. Because there is great demand for continuity, for maintaining the status quo, there is naturally much resistance to change. Resistance to change is why loss and grief are so painful (Parkes, 1972). We experience so much hurt because: there is a sense of loss of control over life; the event itself seems grossly unfair; one cannot bear giving up the past; it is difficult to find one who understands the depth of hurt; and there is a loss of part of the self. Indeed, the fundamental crisis of bereavement is this loss of part of the self (Marris, 1975). And most of all, loss hurts because the fantasy of unending continuity crumbles.

The biggest impediment to the successful resolution of loss is our shortsightedness in recognizing and accepting the painful confrontation for what it is—an *integral* part of living. And this is followed directly by our inability to open up and find someone who is willing to listen and talk about loss on our terms, who will see it through *our* eyes. These two factors are crucial for living with loss, given the fact that beginnings and endings, death and rebirth, the new and the old, loss and gain are part of the cyclic action of life. The pattern is circular as the new and the old, some dying and others being born, come into and go out of our lives *continuously.* Therefore, we need to view this pattern not simply as one which takes from us, but also as one which gives.

GROWTH THROUGH LOSS

How this death has changed me. I feel I have grown from the experience of having a friend die. I know what it is like to deal with many strange feelings and emotions. I have become a stronger person because I know what pain feels like. I had never had to handle this type of pain, then I realized I could handle this terrible feeling. I feel I have been able to express myself better or communicate how I feel to other people. I understand now that it is not bad to cry or discuss how I feel to another person. It is good to express yourself openly and honestly, because now I know it is better to let your emotions out instead of keeping them locked inside to cause you more pain. I have also changed in the sense that I now know that people in any age category can die—that it is not only the old that must die, but a person of any age.

Rita Spaulding, a college senior

Rita's experience with the death of her friend can be treated as a learning experience which developed from the disquieting tragedy of unavoidable loss. As she insisted, her ordeal was a growth experience. Not only did she confront new feelings and emotions, but she learned that she could endure, that she could outlast the pain of loss. In that awareness she realized that grief itself is a process which also cannot be evaded. Grief, too, is inevitable. One only needs to talk with older friends and family members to bear this out. Grief will come as sure as there is life, and pain will change the character and quality of our pain-free moments.

What can we do with this knowledge, this inescapable fact of existence? First of all, each person must acknowledge that, by working hard to remove the painful facts of loss from conscious awareness, one ultimately removes a source of potential assistance in overcoming future unpleasant experiences. If something real is completely suppressed, one has concealed a part of life, a part of reality. Such a person is living in a way which is self-defeating and is ill-prepared to live in the real world.

Most of us are grief-illiterate, knowing little of how grief work fits into life. *We cannot evade change and evolution, we can only attempt to evade the adjustment to them.*

How can anyone ever grow in knowledge, skill, or personal awareness from an experience with loss or the death of a loved one? "Just as broken bones may end up stronger than unbroken ones, so the experience of grieving can strengthen and bring maturity to those who have previously been protected from misfortune" (Parkes, 1972, p. 5). Repeated encounters with loss provide scenarios in which one's self-image and self-confidence are stretched beyond limits as one comes to grips with what seem to be insurmountable odds. Nevertheless, the history of loss always shows that somehow the bereaved make it through the bleakest and most hopeless days imaginable. Looking back, they often wonder how they did it. The capacity of each individual to sustain adversity is immense, and the experience of loss provides them with a sense of strength. It is entirely possible to view the crisis of loss as an opportunity to learn, act, and be tested. We typically fail to take advantage of such opportunities. But such a learning experience is an option. One can choose to continue on despite any burden as Friedrich Nietzsche reminds us: "That which does not kill me makes me stronger."

Therefore, the point of examining the meaning of loss in life is not to encourage embracing loss in some morbid fashion, but to allow the individual potential of each person to unfold, reaching a fuller existence. A major source of growth through loss is the *sensitivity* one develops to the needs of others who are experiencing similar adversity. For example, parents who lose a child are so much more aware of the plight of others when one of their children dies. They provide immeasurable support. The Compassionate Friends, a self-help group for bereaved parents, performs just such a service. It is made up of parents throughout the country who are willing to help others through their trials and grief work. The Widowed Persons Program provides a similar service for surviving spouses (Silverman, 1974). Those who console recognize the needs of others in pain from what they remember of their own experiences. Numerous self-help groups provide this valuable service to others. The same sensitivity and understanding surfaces when the breakup of a love relationship occurs or one's parent dies. Having experienced the severing of bonds in such intimate relationships allows one to empathize better with those struggling with a similar life change.

One of the most frequent life-enhancing results of major loss experiences is the development of new perceptions about the meaning of interpersonal relationships. In particular, the emotional transactions which take place between the bereaved and support persons bring a new awareness of the need for interdependence. In a more critical vein, bereavement frequently makes a survivor evaluate the failures as well as the successes in the relationship with the deceased. We realize just how much we profited from knowing the deceased while at the same time becoming aware of how much more we could have given to the relationship. The result of this inner dialogue is commonly an increased commitment to other loved ones. The analysis of what is valuable in relationships with others takes on new meaning in the context of the reality of death and the frailty of human existence. Most regrettable is the feeling that a loved one has to die before one truly comes to grips with the impact that quality relationships have on life. For others adjusting to loss new relationships are born, new fulfillments are gained in having to develop parts of the self previously neglected. Creativity is sometimes augmented as one finds new meaning in major life changes (Pollock, 1978).

Finally, loss experiences cause one to rethink the deep philosophical questions about the meaning of life and the justice or injustice of it all. Survivors grapple with what loss means and how it fits into their perception of existence. They wonder if their loss is a warning, a part of an ongoing series of losses which are uncontrollable, or part of a universal plan that cannot be fathomed. Nonetheless, having experienced major loss, one emerges with new trials to endure, an awareness of hidden resources that can be tapped, and decisions to be made about a world which has taken on a new look.

Why study, why consider, why dwell on the apparently morbid subject of loss? This is an expected question, given the ethic that pervades society concerning the subject. And it is an important one to understand fully if we are to benefit from an experience which carries with it the perpetual aspect of horror and uncontrolled terror. The essential answer is: because when we peel away the camouflage surrounding the loss taboo, we confront ourselves with the inescapable fact that our study is one of life and living with the knowledge that death is inevitable. It is the study of life as it must go on when loved ones die, when separations occur, when one ages, and when the unexpected happens. It is the study of living one's last few hours or days and escaping the isolation which is so often imposed by a society which lives for the future. Why not interpret the dying trajectory as simply living which takes place in the waning moments of life? What we do with that remaining time, how we relate to the dying, how we go on living as survivors (and we are all survivors), how we talk about and use loss as a stimulus or depressant, is an integral part of life and living. Perhaps most important of all, the study of loss teaches that personal growth is a function of the quality of interpersonal relationships (Brantner, 1977).

Being fully aware of emotions that are normal and natural and which accompany loss will help explain feelings and reactions to many of life's disappointments and sorrows. As a further example, if you choose to love, as all of us do, you choose the pain which is part of the meaning of deep love. The full reawakening of this truth will help mitigate that great sense of powerlessness that engulfs each of us in our response to loss. As Marie said:

> To understand that loss is always a learning experience is helpful when coping. It helps build "immunity" to future upsets. You can delve into yourself best when the pressure is on in these situations. It will be a positive gain of self-knowledge through time.

Thus, loss is the motivator for utilizing one's abilities and assets in ways never before dreamed possible. The "immunity" Marie speaks of is not an "immunity" to the effects of loss but to the inability to deal with the hurt. We learn we *can* cope. If our assumptions about loss and the world around us affect our grief response, then we must take time to question those assumptions. But keep in mind Gibran's suggestion of the relationship between joy and sorrow and that there cannot be one without the other. Sorrow is often the prelude to joy, as joy is to sorrow.

Giving up the old never ends, for the new which replaces the old itself soon becomes old. Or as Mary Beth put it, "I couldn't accept the words 'change is inevitable.' I hated those words, but now I realize how true they are." These examples of self-learning are critical turning points in life. They are part of the establishment of a new identity and a new relationship with the world.

Chapter Two

MAJOR LOSS IN THE LIVES OF YOUNG ADULTS

What types of loss other than death are young adults likely to experience? Are there differences in the way they cope with the same type of loss? What emotions are experienced and do men and women differ in the expression of grief? These questions are dealt with in the pages to follow. This material can help young adults to understand the normalcy of a wide variety of loss reactions because it is based on data provided by their peers. It will also yield insights to guide interventions in the grief work of friends.

> I couldn't talk to my parents about this, and my friends were far away. So I called a professor I'm kind of close with after I'd held it in a couple of days. So I just cried and sobbed and spilled my guts for about an hour or so. I think now that it was very important that someone else know and understand how I felt—and that I got some of it off my chest. Holding it in just makes it worse. Also, I moved. It was important that I be away from that person to cope and deal with what happened.... Don't put everything you have—your energy, your love, your time, your life—into one person, thing, etc., because if you lose that person, you feel like you've lost yourself. You don't know what to do or who to share with. Everything seems meaningless. *You can love someone completely, without loving them solely.*
>
> Jean, a college sophomore

Do you remember the last time you were compulsive, or felt awkward, possessing that strange sense of ambivalence? If you do, then you have captured a hint of the characteristic features of the young adult years. Add to these traits the expressed needs of independence, and at the same time, the practical needs of dependence on parents or other significant adults, and we have a volatile blend within which the loss experience unfolds. It is critical to understand this predicament if we are fully to appreciate the severity of hardships, for young adults are caught between the pressures of dependence and independence and the establishment of a basic human need—identity. The establishment of one's identity is itself problematic and tends to exacerbate the resolution of loss.

In particular, whether one should or should not turn to the support of others, *and in what manner,* is reflective of the dependence-independence conflict which frequently occurs. This often has serious consequences for how the support network is utilized. If one believes that by turning for help to others (or to one important person in her life) she will be perceived as not being strong and independent, she is likely to suppress many feelings. Of equal concern are those who, after a short period of time, believe that they should no longer share feelings with support persons for fear they will be putting too much strain on these relationships.

Jean is an example of a frightened young woman who has become sensitive to what loss can do. She realizes what should be done about loss in order to prevent similar difficulties from occurring in the future. Her final sentence in the description of her breakup of a love relationship— "You can love someone completely without loving them solely"—is indicative of how young adults tend to focus on a single relationship to the exclusion of all others. This practice culminates in (1) minimizing the number and quality of relationships with others, (2) reducing the learning which accrues from such relationships, and (3) narrowing one's support network during times of crisis. Nevertheless, young adults still need to receive feedback about their competencies from peers and adults they esteem in order to help define their future choices. If this need is not satisfied, it will eventually surface in later attempts to adjust to major changes in life.

TYPES OF LOSSES

At the core of the study of thanatology (the study of death) is the central theme of loss in contemporary living patterns. Regrettably, formal and informal education about loss is woefully inadequate. However, the one predictable occurrence in life is change; some people see change as "development," others see it as "loss." If it is change imposed by loss or gain, it carries potential for positive results in understanding our capacities and frailities. Expected and unexpected loss abounds, just as does expected or unexpected gain. Examining a typical list of losses highlights the progressive, lifelong character of the experience.

Some Expected Losses

Loss of the comfort of the womb at birth

Weaning from bottle or breast

Temporary separations from mother

One's first baby-sitter when parents take temporary leave

One's first day at school—separation from home

Loss of youth

Graduation from elementary/high school

Going off to college

Marriages ("loss" of a daughter or son by parents)

These are expected losses by separation from people or objects which were strong symbols of security. Such losses are more or less traumatic experiences surrounding normal events. It is the unexpected losses, however, which are usually much more traumatic since they come with suddenness or little warning.

Some Unexpected Losses

Loss of money

Loss of a job

Loss of an ability

Loss of a limb

Loss of self-respect

Loss of faith or trust

Divorce

Loss of a love relationship

Sudden death

Loss of a friendship

Loss of material goods

Being dropped from school

This partial listing gives some indication of the universality of change. The effects of this continuous process must be assimilated into life. Each individual must answer the question: "How does one confront rapid change?" And, "How does one accommodate the new and give up the old?," must also be dealt with.

Losses, whether expected or unexpected, become major sources of stress and anxiety throughout life. They spawn fears of additional difficulties or create new circumstances and responsibilities that make heavy emotional demands.

The classic study of Holmes and Rahe (1967), frequently mentioned in psychological literature, points up the impact of loss on stress levels. This analysis of life crises and their effect on adult subjects ranked death of a spouse as the single most threatening life change of the 43 events listed. The first 10 crisis events listed in order of impact were:

1. Death of a spouse
2. Divorce
3. Marital separation
4. Jail term
5. Death of a close family member

6. Personal injury or illness
7. Marriage
8. Being fired at work
9. Marital reconciliation
10. Retirement

Notice that the top five events deal with separation. Separation anxiety and its resultant stress are at an unprecedented high in our society. They often lead to a variety of emotional and physical illnesses which are disabling (Lynch, 1977). Careful examination of this list illustrates the effect of death experiences on survivors, the effect of poor interpersonal relationships, the importance of high quality human interactions, and the need for a new loss awareness built on a belief system which recognizes loss as a constant in personal growth and development.

Turning to losses among young adults, we find much similarity as well as some differences in their loss experiences in comparison to persons in older age groups. The most striking characteristic is that nearly three-quarters of all major losses reported by young adults have to do with another significant person in their lives (See Table 1). As shown, the two most frequently occurring separations for this age group deal with the death of a loved one or the breakup of a love relationship. There are also broken friendships which occur when one leaves home and interests change, when one has gone to college, when friendships are strained because of a third party, or when a disagreement occurs which cannot be amicably settled. It is not unusual, for example, for two students to side against a third in a dispute about living quarters. As the conflict continues, the third student may move out, having been rejected by the other two. This rejection is difficult to accept. Divorce also creates major changes in the lives of students, whether it is initiated by the male or female partner. The divorce of students' *parents* is equally catastrophic, leaving emotional scars of long duration.

Totally forgotten by the general public and the college community are the long-term complications of unresolved grief due to separation, regardless of the cause. A 20-year old college junior, Margaret, struggled with her confused thoughts for three years and found some solace in a paper she wrote for me as a class assignment entitled *My Most Recent Loss:* " . . . it probably seems as though I am really confused about my thoughts and feelings concerning her illness and death," she acknowledged. "I have been confused about them myself. Mainly I have wondered why I didn't cry. I guess I thought it wasn't normal not to cry, and that it meant

Table 1.
MOST RECENT MAJOR LOSSES OF 3,510 YOUNG ADULTS

Type of Loss	Female	Male	Total	Percent
1. Death of a Loved One	626	377	1,003	28.5
2. End of a Love Relationship	525	329	854	24.3
3. End of a Friendship	264	91	355	10.1
4. Separation from Loved Ones	259	86	345	9.8
5. Loss of a Good Grade (Failure)	142	120	262	7.5
6. Loss of a Cherished Ideal	67	38	105	3.0
7. Loss of Self-Respect	57	36	93	2.7
8. Loss of Material Goods	33	47	80	2.3
9. Loss of a Job	22	37	59	1.7
10. Loss of an Ability	20	29	49	1.4
11. Divorce	28	20	45	1.2
12. Loss of a Body Function	17	16	33	1.0
13. Loss of a Pet	8	2	10	0.2
14. Other Losses*	133	84	217	6.2

*For a complete listing in this category write the author.

you didn't care if you didn't. Well, while writing this paper I cried—the only tears since I saw my mother in the hospital. I think writing this has helped me understand some of my own feelings. For example, my guilt about her death. I am really glad I had this chance to express how I have felt for all this time." This is a tragic example of someone not knowing how to deal with her emotions, and equally tragic, unable to find someone in three years who could help her deal with the common reaction of guilt.

College freshmen, in particular, find their initial year away from home both comforting with its new-found freedom and, at the same time, saddening because of separation from hometown loved ones. Sometimes the inability to adjust to this separation, as well as the demands of academe, combine to create stressors for younger students which show up in poor grades and many telephone calls home. Some students even choose to leave school and return home.

In some cases, the stress of academic life is the result of having had success in high school but finding that the competition for good grades is more intense in college. Others come to school thinking that parties are first and everything else is second. By the time they realize the commitment needed to survive in college, it may be too late or they may be unable to surmount the grave difficulties of overcoming a poor start. Still others, expecting to be at the top of their class as they were before their college experience, now are up against other A students from even more rigorous high school programs. This fact, combined with a limited social life, causes much unhappiness. The final straw for such a student may be failure in a particular course: This is a common major loss. The results of such failures are grief experiences, some with extreme consequences such as drunkenness, despair, feelings of being cheated, total rejection, quitting school, and, in extreme cases, suicide or attempted suicide.

Losses dealing with self-respect or a cherished ideal are the foundation for additional problems. Conflict with parents, when lines of communication are destroyed, is another. Confrontation with opposing points of view challenging dearly-held beliefs, sexual behavior not previously engaged in, abortions and the loss of confidence or trust in what was previously a part of one's value system are examples of major losses reported. Less frequent in occurrence, but still deeply moving, are losses of material goods—a stolen stereo set, a burned-down home, a wrecked automobile, or lost wallets. Some young adults quietly endure these losses, while others experience much pain as they go about the business of restructuring their lives.

Of particular interest is the reaction of people to losses involving pets. It has long been known that the elderly have strong attachments to pets. The meaningful relationship between a pet and its owner can be a bond of friendship as strong or stronger than that between two persons. A similar relationship seems to exist between young adults and their pets. Terri describes her reactions to the events leading up to and including the death of her puppy which she had obtained from the local Humane Society near the college.

> My emotions were more than sadness. I was also full of anger at the vet who couldn't tell what was wrong with her. As a matter of fact, I hated the vet I brought her to.... After they had taken Meg out of my room, I cried myself to sleep. When I woke up a couple of hours later, I started crying all over again. My head was pounding, my eyes were swollen, and I was extremely tired.... Many people would think at my age it's a little crazy to get so upset over a puppy. Meg meant a lot to me. She was the first puppy I had owned.... The girls I lived with helped me accept her death.

Horses and other pets also have very special meaning to students, causing much heartache if they are injured or have to be destroyed. The long-term effects of the loss of a pet are illustrated by Derek in the following:

> Since this situation happened while I was in college, I could handle it better because I wasn't being constantly reminded of the death. When I go home I have trouble handling the situation because I think of all the things my dog and I used to do (like jumping up on me as I walked into the room).

Health problems are additional sources of major loss on many occasions. Heart attacks of parents, cancer, miscarriages, mental illness or disease in relatives or friends, and loss of a body part or function are examples of health-related impairments which young adults cite as major loss experiences in their lives. Not to be overlooked are the health problems of parents or relatives which reduce potential sources of financial help for the student and which can cause financial strain in meeting the essential costs of a college education.

A rather small number of young adults are sometimes subjected to a series of significant losses. It could be the death of several friends and relatives, or a combination of separations, deaths, and the breakup of a love relationship. In a period of about one month, "I have experienced six deaths ranging from natural deaths due to cancer, to car accidents and a suicide.... All these deaths affected me on various, different emotional and acceptance levels," said Monique. The breakup with a boyfriend or girlfriend, coupled with failure in a course, is another combination with long-term consequences.

Ray experienced the deaths of three close friends in the period of one year, the last of which involved an accident in which he talked to his dying friend. "As one member of our group went for help, I sat there and talked to him for about twenty minutes until he died. The whole thing seemed like it was about two hours; everything was in slow motion. After it was over, I felt as if he was trying to tell me something or give me a message from up above. I ended up leaving school; for two or three weeks, I couldn't think right; I lost weight, couldn't sleep, and had a lot of dreams." It is at these times that young adults are extremely vulnerable and in need of much understanding and compassion from those closest to them. Ray's explanation that "after it was over, I felt as if he was trying to tell me something from up above" is an example of a paranormal experience which, unless discussed, may increase anxiety. Because the accumulation of intense feelings arising from a series of major losses is so overwhelming, professional assistance is often necessary. This also holds true for many love relationships which come to an end.

The breakup of a love relationship is one of the most common and devastating losses during the college years. However, it is also the least understood by others in terms of its impact on the individual. Erik Erikson has characterized the developmental stage of the young adult as a time of intimacy and self-absorption (1963). The discrepancy between intimacy and the deprivation posed by a breakup is a monumental source of grief, because such relationship losses occur at one of the most vulnerable periods in life. Romantic attachment is of prime importance. To understand more fully the way this type of loss affects one's life, examine the following description of David's severed relationship which began in high school and ended in college.

> I cannot express how emotionally hurt I was when I heard she wanted to see other people.... Looking back on the situation, I can honestly say that it affected my lifestyle for almost three full years. I did not act like myself in many ways and my ego was shattered. I was not the confident person that I once was.... I was aware of this but could not control it....
>
> I can remember becoming very obsessed with her. I had pictures of her hanging up all over my dormitory room. I thought about her constantly, trying to figure out ways to get her back. I can remember becoming extremely emotionally upset when I heard a sentimental song on the radio that reminded me of her. When I returned home for vacations, I can recall getting a very strange feeling inside of me. It was indescribable. When I occasionally saw her on my breaks, my stomach would just about turn inside out and my voice would sound rather shaky. I could not control it. It is even quite strange thinking about it now....
>
> I tried very hard to forget her, and I would be very successful for a while, and then something would trigger a memory, and I would fall back into the trap. I guess what hurt the most was that we were also best friends. We spent a lot of time together and we told each other everything. I guess what I wanted to hear the most was that she still cared about me and did not hate me for all that I had done to her. I needed to hear this above all else in order to relieve my guilt feelings.

The breakup of a love relationship is, for at least one of the two persons involved, seemingly a total rejection—the most damaging blow to the ego. The resulting loneliness becomes an emotional crisis in itself; one's identity is shattered, and this is why some students equate this type of loss with death itself. The rejected lover consistently reports intense emotional and physical reactions, many of which are of a long-term duration. This occurs regardless of sex or age. It has been noted elsewhere that the roles of rejecting lover and rejected lover bring differing emotional responses, ranging from relief to depression, and that, generally, the partners' reactions are inversely related (Hill, Rubin and Peplau, 1976). Nonetheless, it is also clear that the rejecting lover often feels guilty for having caused pain to another, and although relieved that the relationship has ended, experiences great emotional turmoil. We shall see in the pages to come the unique differences in coping styles between males and females with regard to this loss of love, and the way it changes the course of one's life.

Associated Losses

Major loss frequently triggers a series of secondary or associated losses which the griever mourns along with the major loss. It is the secondary losses which add to and intensify grief responses in most instances. In examining the breakup of a love relationship, we find that for some young adults the loss is not only the end of the companionship of one person but of many other social contacts as well. There may be a loss of transportation to and from school, loss of a study partner, or loss of one's welcome at certain parties and social functions requiring a date. Depending on how dependent one person was on the other, a whole host of routines come to an end. Each of these losses must be addressed. Combined, they yield a number of stresses in addition to the major stress from the breakup.

The loss of a *body part* also brings with it a series of additional losses. One not only loses the function of that part but also the special abilities or skills it may have provided and the many opportunities for social interaction through competitive activities. One believes he or she is "different" as the perception of the self is altered. It could mean that an individual would have to switch majors, terminate preparations for a military career, or even change schools. These losses may end a part-time job that was helping to meet the costs of education. Similarly, death brings not only the loss of the loved one but the loss of all that person did, the way he or she affected the lives of others. This commonly includes loss of a critical resource for problem solving, support in times of failure, and motivation in pursuit of career goals. Death may also bring associated losses in the form of having to move from a home to an apartment, or even a geographical move to another community or state. Associated losses may be many or few, each having a greater or lesser impact depending on individual circumstances. They are predictable in some instances and unpredictable in others, depending on their nature and meaning to the bereaved. The symbolic meaning of any loss will cause some people less tangible but more intense feelings of a deep emotional nature. For example, the loss of one's home by fire may be interpreted as the loss of a tradition, of generational continuity, of one's roots, or past. On one occasion, after a lecture on grief to a group of teachers, a young woman came up to me, thanked me for the presentation and said, "After my apartment burned and I lost everything, I went away for a week to get away from it all. It's almost like a part of me died." The part of her that had died was represented by the cherished family heirlooms and furniture which were completely destroyed. The symbolic destruction of links to one's past often necessitates an extended grieving period. As associated losses are resolved, the major loss is more readily accepted. We seldom think of associated losses until they occur and have to be confronted in the process of restructuring day-to-day routines.

UNDERSTANDING DIFFERENCES IN RESPONSE TO LOSS

> Once, when I was having a horrible argument with my mother about their separation, I was to the point where I couldn't stay in the house. So I called one of my best friends and she came over and picked me up and got me out of the house. Many times I end up running out of the house to take a walk and I don't feel as though I'm running away from my problems, only getting away so I don't say anything I may regret later.
>
> My problem is that my loss is ongoing and I am still trying to cope with it.
>
> Julie, a college sophomore

Not infrequently, individuality is misunderstood vis-a-vis many problems and afflictions. The subtle differences between someone acting as a member of a group and as an individual, and within a single individual at various times, are overlooked by many well-meaning people. Julie's behavior when confronted with her mother could be interpreted by many people as a poor way to solve a problem. But we need to know much more about her conflict before making such a judgment. Her response to the stress of her parents' marital problems may or may not be appropriate. Understanding the unmatched individuality of each person will be a giant step in helping with any crisis, be it alcoholism, divorce, or death. It will also help you manage your own loss experiences as you realize you must grieve in your own way, not as others suggest.

Individuality in the perception and management of life-and-death stressors is a determining factor in whether loss is resolved or reacted to pathologically. The degree of stress experienced is in large part a matter of how one interprets the stressor (Selye, 1979). The implications for dealing with anxiety, and/or providing support and empathy for someone else, are many. For example, overgeneralizing how people should react to loss and advising a person to get on with the job of living not only oversimplifies a complex human experience, but also sows the seeds of miscalculation, leading to added anxiety and misunderstanding between grievers and caregivers. Biological, psychological, and physiological differences suggest variations in all forms of human behavior, including loss experiences. By refusing to respect our own or someone else's individuality, we place unreasonable demands on ourselves and friends, distorting the means for creating support systems and understanding emotional responses.

Therefore, one's ability to adapt to the loss depends on personal variables which shape the meaning of a given loss to the survivor, the environment in which the loss occurs, and the personal strengths an individual brings to the confrontation. *Loss, like beauty, is in the eye of the beholder;* it takes on different meanings for different people. It follows that grief is not generalizable but a product of age, temperament, genetic endowment, personality, and life-experiences. Some people are better able to adapt than others to the same type of loss under very similar circumstances. Why is there such a divergence? In addition to the reasons already suggested, previous loss experiences play a major role. The manner in which previous losses were resolved (either successfully or not) influences how one perceives the next loss confronted. Thus, an abbreviated list of variables affecting coping style and outcome would include: personality, sex, the type of death (sudden vs. expected), the timeliness of death, the quality of relationships with family and friends, any unfinished business, guilt, and one's dependence on drugs, etc. The subjective magnitude of any loss depends largely on a host of variables such as these. (For an in-depth discussion of factors influencing grief reactions see Rando, 1984, Chapter Three.)

Another factor in response to loss is the type of loss experienced. While there are distinct similarities in how individuals respond to major loss experiences—the flood of emotion, physical consequences, yearning for the return of the lost object, denial of the event, anger, searching—there are also differences based on the nature of the loss. Death, for example, may be viewed as having cheated, destroyed, or stolen a loved one, while at the same time providing a grim reminder that other loved ones may die ("I don't know what I would do if my parents ever die"). It may also be viewed as a redeemer. Furthermore, it may lead the bereaved to idealization of the deceased.

Divorce and the breakup of love relationships provide a different background in which loss is interpreted. First, one of the partners realizes that the other consciously chose to separate. One's healthy husband, lover, or friend chose to be with another. Therefore, strong feelings of inadequacy arise. Second, this type of interpretation usually leads to a greater loss of self-esteem. ("You are not a widow, you are a reject.") Third, one seldom receives the type of sympathy and condolences that a death brings, except from the few who may have experienced the same type of loss. Fourth, closure may be more difficult for some because of the constant reminders of the children or friends that seem to bring memories that the other partner is still alive and one has been abandoned. Even in the breakup of love relationships young people are devastated at seeing their former friend in a new relationship and are revisited with feelings of inadequacy. Finally, there is almost an absence of ritual to assist the transition from married to divorced (Freund, 1975). The fundamental difference in losses of partners through divorce or breakups and death is the absolute finality that accompanies the latter (Pincus, 1974). Postdivorce support and counseling is needed by the divorced, including children, as much as it is by survivors of a death.

Again, I would like to remind the reader that one's perception of the loss event heavily influences modes of response. Perceptions are the meanings we give to experiences. For example, I know exactly what I want to write about loss in this book. I know what the words mean to me. However, you may read the very same words and draw different meanings from them. You will see them as I do, but you may *perceive* them differently. The word *perception* implies great individuality; hence there can be wide variability in responses. Perceptions are the result of a multitude of variables: age, the nature of the physical organism, past opportunities to perceive, the self-concept, goals and values, the experience of threat, and current needs (Combs, 1962). Attitudes toward loss will therefore vary immeasurably. Let us develop this further.

Beginning with anatomical variations, one need only consider that no two people have the same fingerprints or voiceprints. When you consider the millions of people in the United States alone, this is a truly amazing fact. Consider the differences in taste for foods. Some people like salty food, while others abhor it. Fish is a delicacy for some and poison for others. Tastes in clothes are sharply diverse, depending on one's custom, culture, and family influence. The same temperature affects people in rather contrasting ways. Two individuals may consume identical doses of a drug, but with different side effects—one person may break out in a rash while the other becomes nauseated. Pain thresholds are uniquely individual, ranging from supersensitivity to feeling only mild pain, given the same surgical procedure (Williams, 1971). Learning styles vary—some people are visual learners, some are auditory learners, some are tactile learners, while others may learn through various combinations of these three modalities.

You are the only you in the history of the world. The more you can penetrate your own personal complexity by learning about your reactions, the more you can appreciate and enjoy life. Developing respect for differences, so needed in understanding loss behavior, will help you to help others in time of crisis. Just like many other forms of human behavior, grief is often misunderstood. Some people do not cry or follow rituals as expected. Does this mean they are not grieving? There are those who possess a deep fear of going to a funeral home and find many excuses to avoid it. Does this signify they are indifferent to survivors? The answer to both questions is a resounding "no," although the general public would think differently.

Individuality necessarily implies that the advice received from others will reflect the helper's beliefs and expectations. You will receive many messages with opposing viewpoints. A friend may say, "Get away from it all for a while." A parent may suggest, "Time will heal. Try to immerse yourself in your studies. Focus your thoughts on what you still have." A teacher may implore, "You've got to forget about what has happened and go on with your life." All these directives are well-intended, but none may be of any use to you in your hour of need. You and you alone must weigh your next step and choose the direction in which recovery will move. You are always free to search for those persons who will let you be who you are, who will offer their presence as their primary gift, as you progress through readjustment.

Regardless of the nature of individual differences, I am convinced that we all possess the inherent capacity to cope with the most difficult losses imaginable, especially if we are assisted by people who will allow us to share feelings with them and who will not give up on us. With good friends furnishing that kind of long-term caring, the most tragic losses can be overcome and transformed into bridges to new beginnings. We all have that untapped potential to endure and "make it," even when the worst of circumstances casts its shadow. Every person possesses the inner strength which is sometimes activated by the support network or initiated through her own efforts.

DIFFERENCES BETWEEN MALE AND FEMALE COPING STYLES

> The people most helpful were my own friends and the friends of my boyfriend who died. I saw them carrying on as usual and knew that I had to also. I don't think guys show their emotions as much, which is bad for them, but it was good for me.
>
> Terri, a freshman

Friedrich Nietzsche wrote: "The same passions in man and woman differ in tempo; hence man and woman do not cease misunderstanding one another." What Nietzsche calls "tempo" is, in fact, the product of growing up in a specific way with culturally-determined expectations and pressures that shape the individual response to one's environment. One of the additional tragedies of loss experiences lies in the misunderstandings which prevail between the sexes because of the tempo, or more appropriately, the expression of emotions associated with loss. This misinterpretation of acceptable grieving behavior causes grief work to be prolonged for some, and its intensity increased for others. This is especially notable when parents grieve the loss of a child. Because each person grieves differently, and neither marriage partner comprehends why this is so, the additional trauma stemming from the death often results in the couple's separation and divorce. Similar rifts occur within families, romantic relationships, or between grievers and support persons of the opposite sex.

Young adults should be aware of the contrasts and subtleties between male and female coping styles, particularly within their own families. This is most helpful in preventing conflicts in both male and female behavior following a major loss, as well as in ministering to the individual needs of the bereaved. Men who attempt to provide support for women are sometimes stymied in doing so because they are perplexed by feminine grief reactions—i.e., an increased intensity of emotions displayed and a longer grieving period. Women caregivers, on the other hand, are often frustrated in their attempts to help men when they discover that men hide their feelings, often appear to shun reminders of the lost relationship, and invariably seek to return too quickly to their normal routines of living. This does not mean that men are not grieving; it does indicate they may not accomplish the tasks as successfully as women.

Popular exercises which attempt to compare differences between the sexes rarely achieve clear-cut results. However, there are sex-related differences which have a sound basis in research and tend to be ascribed to one sex more than the other. For example, while environmental or social influences are thought to be the basis for most sex differences, there is evidence that neurological constitutions contribute to the differences (Goleman, 1978). In other studies, it has been found that the way certain tasks are processed by men and women may be more the result of how the brain controls certain functions than what one learns as a young girl or boy. Nevertheless, of more concern to us is the realization that ascribing certain traits or behaviors to members of one sex does not mean that the same traits are absent in members of the opposite sex. Nor do we imply that all members of the same sex necessarily exhibit the same traits. However, what can be said with conviction is that frequently there are role reversals. That is, some women may assume the role of the "strong one" when major loss occurs, and some men may openly and freely show their emotions.

The findings of psychological research strongly suggest that women, as compared to men, possess stronger verbal abilities and are better in manual dexterity and tasks of fine motor coordination. Men, in contrast, excel in visual-spatial and mathematical skills and have the edge in gross motor movements (Goleman, 1978). Put another way, men are more analytical and have faster reaction times. Women use their intuition more often. When this is coupled with an orientation towards people, the result is that women are generally more empathetic than men. There is also some evidence to suggest that men and women process information differently (Weintraub, 1981). That is to say, they think differently. This may well be reflected in the unique characteristics of their interpersonal relationships: men look at loss and grief in a problem-solving way, whereas women are more in need of exploring feelings and having their emotions recognized as legitimate by others. Here a major conflict emerges. It occurs when men try to provide answers to women's grief analytically, while women are simply searching for someone who will *listen* to and legitimatize the breadth and depth of their feelings of pain.

The nature and quality of interpersonal relationships have a direct affect on the coping styles of men and women. It is often the case that men do not have close interpersonal friendships with other men. They usually refer to other men as "buddies," and many of their interests throughout life revolve around activities, doing things. At an early age, boys learn to play with cars, to build structures out of blocks, and to build forts or tree houses. Later, they focus on hunting, fishing, and participating in sports, and they join clubs. Oh yes, men have friends, but the associations are usually superficial and not deeply emotional. On the contrary, they usually compete with one another or in groups, and this precludes an admission of fear or possible weakness. One never shows weakness to a competitor. Conversely, women are often encouraged to cultivate a sense of helplessness and powerlessness (Miller, 1976). In addition, social custom dictates that men must not show affection toward other men. This taboo, a constant throughout life, is reinforced early by the male fear of being labeled a "fag"—a derogatory term denoting homosexuality.

"Masculine" expectations often create restrictive sex-role pressures in men. This is reflected in hospice survivor groups and Compassionate Friends meetings. When these groups are mixed, with both men and women participating, men are generally unable to express feelings about the death of their loved one. Social conditioning obviously plays a major role in the development of interpersonal transactions with members of both sexes, women not excluded. Women are expected to act "lady-like" and fit into a mold fashioned by society. As a middle-aged woman recently explained: "It is more acceptable for men to take care of business and women to mourn."

Unlike men, women have many close relationships with other women. They have friends in the true sense of the word—other women they can confide in with their most intimate thoughts. Most women appear to have more than just one other woman with whom they share feelings, which springs naturally from the degree of openness which is a hallmark of their friendships. The intimate, trusting relationship is a part of early childhood training in females and their orientation toward people. They learn that becoming vulnerable is a part of sharing relationships. Although astute readers of the emotional components of human activity, this strength has been downplayed as an impediment instead of an aid to understanding (Miller, 1976). It is the communication patterns established in this open climate of exchange which prove to be a most important asset to women meeting the crises of later life. Generally, women are more honest with their emotions; men are forced to be more deceptive with theirs.

Both men and women, then, meet major loss experiences in the context of their respective sex-role conditioning. Women appear to be better prepared to deal with their emotions, whereas men search for ways to maintain the stoic approach in the face of crisis. Both sexes have their sex-roles reinforced by the media, especially television, where the virile, manly image and the gentle, feminine image are portrayed again and again in productions beamed at every age level.

Traditionally, males have been thrust into the role of provider and pillar of strength in time of loss. While the role of provider may be changing, the pillar of strength concept is still firmly entrenched in western society. Society looks to the male to provide stability and the resources to deal with tragedy, fear, and extreme change. At the same time, men are struggling with similar emotions and feelings as women; emotions and feelings which often need to be expressed. Typically, they acquire fewer support persons to turn to. Suppression and postponement of emotional reactions are therefore employed in the normal course of males' grief work.

My research on male and female reactions to the deaths of loved ones suggests that women experience greater physical and emotional trauma and utilize a wider range of coping techniques than men. Feelings of helplessness, emptiness, and loneliness are reported much more frequently by women. They also experience more anger, guilt, and fear, which may be the result of their life-long orientation toward people. Physically, women report more headaches, exhaustion, numbness, and nausea, and are slightly more prone to insomnia. Finally, women cope more by crying, talking about the loss, and by seeking the support of family and friends than men do. Religious beliefs and memories of the deceased also provide more support for women (LaGrand, 1981).

Men generally appear to be more subdued in their overt reactions to death. However, they too become depressed, shocked, and frustrated, which is often couched in anger. Their physical reactions are less pronounced, although paradoxically they indicate "feelings of weakness" as their chief complaint. The major difference which emerges in coping styles when compared to women is the stronger philosophical stance they assume. ("We have to put it in the past and go on with life.")

Because society tends to focus more attention on women who are grieving, men seem to be overlooked, and this further exacerbates their isolation. Men do cry, but not nearly as frequently as women do; men seem to be embarrassed by this show of emotion. However, if men are encouraged by a hug or by verbal permission, they are more willing to utilize this very important coping mechanism, especially if they are not around friends or family. The "male myth" still militates against the open expression of emotion and encourages its containment and repression as the norm. The myth also accounts for the fact that men report fewer specific feelings and physical reactions to their losses.

The result of these differences in grieving styles is the basis for much conflict and misunderstanding when loss occurs. Communication between men and women is not generally open and is characterized more by silence than by extended dialogue. There is a fundamental conflict between the sexes in terms of how emotional states and approaches to adjusting are managed. Males need more opportunities to unburden themselves, to find outlets in which to channel anger. At the same time, they must learn to understand that the female usually needs to express emotion and talk at length. And most importantly, men must allow for frequent discussion and recollections about the deceased or object of loss. Too often, men try to cope with their loss by avoiding emotional conversations, dismissing the event from consciousness, or through periodic drinking bouts. They expect similar avoidance behaviors from their female counterparts, which are not forthcoming.

Men and women must begin to build bridges to meet each other's needs. Ideally, but impractically, this is best accomplished long before a personal loss occurs, when both are in a position to learn what happens between the sexes during crisis conditions. However, this objective look before the fact is seldom considered in school curricula or in preparation for marriage. Nevertheless, when traumatic change takes place, *members of each sex must never assume how members of the other sex should grieve.* Both must be allowed to move through grief *at their own pace,* and each must attempt to facilitate the healing process of the other. This demands great patience on the part of all concerned.

In order to meet such a challenge, a much deeper awareness of male and female grieving roles is in order. This is most difficult at this point in history when the roles of the sexes are in great flux. Specifically, the masculine image, built upon a sense of aggressiveness, competition, impeccable emotional control, and "taking over" during times of crisis, still prevails and should be acknowledged. Concurrently, males must be given freedom and careful encouragement to grieve, too. In short, this means recognizing that men often work through their grief in behavioral instead of verbal ways. Let them *act out* their grief: let them saw wood, jog, stack lumber, mow the lawn, move furniture, or run errands. And recognize that the physical expression of grief through work may be one of the few avenues open to them, even though they must learn the importance of verbalizing their feelings. Many men do not know how to grieve, as much of their haphazard behavior indicates. Women, on the other hand, need to understand the cultural deprivation men have been subjected to in this regard, just as men must acquiesce to the compassionate listening that women seek during their grief work.

The female image, although recently changing to a more aggressive stance, still maintains a unique blend of gentleness, sensitivity, and intimacy which facilitates and demands a sharing process during major transitions. Thus, women have much need for the dialogue usually provided for them by other women friends willing to listen.

Young women and young men who seek family assistance with their losses usually find that their mothers provide this support more often than fathers. However, women's need for much longer periods of emotional release must be understood within the framework of their social roles. It is important to realize that it is the *process of expression* relating to loss-events which differs dramatically between men and women, not the innate feelings which either sex possesses and utilizes in its grief work.

REACTIONS: EMOTIONAL, PHYSICAL, BEHAVIORAL

> I was in Europe for a semester, so my friends were new friends, and I wanted to be alone or with my family and old friends. Since they were thousands of miles away I just had to be alone and cry and cry.... For me, one thing was I had unfinished business with him and there was something I planned to tell him that week in a card and I never got to tell him. So I guess letting people know how great you find them before you *can't* let them know, would prepare you for loss.
>
> Alice, a college senior, on the death of her grandfather

What happens when expectations are not met, when someone who has always been there is no longer there? Dealing with the sudden twists of fate, the panic which overwhelms, the realization that what was expected to continue forever is now changed forever, brings thoughts and behaviors which are wide-ranging and complex. And, as in Alice's case, there is frequently unfinished business when loss involves the death of a loved one. This always heightens one's emotional response, prolonging adjustment. Unfinished business is an occurrence which dramatically illustrates the problem of viewing relationships with others as never ending, as it deludes one into withholding expressions of love until it is too late. This is one factor involved in whether grief reactions are immediate or delayed, intense and erratic, or short-term or long-lasting.

Emotional Reactions

The veritable explosion of emotion which usually accompanies major loss experiences carries implications for the body as well as the mind. Like other bereaved people, youth are subject to a variety of bodily changes which are energy-sapping and which heavily influence progress toward resolution of loss, especially when these effects are allowed to continue unchecked. Emotional and physical responses also interfere with study and work schedules, health habits, and class attendance in many cases. However, young adults say that a larger factor in their overall responses is the lack of warning or useful information about what follows any loss experience perceived as major.

Heather's first confrontation with death suggests this lack of awareness and its resulting impact. On seeing her grandmother at the funeral home, and realizing that she was dead, Heather was finally able to let out emotions which had been bottled up for three days. She cried so hard she vomited. On looking back at this experience she writes:

> I feel that one of the major reasons why my first funeral was so hard to accept was because I was never informed about death when I was little. To wait until you are eighteen years old to experience your first death can be devastating! Death was one of those hush-hush topics in our home. My parents wanted to protect me by sheltering me from the reality of death. Now they realize it was wrong of them, and my little sister is now exposed to the topic of death.

It is important to emphasize here that Heather's observations are not the exception, but generally the rule. The protection of young people from loss experiences by well-meaning adults is a significant factor in their inadequate responses to traumatic change.

But feelings and reactions of this magnitude are not limited to losses imposed by death. Severed relationships, such as divorce, the end of a long friendship, or the breakup of a love relationship, take an equal emotional and physical toll, and in some instances are even considered as devastating as the death of a loved one (LaGrand, 1983). Kate's boyfriend of several years ended a relationship which had many deep roots and commitments. Her reaction was complete estrangement from all.

> It's been really tough, and at times I had my doubts as to whether I was going to make it. There were days I didn't even want to get out of bed because I didn't want to face things anymore. I just wanted to curl up into a ball and hide....I became extremely depressed. I was unable to eat properly and never able to sleep or do any kind of work.

Consider the impact of parental divorce on Fred:

> I used to be part of a very close (I thought) family unit. My parents' divorce seemed very sudden. I was extremely upset, not at them but at the situation. I think I coped by changing my whole character. I used to be very content with being an individual. Now I need to be one of the group (which I regret deeply). Something which I thought was so secure was so suddenly shattered. I've lost confidence totally with anything I thought was secure. When I visit the friends that I used to be very close to, I don't fit in, for they are individuals, and they don't want to do the things "everyone does."

The sense of isolation, of being different, is quite common in loss by parental divorce. In terms of loneliness, parental divorce is more detrimental than the death of a parent (Rubenstein, Shaver and Peplau, 1979). Like death, parental divorce may lower one's feelings of self-confidence.

Deanne, who was undergoing a three-month separation from her boyfriend because school was over, reacted in the following way:

> I sat down and started talking to my Mom. After ten minutes, I was engulfed in tears and sobbing, wondering how I would ever make it through the summer. My head ached, my stomach was upset, my eyes were all reddened and swollen, my nose was running and stuffy and, by now, my whole body felt physically exhausted. I felt like a mental wreck. I was so afraid at this point that these feelings would last the whole summer through.
>
> I had never felt or known this kind of love with anyone before this. The feelings that accompanied these emotions were so foreign to me. I felt depression, like I had suddenly been left alone in the world. I was scared—I thought I might lose Rick with such a long separation—or was our love enough for each other to keep us together? I felt hostile. Thoughts came to me, "What could I do to overcome this grief—what is ahead?"

When reading this reaction to separation you may chuckle and snicker at such a display, given the nature of the loss, because you are judging from your perspective, not Deanne's. But this scenario is real—and threatening—and must be understood from her frame of reference. In order to appreciate the impact of loss on individuals at a particular time in life, we must be attuned to their *beliefs* and *perceptions*. At such delicate times, friends, family, or relatives will either affirm life and provide support for the bereaved or cruelly dismiss the reaction as childishly immature. Fearsome apprehension is a condition which prevails in many of the changing scenes of life and should be acknowledged as acceptable.

Table 2.
FEELINGS ACCOMPANYING LOSS AS REPORTED BY 3,510 YOUNG ADULTS

	Female	Male	Total	Percent Experiencing
1. Depression	1,673	907	2,580	73.5
2. Anger	1,254	677	1,931	55.0
3. Emptiness	1,310	606	1,916	54.5
4. Loneliness	1,211	553	1,764	50.2
5. Frustration	1,135	625	1,760	50.1
6. Disbelief	812	455	1,267	36.0
7. Shock	806	452	1,258	35.8
8. Helplessness	827	390	1,217	34.6
9. Loss of Self-Confidence	689	359	1,048	29.8
10. Guilt	705	328	1,033	29.4
11. Fear	677	217	894	25.4
12. Rejection	560	249	809	23.0
13. Self-Pity	527	217	744	21.1
14. Hatred	444	178	622	17.7
15. Denial	395	187	582	16.5
16. Lost	419	154	573	16.3
17. Other Feelings*	147	73	220	6.2

*For a complete listing in this category write the author.

With some insight into the types of reactions possible, a more thorough understanding of the kinds of feelings that surface is found in Table 2. Remember, we are not abnormal if we experience any of these emotions or the physical reactions which are their counterparts. Unexpected as they may be, they are really quite common. Topping the list is the feeling professionally described as "reactive depression." There are many variations in the length and intensity of depression from "mild" to "severe," or even "psychotic." Most of the depression due to major loss can be worked through, *is normal,* and must be understood with patience and persistence by loved ones. For too long a period of time depression has carried the stigma of being something inherently evil, whereas, in fact, it is the common denominator of drastic change. Loss is a personal form of radical transition; depression is its common companion. And radical transition is a life event with which few are prepared to deal. Yet these events are both random and broadly predictable to some extent. Our penchant for the familiar and our resistance to transitions combine to cause great unrest, even though life demands loss *and* gain, as a rule, not a choice between them. Hence, everyone is susceptible to depression, a reaction which mirrors our unwillingness to accept change which cannot be controlled.

This in no way should be misconstrued as romanticizing loss or death. There is no intent to suggest that a sugarcoated version of depression is either desirable or useful. On the contrary, this is an attempt to remove a negative stereotype which may well hinder the way we relate to those who are depressed.

Intensity of Reactions. Immediate reactions to loss vary from physical collapse:

> He started crying rather hard over the phone, and this triggered me to cry also. After hanging up, a wave of heat seemed to swoop over me, and before I knew it, I had hit the floor. My roommate revived me and comforted me as I cried for about two hours. Thank God she was there for me. She was great support, and just listened as I went on and on about how unfair this was and how much I cared for him.

To the typical headache and nausea:

> Physically, I can recall, upon hearing of my grandmother's death, a feeling comparable to that of falling off a high building. My heart began to beat irregularly and rapidly, my palms began to sweat almost instantly, and I think I also had a headache and vividly recall the butterflies in my stomach.

To the typical shock and numbness:

> When I hung up the phone, I was allowed to release my real reaction to the situation. I threw myself down onto my bed and carried on a howling crying session. I think, at this point, I felt numb and shocked by the news. The hardest thing was not knowing how this had happened as no details were known yet.

Sudden losses often accentuate responses.

Strong emotional reaction, a hallmark of most meaningful losses, can be both poignant and confused, lasting for long periods of time. Colleen, who had dinner with her friend two days before he died, was overcome with anger, unable to find an answer to her question, "Why?."

> I was always on the verge of breaking down in front of anyone or anything that reminded me of Bob. Emotionally, I was a mess. My biggest problem was I hated God. I couldn't believe that He could take such a good person, someone who enjoyed life so much and who lived each day to its fullest. Why? There are so many bad people in the world—so many unhappy people, some who cannot

love, others who don't even want to live! Why was it Bob's turn to leave us? I no longer believed in God. He was evil as far as I was concerned.

Guilt. Of equal significance are the very personal feelings of responsibility for the death of a friend, lingering for long periods of time, as suggested by Tina as she explains her thoughts at the wake of her friend Lee.

> I still felt guilty about the accident and my part in it. I saw Lee in the casket and asked for her forgiveness because I thought that I had done something wrong. I kept thinking that I should be the one in the casket or in the hospital. I felt the same way when I went to see Joanne in the hospital. I wanted to tell her that I was the one that should be investigated by the police and not her. Slowly I realized that what happened had happened, and there was nothing that I could do about it. I still think about the accident from time to time. . . . The sight of Joanne's car lights going over the embankment is still imbedded in my mind and I think that it always will be.

Guilt surfaces in many forms and frequently is based on the inability to control specific events associated with the loss. Take the example of Helen, who made a promise to herself that she could not keep, resulting in a serious social and emotional toll.

> When we got to the hospital it was too late. I then began to feel very guilty. I had made a promise to myself that I would be there when he died and he wouldn't be alone. I cried very hard not only for the death of my father but for not being there and never telling my father that I loved him before he died. I was allowed to enter my father's room to see him. I walked into his room and just stood there at the foot of his bed in a state of shock. He looked terrible. He had tubes still connected to him. I got very mad at the nurse for letting me see him when he looked so terrible. I thought it wasn't my father on that bed. It was someone else who just looked like my father. My mother came and got me out of the room.
>
> I cried like I never had before that day. I felt like a part of me was missing. I wanted one more chance to see my father. I had so much to say to him. I left too much unsaid. I felt very sick to my stomach for many days. I couldn't eat. I wanted to talk to someone. I tried to talk to many people, but no one would listen to me. I wanted someone to just listen and not give me advice. No one could understand anymore. If I ever tried to talk to someone, I always ended up hearing their problems. My father had died and it seemed that no one even cared. I couldn't understand why the world wouldn't stop. I was out of place. My boyfriend broke up with me because I had changed so much. I didn't like to have fun anymore.

Helen finally found someone who, instead of judging her feelings, allowed her to discharge her guilt. She began to understand that others had not wanted to listen to her because they could not relate to the situation or her feelings; they did not want to add to her hurt. Her belief that "no one even cared" is shared by many others in their struggle with loss. However, there are other guilt feelings which are ill-defined, where the individual is not fully aware of the source of her guilt. Eileen explains:

> My most profound emotional reaction experienced was the guilt I felt shortly before and after my father's death. I expected to feel sad, and maybe to be depressed, but I couldn't understand why I felt guilty. Now that I can reflect back on those feelings, I think there were two factors involved in my guilt. First, I began to look back at the relationship I had with my father throughout my life. We had never been close, and I think as death approached I began to realize what I had missed and regretted it deeply. I began to wonder why I had wasted all that time arguing and defying him.
>
> Secondly, after his death, I think the guilt resulted from my not being there when he died. I felt the worst that could happen is that he could die alone. By the time we got to the hospital that morning he had already passed away. I felt I should have been there holding his hand, letting him know that I really did love him — I just never knew how to say it.

The feeling of guilt, as Eileen described, is deceptive because one is unable to define it clearly. This kind of circumstance demands much support and understanding, and in some instances requires the assistance of a professional counselor. That Helen became angry at the nurse for not removing the tubes from her father's body was clearly justifiable, inasmuch as anger is one of the most predictable reactions in such circumstances and loss frequently evokes anger in the bereaved. This is due to the fact that one usually perceives loss, and events accompanying it, as demeaning. Hostility and anger are the natural responses to the lowering of self-esteem (Layden, 1977). The source of anger is self-centeredness, but its expression is healthy. Because so many people have been taught that anger is improper, it frequently leads to guilt feelings once it is expressed. Anger is also associated with feelings of dependency, depression, and frustration, and should be considered a coping response. It is altogether acceptable to put anger into words; it's alright to say something is wrong, that one is hurting. As opposed to its violent expression, the normal discharge of anger is to be encouraged.

Anger, guilt, and depression are three emotions which are most commonly associated with relationship losses. We will examine them more closely in Part II in our discussion of the grief process. A final comment on guilt as experienced by Helen and Eileen: Both of these young adults were absent when their fathers died and felt guilty about it. This frequently happens, especially when one dies in the hospital instead of at home. Such ensuing guilt is *not* true cause-and-effect guilt, but it continues to be the source of much unnecessary suffering for people of all ages.

In addition to the feelings listed in Table 2, numerous descriptions of one's emotional state surrounding loss appeared in the data in handwritten form. They included self-portraits of bewilderment and deep hurt as suggested by words such as numbness, confusion, injustice, bitterness, apathy, and intense sadness. Others described feelings with words such as: suicidal, vengeful, aggressiveness, jealousy, deceitfulness, and anguish. Still others responded with "my 'everything' died" or "I was stunned even though the death was eventually expected."

These encounters with loss are major transition points in the lives of young people. They learn much about themselves and the fragility of life, developing new perceptions and meaning from existing interpersonal relationships. Cindy put it this way:

> Since this tragic death, I have treasured each day. I am thankful for each day I can live and am able to share fun times with my family and friends . . . When I know that someone has a problem and needs someone to talk to, I want to take the time to listen.

Physical Reactions

Hippocrates wrote: "The chief causes of disease are the most violent changes in what concerns our constitution and habits." Physical reactions of young adults to loss range from insomnia, headaches, and digestive disturbances to gaining or losing weight, dizziness, rashes, and general tiredness. In Table 3 we find that crying is a most significant physical response to loss, although males tend to repress their tears much more than females, believing it to be a show of strength if they do not cry. But crying is probably the most helpful physiological response for the body. It is a pathway of release for emotions gone awry. Crying must not merely be permitted, it must be encouraged.

Next to crying, sleeplessness, fatigue, and digestive disturbances are often combined in many physical responses to major loss. ("I had all the classics: stomachaches, insomnia, loss of appetite, and loss of concentration when it came to anything else but thinking about my girlfriend.") The extremes of this physical triad appear in vomiting, hospitalization, and the use of tranquilizers or barbiturates to induce relaxation and sleep. Illness and disease resulting from major loss are themselves cop-

Table 3.
PHYSICAL REACTIONS ACCOMPANYING LOSS
AS REPORTED BY 3,510 YOUNG ADULTS

Physical Reaction	Female	Male	Total	Percent Experiencing
1. Crying	1,730	497	2,227	63.4
2. Insomnia	843	442	1,285	36.6
3. Headache	896	252	1,148	32.7
4. Exhaustion	744	273	1,017	28.9
5. Digestive Disturbances	465	216	681	19.4
6. Weakness	416	232	648	18.4
7. Nausea	401	135	536	15.2
8. Numbness	231	50	281	8.0
9. Chills	151	50	201	5.7
10. Cold	142	41	183	5.2
11. Backache	101	46	147	4.1
12. Labored Breathing	68	32	100	2.8
13. Vomiting	71	24	95	2.7
14. Skin Rash	46	13	59	1.6
15. Other Physical Reactions*	202	131	333	9.4

*For a complete listing in this category write the author.

ing behaviors, expressions of emotional turmoil. Therefore, it is not unusual for old injuries or conditions to flare up as a part of one's loss response, or a present illness or disease to become worse as one is unable to respond to treatment. Young adults in this study also reported such physical problems as colitis, extreme weight loss, fever, stuttering, and uncontrollable bowel movements as a result of confrontations with loss. These physical responses pointedly demonstrate the acute impact of major loss experiences.

There are literally hundreds of aches, pains, and physical responses associated with loss. They vary in intensity, depending on the personality and biological characteristics of the individual, together with the unique perception of the loss event. Reports of backaches, "a lump in my stomach," a choking feeling in the throat, labored breathing, spasms in the abdomen, stiffness in the neck and back, and shaking capture the scope and diversity of the physical experiences which generally accompany major loss. A minority of young adults experience severe reactions: vomiting, vaginal infections, mandibular joint (jaw) syndrome, viral infections. Once again, we should be reminded that to experience some of these physical changes is quite normal. On the other hand, there are some individuals who experience relatively few physical symptoms.

Does this mean they do not care as much as someone else experiencing the same loss? Not at all. Individual behavior is a product of numerous biological and psychological variables, often quite difficult to assess.

Behavioral Reactions

Behavioral changes arising from major loss experiences can be examined on two levels: immediate changes due to shock and the onset of grief, and long-term change resulting from a different perception of life and loss based on having endured the process of adaptation. Therefore, behavioral responses include both the poignant and the bizarre. Generally, the shock and disbelief following news of the event bring normal routines to a halt. Specifically, time barriers no longer exist: conversations go on for hours concerning the loss, close friends and the bereaved may stay up all night unable to sleep, while other survivors have to travel hundreds of miles to their homes or to be with friends and relatives. Some individuals are so stunned that they are immobilized and withdraw to be alone. ("Then I wanted to cry. When I went to my room I was glad my roommate wasn't there because I didn't want to say anything.") Aimless behavior often predominates. Recall what Mike said in the anecdote on page 5 when his girlfriend told him she wanted to break up. "I hopped in my car and just started driving. . . . I drove around for another four hours."

Many people do not remember what they did during the early hours of grief, although they remember how they felt. Nick advises, "It is interesting that we really are not all that aware of what we are doing and feeling when we experience a great loss. My methods of coping are very clear to me now, but when each was being used, I was too wrapped up to recognize."

Later in the process of grieving, avoidance behavior is commonplace. Avoiding the site where the loss event took place is prevalent: refusing to return to the scene of the fire; an unwillingness to drive past the street corner where the accident happened; declining an invitation to attend a social event because one's ex-boyfriend may be in attendance. Going home on weekends or to visit friends in order to escape painful reminders is usual. Long after the death of a parent, some young adults who are back at school delay returning home on weekends or holidays because they fear facing an "empty" house.

Behavioral changes also take place, affecting the quality of work at school or on the job. It is not unusual for the depressed student to stay in bed and miss classes, especially in the morning. Not infrequently, those students suffering from major loss who do attend classes, or return to work on a part-time basis, are unable to concentrate. From an academic perspective, some individuals are so involved in their attempts to deal with loss that they are forced to drop courses and, in rare instances, withdraw from school. These conditions are exacerbated by instructors who interpret poor attendance or lack of enthusiasm as signs of irresponsibility or little interest in academic excellence. This misunderstanding, coupled with the deteriorating student-teacher relationship, introduces additional stress into the recovery process.

Long-term behavioral changes revolve around the particular meaning that is accorded to the loss by the individual. The death of a loved one frequently brings the person to confront feelings about his or her own death. ("Tom's unexpected death caused me to think long and deeply what it would be like if I was the one who had died, about how vulnerable each and every person is to death, and about the temporary condition we call 'life'.") Often new emphasis is attached to living and the daily routines normally taken for granted. Many loss events highlight the importance of honesty in dealing with dying, grieving, or support persons. Breakups usually include a feeling that dishonesty was involved. ("In addition, I felt she used me. I felt she just wanted to go to the senior prom with me, which she did, just to go to a senior prom.") The significance of honesty, trust, and openness is constantly seen as a key factor in resolving loss or complicating it. Much is learned about the importance of these virtues, and vows are made about practicing them to a greater degree in one's life. However, there is no hard evidence that this actually occurs. My personal view is that, in most instances, a more positive, enriched lifestyle results from young adult's confrontations, and loss and honesty become highly valued.

Chapter Three

COPING MECHANISMS

In the previous chapter we discussed the many types of loss encountered by young adults and their responses to such loss. In the following pages, analyses of coping mechanisms employed and differences in coping patterns will be examined. From both a social support and philosophical perspective this material can prove useful in comparing and evaluating one's own coping repertoire. At the same time, it will prove useful in understanding the psychological framework within which support from others is utilized.

> The support of my family helped me to cope with the loss of my father. Also, the support of my friends and getting back into my old routine to make things feel as normal as possible. I was glad to have school and other distractions to take time away from sitting around concentrating on my loss and feeling sorry for myself. I also feel my religious beliefs gave me a certain strength and courage.
>
> In my case, my father was sick with cancer for six months before his death. That was time to prepare—but I still believe that no matter how long you know its going to happen, the finality of it still is shocking and hurtful. My sister and I used to always ask each other, "How do you think you'll react when Dad actually is dead?" Well, we reacted just as expected. We all broke down and cried together—as a family—and I think that togetherness and comfort with each other was very important.

Margaret, a college senior

This discussion began many pages back by indicating that loss is a fact of life which accompanies all of us on our journey through growth and development. One question which derives logically from the material we have studied on loss is "How do young adults choose to cope?" While other sections of this book will examine coping with one's own loss experiences and helping others cope, it is of importance at this time to become familiar with the range of coping mechanisms employed during the grief process by one's peers. As in Margaret's case, your peers can provide much insight into confrontations with change and adjustment which will prove helpful in one's own processes of adjustment.

To begin with, everyone has died a thousand deaths by way of the rejections, disappointments, failures, and unexpected turns of life. Along the way, in dealing with these "little deaths," a variety of ways to manage the ensuing emotions and behaviors has been adopted. I do not mean to imply that this adoption of coping techniques is easy. It is not. On the contrary, depending upon early nurturing and how positive or negative our grief models were, as well as how they helped us understand the mixed emotions being experienced, the task of readjustment is widely diverse. Margaret's ability to cope with the death of her father is reflected in the diverse repertoire of coping resources to which she could turn: family, friends, religious beliefs, keeping busy at school, her open expression of emotion, and a sense of togetherness. Not everyone is as fortunate as Margaret in possessing such a broad assortment of resources.

Keeping in mind that there are as many coping styles as there are grievers, let us examine the coping techniques young adults most frequently utilize as shown in Table 4.

The list depicts a wide range of coping techniques, indicating great variation in how loss is resolved. It is important to realize that more often than not a combination of techniques or approaches is used in adapting to changes imposed by any particular loss. Each individual possesses a very personal coping style. Although acceptance of the loss is the first task to be undertaken in the adjustment process, talking about the event is the single most frequently utilized approach in coping with it. This has salient implications. For instance, who will listen? What will be talked about? What should listeners do? What should they say? Will the griever discuss deep personal feelings, and with whom? Do one's previous skills in communication influence how one grieves? These and other questions will be addressed below. The central point here is to call attention to the lofty position that dialogue holds in the resolution of loss. Regrettably, the shattering interpersonal exchanges between survivors and those who fail to understand the impact of that loss form a common and cruel element in the experience of young people.

We see here a paradox present in many loss experiences. Friends and loved ones are frequently both the object of grief and the keys to coping successfully. The loss of loved ones brings profound sorrow into our lives. At the same time, it is our friends and family who have established close ties with us, who try to understand our sorrow and behavior, but who will also be the subject of our tears when we are separated from them (Brantner, 1977).

Table 4.
COPING TECHNIQUES EMPLOYED BY 3,510 YOUNG ADULTS

Coping Techniques	Female	Male	Total	Percent Using
1. Talking about the Loss	1,733	781	2,514	71.6
2. Gradually Accepting It	1,359	754	2,113	60.1
3. Crying	1,587	403	1,990	56.6
4. Through Support of Friends	1,327	540	1,867	53.1
5. Time	1,180	631	1,811	51.5
6. By Keeping Busy	948	491	1,439	40.9
7. Thinking of All the Good Things	885	401	1,286	36.6
8. Through Family Support	807	338	1,145	32.6
9. Developing New Relationships	648	305	953	27.1
10. By Religious Beliefs	461	219	680	19.3
11. By Writing about My Feelings	526	141	667	19.0
12. Developing New Interests	386	189	575	16.3
13. Replacement	325	199	524	14.9
14. By Philosophical Beliefs	159	138	297	8.4
15. Learning to Relax My Body	139	94	233	6.6
16. By Drawing My Feelings	42	32	74	2.1
17. Coping by Other Means*	180	143	323	9.2

*For a complete listing in this category write the author.

SOCIAL SUPPORT SYSTEMS

Family, friends, counselors, clergy—people—play powerful roles in the resolution of loss in the lives of the young. In time of acute crisis, the bereaved need to talk to someone with whom they feel secure, support persons who will not cause feelings of self-consciousness or increased vulnerability as emotions surface. This concept is well illustrated by Jody:

> Between my husband and myself, we lost three grandparents within six weeks, *all suddenly.* At first I/we were numb, and after the third death, my feelings were anger at such an "unfair" sequence of events. I guess it was the days following the funerals that we, as families, could share and support each other. My husband and I talked, *and talked.* I feel that openness and *listening* can help people cope with their losses.

It is significant to note that when away at school, close friends most often provide for immediate needs, as Joyce indicates in talking about the day she broke up with her boyfriend. "I feel that my close friends were of most help to me in coping with this loss. They were very supportive of me and kept me going." Allie explains: "My boyfriend and people in my dorm helped me the night she died through just being there, not really saying much. My family and friends at home helped at the wake and funeral." Regardless of the nature of the loss, talking to another person about it is the most common and natural response to a crisis, whether the crisis develops suddenly or was expected. Available support persons are salient factors in the resolution of loss, especially if they possess strong listening skills.

Social support systems provide the following functions for young adults: (1) they act as a listening post to send messages about feelings, ideas, and decisions in an attempt to gauge *acceptance* of emotional behavior, (2) they provide a sharing of loss to unburden one's self, (3) they may act as a replacement for severed relationships, (4) they offer sources of motivation to continue with one's responsibilities and a strengthening of the self-image, and (5) they help one review the relationship with the person or object of loss. This review process, the recollection of memories, is a crucial factor in recovery and reinvestment in life, both during the early phase of the grief process and for months and years later. There is a need to plumb the depths of emotion in the delicate interaction between griever and support persons. It is frequently experiences with others that affect how the bereaved feel about themselves at any given time. Those in the company of others who are empathetic find a haven of security.

Time is another pivotal factor in young adult coping styles. When loss occurs, time loses its unidirectional flow; it stops, it drags. Day and night merge into one continuous time; normal circadian rhythm vanishes. Time has long been considered to be a key component in the resolution of loss. But the cliche, "time heals," is only partly true. Time can be a *negative* as well as a positive force—depending on the individual and the circumstances surrounding the loss. For most young adults, it brings healing and respite; for those who refuse to let go of the person from whom they are separated or whom they cannot give up, it brings additional pain. Failing to become fully involved in the reality of the situation nurtures the hurt for seemingly infinite periods of time. This happens when loss is continually denied. In this vein, it is important to understand that time does not always heal, particularly in losses which involve conflict concerning the person or object of loss *before* the actual loss occurred. Time often does become a healer when influenced by one's religious or philosophical stance, however.

RELIGIOUS AND PHILOSOPHICAL BELIEFS

Religious and philosophical beliefs are the bedrock on which acceptance of loss is commonly built. What seems to maintain a link to self-worth, giving a modicum of stability, is the degree of faith in a power outside of the self or the belief that the loss is a part of life and must be accepted. As one young adult remarked, "All you can do is have faith that God will get you through that loss when it occurs." Prayer is direct communication with God. Prayer, religion, and belief in God are utilized often in dealing with the deaths of loved ones and other relationship losses. One of every three young adults indicated turning to God as a valued way of coping with the death of a loved one. This is especially true if the deceased was a parent. The belief in an afterlife is especially helpful in accepting a death. Lynn, a sophomore, said:

> I went through this loss very alone. I knew that my father was happy because he was not here on earth with all the hate and suffering. Someday I would join him in heaven. I knew he was in heaven and I could now strive to get there. He was reunited with my mother, who was in heaven too.

One's relationship with God becomes a critical pathway for internal dialogue. Faith in a personal God is, for substantial numbers of young adults, a form of communication in which nothing is held back and from which peace ensues. The search for meaning in the death reaches a conclusion.

Belief in God, when shared by others who are grieving, is another factor in support through religion. This is suggested in Dennis's remarks.

> It was helpful for me, as a Christian, knowing that my grandad was a Christian. The support I felt from God was tremendous. I couldn't have made it without Him. Just knowing that my grandad was in a much better place, and that he didn't feel any pain, but was now with the Lord, was very comforting. Also, my toughest moments were a couple of weeks later when it really hit me that my grandad would not ever hold my child. I went through some emotional stress. But talking about it with my brother, who is also a Christian, was very comforting.

There is a special sense of security in the awareness of mutual beliefs, just as there is when one realizes that he or she is not alone with grief, and others are grieving in a similar fashion. Strength in numbers gives solace and comfort.

All of this does not mean that faith removes depression, shock, and all the other psychophysiological reactions. Not at all. But religious faith does provide a sound basis for acceptance of and working through grief. It is a window through which a sense of continuity emerges. The synthesis between faith and knowledge has a profound effect on the resolution of loss. Religion and immortality have always been means of transcending death (Kalish, 1985). However, the strength of belief, independent of a particular religious persuasion, is the force which helps one manage death fears and anxiety. This is dramatically illustrated by people who report having near-death experiences (Moody, 1975).

Philosophical approaches to coping with loss are utilized both in conjunction with religious beliefs as well as independently of religion per se. Writing on the death of a loved one, a music major closed with the following advice:

> I have discovered that it is good to learn to realize that everything happens for a particular reason, and usually it is a good reason, but you don't always see that right away. It also helps if you can accept everything that happens to you as just being part of life and developing you as a person, which makes it a lot easier to handle. All of this takes time, but it can be done if you put your mind to it.

This statement clarifies the potential value of recognizing loss as a developmental experience, as being unavoidable and ongoing, and yet also tragic and devastating. It also highlights the fact that major life changes and accompanying grief take time to assimilate and accept. It is this time period which demands determination from the griever and support persons.

Losses are lessons. Much learning can occur following a loss. It is frequently discussed and elaborately thought out as one forms a rationale for acceptance. In ending a love relationship, Jennifer wrote:

> One should be taught that even though you may lose something of great importance to you, life still goes on. Losses are a part of life and we must realize that nothing is immortal. We must accept the fact that losses *can* be overcome and compensated for in a separate domain of our lives. Never give up hope.

Such a philosophical stance becomes a strong force in the healing process.

That life goes on is illustrated in the large number of young adults who indicated the importance of keeping busy, of reengaging life. Keeping busy most commonly involved returning to study or work. This redirection of energies was especially useful in coping with feelings of self-pity, mild depression, and despair. *Plans* for getting back into the mainstream of living were critical in any approach to coping with change, as immobility and withdrawal reinforce feelings of helplessness and despair. Thus, specific activities engaged in included, but were not limited to, painting, reading, playing racquetball, attending concerts, doing volunteer work at the hospital, going shopping, visiting friends, and making preparations for an upcoming holiday. Planned activities of this type were important adjuncts to the coping repertoires of more than 40 percent of all young adults. The creative motif as a part of keeping busy is best illustrated by Bonnie's description of how writing helped her cope with the death of her next-door neighbor, whom she loved very much.

> The next semester, I took a Creative Writing course. While in the course I often wrote about him. We had to write a fairy tale; mine was about my past with him and waking up to realize that he was dead. The writing really helped me cope with his death, and my teacher seemed to understand this because she always wanted me to give more details about him.

Bonnie's writing not only allowed her to review her relationship with her friend and express her sadness and love, but it also helped her to realize that his death was real.

GEOGRAPHICAL CHANGE

Should one grieving a major loss get away from all the reminders through travel, vacationing, or simply by taking short trips to visit friends or family? This is a question which has long been discussed and debated over the years, the consensus being that seeking geographical change is akin to running away from problems. However, there is very little reliable evidence to support what is commonly agreed upon by the general public and some professional counselors. In an analysis of this issue based on the reports of young adults, it appears that geographical change, under certain conditions, is a very useful coping tool; it should not necessarily be considered as running away from problems.

Young people grieving the deaths of loved ones, for example, echoed the belief that being able to come back to school after several days was very helpful to their emotional disposition, as it forced them to take up their studies, become involved with responsibilities as students, and keep busy. Also, they came back to friends who, with few exceptions, were supportive. Their return to school gave them a respite from being in the familiar places which constantly reminded them of their deep hurt. Gloria gives us an example of the importance of geographical change in her return to visit friends at the college from which she had withdrawn.

> Returning to the college I went to before, to visit friends, was helpful because I was able to be away and discuss my father's death with someone other than my family or people in my hometown. It was real important for me to talk about my father. And even if I knew it might be awkward for people at first—I simply wanted them to acknowledge it and not pretend it didn't happen. Asking me questions about *how* it happened was too hard to talk about in the first few months—but not now.

Geographical change from school to home worked with other types of relationship losses which occurred on campus; many young adults indicated that the summer break was an excellent opportunity for a change of scene, a rest from the stresses of breakups or severed friendships. In an extreme move, relationship losses occurring at home were met in part by moving to another city, community, or state in order to ease painful reminders of separation. One of the most useful geographical changes involved leaving campus on weekends as a relief from the possible confrontation with the estranged partner and impending loneliness.

Obviously, geographical change (escape?) is not for everybody, particularly if one views the change as the solution to all problems. However, it does provide an opportunity for an unencumbered review of one's loss and plans for coping with it. It can also be a source for regaining energy, initiating new relationships, for encouragement from friends at home, and for motivation to continue to endure the pain involved in the transitional stages of grief. Those who seem to profit most from geographical change usually have relatively little hostility; are able to visit someone who is supportive; possess a relatively positive self-concept, given the existing circumstances; and do not harbor illusions that getting away from it all is the only way to cope. Again, one's perception of this change as a reprieve, not a cure-all, is essential. In my judgment, geographical change, when preceded by discussion of its purpose with a trusted friend or counselor, is quite effective as part of one's coping pattern.

Coping Opposites

There are also a number of coping techniques which seem to be contradictory but whose effect many young adults consider to be quite positive and helpful. I have called them "coping opposites," meaning that they are used by some young people, while others cope in a *completely opposite* manner. The distinction is strictly an individual preference, assisting the particular person's adjustment and conflict of emotions. They are opposing behaviors which facilitate healing. For example, after the breakup of a love relationship, the question arises as to whether to continue being "just friends." Many young adults said that completely avoiding the ex-boyfriend or ex-girlfriend was essential in coping, although others insisted that being able to talk with one another was equally necessary. In the latter instance, dialogue constitutes a way of reducing anxiety and complete rejection. However, those who believed that avoidance was essential felt that in order to make a new start they could not be reminded of their loss by seeing and talking to the other person again and again.

In dealing with the death of a loved one, visiting the cemetery or not depends upon individual needs and interpretations of the symbolic meaning of such an act. One person may view the visit as a way of paying respect and remembering the deceased, while another may see it as the path to opening old wounds and causing new emotional hurt.

As indicated earlier, we frequently hear the phrase, "Time heals all." This is probably true for many people, but not according to Tom, who said, "I can only adjust to the loss over time. I won't completely heal." Most individuals see time as a healer, others do not. Another coping opposite is seen in a minority of young adults who said they dealt with some losses alone, without help from others. This was usually because they did not think others would understand, or they were too embarrassed to seek assistance. However, the vast majority express the belief that friends and family pulled them through the critical periods of grief. Without the love and care of others, they were convinced they could not have come through the loss as well as they did. These and other coping opposites capture the complexity of utilization of techniques based on their individual meaning for the young adult.

PROFESSIONAL HELP

Young adults are not afraid to seek professional help. They turn to the college counseling centers, which are a part of student services available on most campuses, or to community mental health centers. A few seek out trusted teachers, whom they judge to be experienced in helping other students and whose reputations have grown because they are known as being "student-centered." These resources, I regret to say, are in the minority. Psychologists and psychiatrists also play a contributing role in the coping process. And last, but not least, are the clergy. Often young adults turn to these professionals when depression has not lifted and when they feel their state is hopeless from other standpoints.

It takes courage to seek professional help, especially with the stigma that still prevails about mental illness. But acknowledging the need for professional assistance is extremely important, particularly if one has had a history of emotional problems, feels isolated with no one to turn to, has repeated bouts of depression, or has become dependent on a drug. Loss precipitates behaviors in some young adults which only professionals can fully understand; and, because they understand both the person and the problem, professionals are often able to assist in the transitions which must be made on campus on in the community.

NONADAPTIVE COPING BEHAVIORS

Alcohol, the number one drug of choice, plays a surprisingly strong role in the confrontation with loss for some young adults. In conjunction with the alcoholization of the country, the rise of "coping mechanism drinking" has increased as a significant way to deal with anxiety (Parry et al., 1973). Alcohol has long been used to escape emotional discomfort and pain. It is used commonly in coping with separation anxiety. Frequently, the grieving young adult is invited to drink by well-meaning friends or roommates "to forget what has happened." The most common scenario is the drinking bout which follows the breakup of a love relationship or the failure of an examination or a course. Attempting to give solace and comfort to the individual in some way, friends take the young person on a tour of bars and restaurants with the goal of becoming intoxicated. In my interviews with bartenders, they agree that sudden change, failure, and loneliness resulting from loss experiences often are antecedents to alcohol abuse. Peers also bring social pressure to drink—a key factor for many people in their abuse of the drug (Mecca, 1980).

The use of alcohol to deaden the emotional pain of separation or rejection is prolonged in some situations, causing additional problems. On returning to school after the summer break, Cathy was shocked by the sudden and callous way her boyfriend told her that he didn't want to see her again. She writes:

> I also started to drink very heavily. For the first month of school, I was out every night downtown or at the campus pub—even on Sundays. Everyone kept telling me they could not believe how well I was coping. . . . Also, during that month I did not eat at all. Every time I tried to eat I would get really sick to my stomach and sometimes I got headaches, probably from not eating or being hung over.

The use of alcohol or other drugs seems to be an accepted way of coping with loss, although most young adults eventually realize it simply is time consuming and does not eliminate the reality of loss. It is a temporary, stop-gap measure at best.

Alcohol may also be used as a release for repressed emotions, particularly anger, as Don indicates in the following reaction to his grandmother's death:

> I continued to hold my feelings in, until one night when I had been drinking with close friends and relatives. After a number of beers, I began to cry uncontrollably. I explained everything to my friends and they listened carefully and quietly. However, after this night I returned to holding things in. It became a problem that I dealt with by myself. I realized that my grandmother was satisfied and peaceful in her death. But I could never understand why I never cried unless I was drunk. . . . On occasion, alcohol became a form of coping mechanism for me. I used it as an excuse for breaking down on occasion. I now realize how often I did this.

It is well-known that alcohol releases inhibitions, allowing one to speak and act with very little restraint or self-control. Men, in particular, who suppress feelings, seem to act out in their behavior what has been held in for long periods of time.

Alcohol or any other drug does nothing to remove the source of pain. It does help to modify symptoms of emotional discomfort, or it would not be called on as frequently as it is. Its transitory effect is to numb pain and provide temporary relief. However, one cannot escape discomfort indefinitely. It is the ransom normally due the emotional investment made in others. What is so difficult to overcome is the belief that the pain will *never* end and that adjustment is impossible. It is during that critical period that alcohol replaces people as a way to help the bereaved endure. The temptation of immediate relief is understandable, but it is the caring other who facilitates a lasting adjustment.

In addition to excessive use of alcohol, other nonadaptive coping behaviors were employed by a small minority of young adults. They included suppression of emotions, trying to be "strong for others," blaming others, sleeping to escape, hating the object of loss, "chasing other women," quickly starting a new romance, and refusing to accept that the loss occurred. Other health-risk behaviors included refusing to eat, overeating, smoking marijuana, and using tobacco.

COMMUNICATING HURT

In an assessment of the meaning of each coping technique, quite frequently the importance of communicating feelings to others is brought out. At some point, most people seek ways to share their oppressive thoughts with others. The consistent need to talk about what has occurred with someone trusted, someone who is a friend or a family member, commonly surfaces. Depending on the particular loss, the quality of relationships with others, and timing of the situation, a trusted person is sought out. Occasionally, a stranger becomes the listener on a long train, bus, or plane ride. The anonymity provided by a stranger reduces the shame and embarrassment that one feels following a loss. But the goal is clear: letting others know what is happening inside. One searches to find someone who might grasp his or her dilemma, who will acknowledge the gravity of the loss and what it means. Hopefully, the listener will enter into the sorrowful world of the bereaved and see the devastation that has occurred. One can exclaim, "Look what has happened to me!" This is not boasting. Rather, it is a need to share the feeling and dimensions of personal confrontation.

There are other ways of communicating feelings, of letting out pain which seeks release. The written word often becomes a medium of expression, a channel through which release from sorrow begins. Letters to close friends or relatives play critical and healthy therapeutic roles as they allow for a more searching and thoughtful means of conveying emotion. Denise, a junior, described it this way as she looked back on the severed relationship with her boyfriend: "I have a friend in another school. I wrote to her and explained the situation to her. By writing to my friend, I was able to realize for myself that it's gone and there is nothing I can do to get it back." Diaries give complete privacy, and are available day or night depending on when one feels the urge to express emotion. Putting thoughts on paper assists in accepting, venting, and for some, clarifying their position.

An excellent means of communicating feelings is found in writing poems. Poems usually focus on sorrow, the object of loss, or specific memories. The poem not only allows both friends and strangers to learn how the bereaved person feels but stands as a public tribute of the writer's love. Writing music fulfills similar functions: a song tells the world how the person is struggling with the loss; what the loss means to her; how the object of loss will never be forgotten.

Listening to music with lyrics that have special meaning for the bereaved person reinforces beliefs and provides respite by clarifying thoughts and sometimes introducing options to cope with the dilemma. In this instance, someone else is speaking for the griever. Listening to music is also a means of needed relaxation.

Drawing and painting have always been special ways to transmit thoughts and feelings. In coping with loss, these techniques are utilized to provide a loving memorial to deliver lasting messages, to give meaning to loss, or simply to provide an outlet for tension and anxiety. These modes of expression possess important therapeutic potential by recreating happy memories and channelling energies into constructive pursuits. Later in the grief process, the process of redirecting energy, of reawakening latent interests, is a crucial step in recovery from loss.

THIRD-LEVEL COPING RESPONSES

Thus far we have examined two broad levels of coping responses: primary or personal techniques such as religious beliefs, writing, drawing, drinking, and keeping busy; and responses which evolve from the available social support network represented by the freedom to express feelings in a nonjudgmental environment. These two response levels vary according to the personal habits, idiosyncracies, and learned reactions to stress, as well as the quality of interpersonal relationships an individual enjoys with support persons.

There appears to be a third set of responses which are often unplanned for and generally not under the control of the grieving person. Nonetheless, these responses have a particularly strong impact on grief work and play a major role in resolving loss so that one is able to go on with life. These coping responses may be looked on as chance occurrences. For example, a young woman who was expecting a child learned that her best friend died very suddenly. Their friendship had been very strong and the death was deeply disturbing to her. The turning point in her grief came with the birth of her daughter three months later. "My baby seems to be a sign of her continued life," she said. "She was a girl (baby) and helped to console me." This birth was the single, most influential force in the acceptance of the death for this young woman. Her new baby was a symbol of the endless chain in the continuity of life.

For some grievers, assistance may be found in the simple form of a change in the weather. ("Being outside in spring-like weather, it was very sunny outside that week, helped to boost my mood at this time.") Other young adults may hear a song on the radio which sends them a specific message. For example, there was a recent popular song entitled, "I Will Survive." Sometimes, what seems to be an insignificant comment possesses great meaning for a survivor. ("One of my relatives made a point of mentioning that the deceased person had gotten a chance to eat my homemade soup, made when I last saw her, before she died. This meant much to me.") There are other specific remarks made by support persons which young people indicate helped them cope with the deaths of loved ones or the breakup of a love relationship. Here are some examples, with explanatory notes, as written by respondents.

1. It's time to give him back to God.
2. The love one holds for others never dies. It lives on in those he has loved. ("This is a quote I had heard that was the real clincher to resting my hurt and loss.")
3. A priest said, "If God could forgive me, why could I not forgive myself?"
4. She was so special to everyone and everyone will always remember her.
5. I'm sorry. She's finally at the end of all her pain. She's peaceful and God ended her misery.
6. Life goes on and so will you and me and everyone else. ("This was so crude at the time. It was a shock of reality because I was living in my own little world.")

Keep in mind, that these and other comments were helpful in the coping patterns of some young adults—but they were meaningless to others. The timing of these comments was another uncontrollable factor, one which has great impact on how they are received. With some individuals, these same comments, heard at the wrong time, would be sources of anger and additional hurt.

A large number of paranormal experiences, a subject we will examine in Part II, provide the basis for the acceptance of deaths of loved ones and are key experiences in changing the emotional outlook of young adults. Whether such experiences are figments of the imagination, purely coincidental, supernatural in origin, or simply hallucinations is irrelevant; they heavily influence, usually in a very positive way, how one copes with loss.

As we become aware of the large number of coping techniques which can be brought into use when loss occurs, it is important to consider that those not frequently used are as significant as those commonly used. In our understanding of how others cope we need first to recognize that a combination of techniques is most effective in aiding the griever. And it is not unusual that the griever's skills and interests are the sources for revitalizing lost self-esteem and overcoming injury and hurt. We will examine coping options more fully in the next section. But now let us turn to a critical factor which complicates the adjustment to loss.

NEEDED: A BALANCE OF DEPENDENCE AND INDEPENDENCE

> I think I committed too much of myself in this relationship and in doing this I lost much of my self-identity. Thus when the relationship ended I was lost and disoriented. When I do meet someone again and I fall in love, I'm going to make sure that I and the other person do not lose our own identities. I think that it is possible to have a loving relationship and still maintain your identity.
>
> Megan, a sophomore

Each person possesses dependency needs; one learns out of necessity to be dependent very early in life. Children, must look to parents or other adults to provide food, clothing, and shelter. As they grow older, their needs for education and financial support for education become important necessities. Along the way, one becomes dependent on the emotional support of family and friends in establishing an identity. All of this is quite healthy mental growth but ideally there should be increasing independence and a renewed sense of self-direction as one matures, assumes responsibilities, and makes commitments to others. This is crucial in the development of a positive self-concept and in acquiring the coping skills to deal with a variety of life changes.

On the other hand, how much we depend on others is the result of our self-image, instincts, what we believe our commitment to others in various relationships should be, and whether those who love us are willing to let go and give us a chance to make mistakes and become self-sufficient. How we feel others are perceiving us and our behavior is also involved, as peer pressure forces changes in behavior in order to accommodate others. How far we go in this accommodation is a crucial decision, one which many have difficulty making. There is always the urge to cling to the advantages of dependency while concurrently seeking the freedom from authority and the independence of adulthood. Additional conflict occurs when the emotional needs of parents to maintain a child-parent relationship influence the young adult to maintain the status quo. This pathological pattern forestalls or eliminates the normal change in relationships that must occur if we are to reach the goal of *interdependence* and reduce the creeping lack of self-confidence which destroys the ability to deal with change.

For parents or guardians it is difficult to allow young people to make the same mistakes and suffer the same consequences they themselves have already experienced. The tendency among parents is to spare children the wounds of growing up, to prevent them from learning the hard way. When one is loved or when one loves others it is easy to develop a dependence if love does not allow others to be individuals and grow. It is common to lose one's sense of independence or to fail to understand the need of others for independence. When love or fear motivates and blinds by allowing others to do too much one grows comfortable without having to be responsible.

When dependent on another person or object, one develops a false sense of security. In doing so, he or she loses the sense of inner security. In the dependent relationship we give up our power to grow; our life rises or falls based on another's behavior. It leads one to expect so much from the outside that the tendency is to forget to develop inner resources. Looking back on a breakup that caused a very intense grief response, Sarah states:

> I feel the best way to cope with the loss of a love relationship is to keep your options open. You should never become so totally engrossed in a relationship that, if it ends, you have no "out," nobody or nowhere to turn. Keeping busy afterwards and confronting the fact that the relationship won't last forever (before it ends) is of great help.

How do we keep our options open? *By recognizing first that happiness and self-worth basically come from within oneself* not from searching for security in another person. We need to rely primarily on the self and secondarily on others, fashioning personal goals, developing strengths, and becoming aware of weaknesses if we are to maintain a sense of power and control over our lives. This is not incompatible with love or marriage, as there is in marriage a merging but not a loss of individuality. There is also a need to define ourselves even as we are changed by relationships; although committed to others, we must still grow and develop individually. Couples cannot flourish along identical lines, nor do they possess the same security or risk needs. Unconditional love actually *promotes* individual growth in the other. Conditional love gives rise to dependency.

Most young adults find themselves fluctuating between their yearning to be independent and their practical needs to be dependent on their parents. At times this becomes an awesome predicament for both children and parents alike. When major loss occurs, the feeling that one should face it alone is often in opposition to seeking support needed during such experiences. Members of both sexes must understand that it is important for young and old alike to seek others with whom they can share emotions and beliefs at various times. At the very least, it is essential to find peers who will enter into one's world of grief. To be interdependent—*providing for each other in time of crisis*—is sound thinking, not a sign of a still-present early childhood dependency. Remember: a balance between dependence and independence, one of the signs of emotional maturity, means to recognize that there are times when *each person needs another human being to see her through the dark hours of life*. It is all right to revert back to a parent-child type of relationship temporarily. Most of us need permission to be childlike in our grief. We can be free to use another's strength and, in time, reciprocate that strength when our friend is in need.

In many nongrief relationships, however, individuals often depend on others to supply them with so much attention, affection, and approval that they forfeit their independence. There is a loss of that delicate balance between dependence and independence. As Megan stated earlier, there is a sense of loss of identity because we overidentify with other persons who meet most of our needs. There are some psychiatrists who are convinced that one partner tends to distort the individuality and thwart needs of the other in a love relationship in order to meet his or her own needs. Nobody has every need met and is worry-free, but dependence on others seems to eliminate worries about "who I am and where I'm going," at least temporarily. In the long run, destructive dependencies are costly to the development of coping skills.

Enter separation. Enter divorce. Enter death. What happens when the overdependent relationship is severed? In that case, there is an additional task that must be undertaken: one has to reestablish her identity which was lost in the other, learning new skills and a sense of self-worth.

The bereaved is at once faced not only with separation but also with regaining a sense of independence and assuming responsibilities the other had fulfilled. Furthermore, overdependence usually results in intense anger—often at the person who left and always at the one perceived as responsible for the separation. When a death is perceived as desertion, which often occurs, anger is the essential protest (Raphael, 1984). Such anger may be of long-term duration. The bereaved are despondent and doubtful, never imagining they could feel so insecure.

If you are assisting a friend to cope with a broken relationship, it will help in order to understand the intensity of his or her responses to recognize just how dependent the person had become and that there is a near total collapse of his or her sense of self. The latter is inescapable; the former can be modified if the griever *believes* it is important to do so. You can help point out and encourage the development of self-sufficient behaviors. Even though one may have learned overdependence in relationships as a child and adolescent, that tendency can be slowly reversed. Young adults frequently need independence *before* going off to school and *during* their years when away at school. Such advance preparation will be invaluable to them later in life.

Overdependency limits the development of skills, interests, and other enriching relationships. It causes one's world to shrink without notice— until the relationship is severed. Then, and only then, is vulnerability exposed, and the person realizes how ill-prepared he or she is to deal with the real world. There are many widows and widowers who allowed their loved ones to do too much in their lives, only to realize too late how much more difficult their recovery has been because of undeveloped skills, a sense of inadequacy, and not having maintained a modicum of independence. The trap is real and a very common experience with the young adult involved in the breakup of a love relationship.

After the breakup of a love relationship, most people realize just how destructive their overdependence has been. Here are some samples of what young adults say:

> In my situation I could have been better prepared if I hadn't realied so heavily on him to make me a whole person. Realizing your self-importance and living for *you* first would better prepare you to go on without the person you lose.

> Try not to be so dependent on the one you love. I spent all my time with her and did everything for her. Then when we separated I had nothing left from the relationship and the love I had received for so long.

> It was only through this experience that I am prepared if it should ever happen again. I learned that I was too dependent on one person for my existence; I have also learned to be my own person. I don't think I will be that vulnerable again and my future relationships will be better.

In a sense, one becomes addicted to another person, and nondrug addictions can cause the physical pain of withdrawal just as cutting off one's drug supply would. The big question remains: how does one reduce the overdependence before it becomes destructive? The answer lies in increasing one's level of self-awareness and self-esteem, and in communicating to the other partner the need for balance within the relationship. It is just such an open exchange about mutual growth and independence which will enrich any relationship.

When death intervenes in an overdependent relationship the survivor is especially vulnerable because of the removal of the primary support system upon which he or she always relied. The sense of total inadequacy and powerlessness that follows in the wake of loss increases chaos and panic; one retreats from reality. To some extent this should be expected and tolerated. However, the prolongation of this retreat must be carefully monitored if one is to begin the long journey of building a new world in recovery. An additional burden may be imposed when the overdependent survivor is expected to provide support for other family members. This occurs when the father dies and the teenage son is expected to assume the role and responsibilities of the deceased parent; or the mother dies and the daughter is expected to assume the motherly role.

The overdependent child-parent relationship with its negative consequences for the maturation of the child is well documented in the literature on child development. It has also been suggested that overdependency coupled with ambivalence complicates the resolution of loss in children's and adult's grief work (Rando, 1984; Raphael, 1983; Freud, 1959). The same holds true for the adolescent and young adult. Preexisting ambivalent relationships with the deceased loved one and excessive dependency on that person may cause severe adjustment problems. When the overdependent parent-child relationship carries forward into late adolescence and early adulthood the result in the face of death is intensified fear and anger often resulting in long-term adjustment problems (Parkes and Weiss, 1983). Losses of material goods, failures in school subjects, loss of a job or an ability, and other major life changes are all sources of fear and apprehension in the overdependent individual.

A word of caution: let's not forget that being too independent can also have equally damaging consequences for grievers. People who are totally independent of a loved one may believe that they must cope alone or risk the stigma of being weak. If they have learned to be totally self-sufficient in their lives, a profound threat may develop as they realize that they are unable to control death and other major loss-events in life. They will need supporting others willing to be available to them at opportune times, for such strong independence obviously limits the number of opportunities the griever will have for venting frustrations and sharing emotions. Mount (1983) suggests that America's emphasis is on individualism and on an outlook in which one's worth is measured first by the number of one's achievements, thus exacerbating the fear of death. The emergence of the narcissistic personality, coupled with the absence of a sense of community with others, leaves one impotent and unprepared to deal with the major crises of life.

So far, we have examined the relationship of loss experiences to life experiences and the impact of major loss on the lives of youth: its devastating emotional and physical aspects, the behavioral changes it necessitates, its growth potential, and the variability of coping techniques employed to manage it. In Part II, we turn now to putting theory into practice. We will attempt to show that each person can influence how he or she copes with any major loss, and that in the final analysis, we can choose to persist in the resolution of loss or succumb to the temptation to withdraw to a self-imposed exile.

FACES OF DEATH

Death has many faces and each one we view differently. They range from the very distant face whose features are hazy to the recognizable face and finally the one we feel we know.

To me, the distant face involves people we don't know. It looms in the back of our mind as we read the obituaries or hear of an accident involving people we've never heard of. A name no longer exists or a space is now empty at their table is all that we can fathom.

The face with the recognizable features is the one we see at the funeral of our best friend's father or your great Aunt Fan's wake. Oh, here is the person we've heard so much about. So this is what she looked like or she was the one Mommy had to dress every morning and feed. We are able to associate death with a body that we knew was alive.

Finally, there is the face that is seen almost too clearly. This "death" stands by us at our mother's wake. This "death" walks with us down the aisle at our father's funeral mass. And this "death" holds our hand at the grave site of our spouse. This face of death looks us in the eye at the time of our greatest loss. It confronts us when we must confront the fact that, "Mother is gone, Dad is no longer, my husband is dead." This face is present, is with us, when we are the closest to death — the survivor.

This is my view of death. The idea is always there, always in the back of my mind right beside "How will I cope? What will I do when I am the survivor?"

MARY LOUISE WHALEN
College Student

Part II

MANAGING YOUR OWN GRIEF

There can be no transforming of darkness into light and of apathy into movement without emotion.

CARL JUNG

In this sad world of ours, sorrow comes to all. . . . You cannot now realize that you will ever feel better. . . . And yet this is a mistake. You are sure to be happy again.

A. LINCOLN
(Three of Lincoln's children
preceded him in death:
Thomas, age 18, William,
age 11, and Edward, age 4).

Chapter Four

WHY GRIEF?

The minister talked about those things about a person which are visible and invisible. Even though Grandma is dead and we no longer have those visible and tangible aspects, we will always have those invisible things. We can remember what she gave us and how she influenced us through her love and the memories we have of her. These invisible things are extremely important because in so many ways, she will live on in us. This idea really helped me cope with her death.

Alicia, age 21

There are very few forms of behavior which are more misunderstood than the human response to loss. However, the grief process marks the beginning of adjustment to each of the lifelong series of changes which everyone undergoes. It is a central process of adaptation with most unique individual themes; seldom is it considered a tool for self-understanding, a gift of transition, or a medium through which one's personal world is reborn. It is all that and more, as we shall examine in this chapter. First, in our journey of managing grief several reasons are suggested for why it must be studied. Then, an analysis of the process of letting go is presented, followed by discussion of paranormal experiences of the bereaved which are integral parts of grieving for many individuals.

Our ability to adapt to death and loss is an essential skill in living and a balancing factor in being able to rise above our losses in order to continue to exist and grow. This is the constant theme of aging: one has to learn to confront change in relation to one's innate capacities. The same holds true in any stage of life-span development, for dramatic change is usually accompanied by the universal experience of grief. Learning to live with grief in its many disguises will enhance the quality of life (Cassem, 1975; Simos, 1979); it permits us to regain our emotional balance. How we proceed in the process of adaptation is the basis for healthy or complicated life adjustment. Even though our expectations for coping well often outstrip reality, knowing how we may react under crisis circumstances is valuable in regulating behavior when the time comes as well as for gaining insight into the process of adaptation to loss through the normal channels of mourning.

There are five basic reasons why everyone should become familiar with the dynamics of the grief response. First, there is ample evidence to indicate that unresolved grief has negative health implications (Greenblatt, 1978; Parkes, 1972; Lindemann, 1944; Markusen and Fulton, 1971). Mortality rates of bereaved people are often higher than comparative groups (Rees and Lutkins, 1967; Parkes, Benjamin and Fitzgerald, 1969). Many individuals do experience one or more negative psychological or behavioral outcomes. In this vein, we need to rid ourselves of the still predominant notion that the release of emotion means we are not "strong" in the face of tragedy. Second, we must firmly establish an awareness of the normalcy of the grief response, that emotional trauma is not unusual, and that grieving is a healing force that all must experience when the expected course of life no longer meets our hoped for plan. A third reason for being aware of the grief process is the understanding that the dying are grieving just as their survivors are (except their grief revolves around the loss of many people, not just one person), and they must redefine their personal relationships. We can assist them in their grief work if we can understand how they accomplish such a redefinition in their process of adapting to a vastly different world. Fourth, an understanding of the nature of grief is essential if we are to help our loved ones (and we *shall* all have that opportunity) in their hour of need. Becoming knowledgeable about the depth and meaning of the experience, the types of feelings confronted, and the variability of expression can assist in creating viable support systems for them. How this can be accomplished will be the subject of the final section of this book.

Finally, knowledge about the grief process is applicable not only in supporting others coping with the death of a loved one but also to assist in confronting other major transitions which are part of life. Divorce, separation, illness, material losses, and so many other sudden changes in our lives bring a need to understand the variety of ways that we can cope with and express hidden feelings. "Homesickness is a form of grieving and responds to the same treatment in psychological therapy" (Kavanaugh, 1974, p. 82). We must confront change; there are no alternatives except to suffer unnecessarily. Changes will take place in our lives whether we want them to or not; we have no choices here. But we can choose how to react to such change and how to best utilize our knowledge of how to cope with adversity. *We can ultimately prevail over any loss.* History testifies to the universal truth of this experience.

A Chinese proverb puts the importance of understanding grief in perspective: "You cannot prevent the birds of sorrow from flying over your head, but you can prevent them from building nests in your hair." The emphasis in the proverb is on *you.* The first message is: grief is inevitable. The second is: each individual can prevent extreme, unnecessary suffering. How? By recognizing and accepting that loss is continuous and that hurt and sadness necessarily follow major losses. Furthermore, we must see that grief is the *natural* response to letting go of someone we love very much or something cherished. It is not something dreadful. *Life is a matter of our letting go and beginning again.* If we commit ourselves emotionally to a person, place, object, or belief—when that which was held dear is lost—grief must follow. Grief is an integral part of love which helps us to gently let go or, if we fight it, to forever struggle with ourselves and memories of past transgressions. But why is the typical reaction to major loss that of grief? Because grieving is the only proven means of recovering emotional stability and integrating major loss into life. The process allows for the natural emergence of disagreement with the change that has been dictated. Grief permits one to rail against the suspected injustice.

Generally, the evidence of experience suggests that people usually grow in their ability to cope with loss (Downey, 1983; Bertman, 1983). There are some people, of course, who regress, who learn little from their confrontation, depending on their previous experiences in developing coping skills and beliefs about loss. This is why it is so important to have loving guidance from those who themselves have suffered and loved under stress. Love is a powerful force in resolving loss, but it is relegated to a lesser role by too many lay and professional persons. For it is the love of self and others which helps one to begin anew, and it is this same love that one must nurture on the road to recovery. Said scientist-philosopher Pierre Teilhard de Chardin: "When man reclaims this energy source, for the second time he will have discovered fire."

Where do we acquire our coping responses and our self-love? Just as love is a learned behavior, so too are our coping responses. We learn them from society in general and from parents and experience in particular. We have to experience some things in order to understand and learn from them. Only through loss experiences as children, and the methods learned then to deal with them, is the stage set for the manner chosen to cope with major loss as one ages. Ask yourself: who were your grief models? Your answer may help you understand why you refuse to let your feelings flow freely, why you may have repressed certain emotions, and why you fear having someone see you cry. Perhaps you were ridiculed as a child because you were sad over what some adult thought was an insignificant loss. Sometimes our grief models have exerted undue pressure on us to behave in a stoical manner by their repetition of the notion that "big boys (or big girls) don't cry or get angry." But crying and anger are means by which many losses can be dealt with so do not be ashamed of such responses. In reality, crying is one of the most common ways of venting anger (Madow, 1972). Remember, crisis-solving behavior depends on how we developed our coping skills and managed past losses, although this does not necessarily mean we are hopelessly locked into the same pattern of responses. With help, our coping responses can become more effective.

THE GRIEF PROCESS

> I don't feel there is any way to be fully prepared for death. It is always a shock. But after it does happen, my best advice is to accept it and deal with it realistically.

> Matt, a junior

If grief is to eventually become a life-enhancing force, begin the search by finding out all you can about the process which always follows any meaningful loss. The word conjures up many different images for people. Most often it appears in a negative context: associated with death and commonly thought to be a sign of weakness of character. However, grief is an integral part of the ebb and flow of life. Learning about it is not going to be useful to us just once or twice in a lifetime. The process is occurring daily in someone at work, school, or in our circle of friends; it is within and around us. Learning about it can only result in a greater appreciation for the power each of us possess to endure.

Bereavement, Mourning and Grief

These three words convey an assortment of messages about death and other loss-events which vary in meaning, depending on the individuals using them. Sometimes they are used interchangeably in conversations when, in fact, they possess quite different meanings. Defining these commonly used words will be useful in understanding the process of adapting to major loss.

Bereavement refers to the fact that one has been deprived of, lost, or experienced the removal of a person or object from her personal world; something has been taken away. If you lose your wallet, if you lose your home by fire, or if an heirloom is stolen, you are bereaved of those objects. When a loved one dies, you are bereaved of that person. Bereavement, then, is the objective consequence of loss. It is the state of having experienced a loss. Notably, not every bereavement necessitates a grief response. There are objects lost which mean very little to us—a pencil, an old hat, or a pair of broken sunglasses. But one who has experienced the breakup of a love relationship, a divorce, or a severed friendship is a bereaved person.

Mourning refers to the cultural or ethnic patterns of responses associated with bereavement. These traditional patterned responses vary from culture to culture and oftentimes even within the subculture of a single country. After a death, mourning customs may dictate wearing a black arm band or specific mourning clothes, or it may include following a specific ritual. In these cases, the special dress signals others to approach us as someone in grief, not as just an ordinary member of society.

Grief is the process by which one "works through" or experiences emotion after a significant loss has taken place. It is commonly defined as the *normal* reaction, a positive emotional and physical response, to any meaningful loss. Grief is as automatic as eating, sleeping and breathing (Westberg, 1971). It includes all the uniquely individual responses we experience in coping with massive change. This process is the predictable response to the drastic altering of relationships with the lost person. It is the result of truly cherishing an object or place. Therefore, grief comes in many forms and follows the developmental and situational losses which occur throughout life. Accordingly, we are affected socially and spiritually as well as emotionally and physically.

Each of us is subject to death and rebirth, to giving up or losing many cherished people, places, or things during our lifetime. We will grieve our own death as we become aware of our own dying. Consider the hours, days or months that were spent lamenting about, adapting to, and coping with the new as it overcame the old. These were times of grief—grief we conveniently forget and from which we frequently fail to learn. Recall in the first section of this book the list of the types of losses that some have said were major losses in their lives. All these persons searched for ways to adapt to transitions in living, a way to adjust to dramatic change. This is the meaning of grief: a powerful agent for meeting change. Grief most frequently follows immediately after loss occurs although it may be delayed. Some people are able to deny their feelings for a period of time, but this only delays grief work which must be done if they are to become fully functioning again. Grief, delayed or not, can last for a short period of time, or it can go on for years. For example, sudden deaths from accidents have shown to prolong grief in survivors from four to seven years (Lehman and Wortman, 1985). Grief can be extremely intense or relatively mild; it can be sporadic or continuous. The course it follows varies greatly from one person to another and even within a given person from one occasion to another. Meg, a senior, expresses her long-term grief:

> My brother died 5 years ago from a chronic disease. He was 2 years older than I, and was a very important part of my life. Although his death was expected, it was a shock to all of us and was difficult to accept. Our family was close and always gave support, and friends shared our loss. I still have difficulty coping with his loss. I wish I knew how to cope.

Frequently, grief begins long before a death occurs, such as with Meg's brother when there is a forewarning of loss. Grief may begin before the divorce is final, before the geographical move is made, before the eviction occurs, or the separation from loved ones happens. This is referred to as anticipatory grief. Anticipatory grief is generally healthy and can be shared with friends in whom you have full confidence. It can be unhealthy if it results in the absence of a family member from the bedside of a dying person due to a premature "letting go" (Fulton and Fulton 1971). We may experience many emotions which need to be discussed with a trusted friend; do not stifle them. These responses are often shared by the dying person and other family members and are very similar to those which occur after the death of a loved one (Kubler-Ross, 1969; Fulton and Gottesman, 1980). Although many emotions can be involved in anticipatory grieving the death of a loved one, there is often depression, increased concern for the dying person, rehearsing the death, and attempts to begin adjusting to the consequences of the death (Fulton and Fulton, 1971). We may need to find someone who will listen to us air our grievances, one who will not blame or trivialize our feelings. Beginning the necessary grief work *before* the major loss is final is appropriate, if we feel the need to do so. It is not a sign that we cannot cope with the inevitable or that we are unable to deal with hardship if we discuss our grief openly. This may well assist us in the final acceptance of loss. Anticipatory grief is a sign that one is coping with a major change in a very healthy way. It may or may not reduce the intensity of our grief work when the loss if final. That will depend in part on the nature of our past relationships with the deceased and our belief system.

There has been a good deal written about the various stages which one passes through in the grief process (Bowlby, 1980; Parkes, 1972; Lindemann, 1944). In looking at the normal progression of grief, we must be careful to avoid thinking in terms of stages, although a stages model helps understand complex behavior. Stages typically imply mutually exclusive parts. However, the drama of grief includes the overlap and repetition of emotions where people obviously do not react in anything remotely resembling "stages." If one mistakenly uses a model involving stages as the sole means of understanding human responses, clear-cut characteristics do not always emerge. Combinations of emotions and behaviors sometimes are confusing or absent and reflect the complexity of events. For example, one may move back and forth between denial and anger.

But we can identify common elements that frequently surface and accompany reactions to loss. *Not everyone experiences all the feelings or so-called stages associated with grief, nor is the physical and emotional pain always intense.* Grief appears in many different combinations of emotion and behavior, all of which can be healthy, although to the casual observer they appear to be very unhealthy. The pace of the grief response appears to follow a four-fold progression: early shock (numbing) and protest, yearning and searching, disorganization and despair, and gradual reconstruction and reorganization (Bowlby, 1980). Let us examine this ongoing adaptational sequence in detail, keeping in mind that the combinations in which the following appear are countless.

1. SHOCK AND NUMBNESS

The initial reaction following a significant loss is often described as feeling a sense of unreality, that what has occurred is somehow only a dream, a fantasy that can't possibly be true. The tragedy *has* happened, but still it couldn't have happened. There is tension; breathing is labored. Bodily reactions parallel the emotional strain. One feels as though placed in a state of suspension. The first words spoken may be, "I can't believe it," or "no, it's not true." The bereaved seem temporarily without the ability to acutely sense what is around them. The shock of what was heard brings numbness. One goes through the motions of responding, but moves as though in a trance. Days later numbness frequently is converted to intense feelings of separation (Osterweis, Solomon, and Green, 1984).

Mary, whose close friend drowned in a freak accident, described her reactions upon hearing the news: "I was stunned—there was some sort of mistake. Jean was just fine when I left her. I tried to think. . . . I could only picture white space inside my head." Separations from loved ones, whether permanent or temporary, whether expected or unexpected, are events in which what is known is replaced by the unknown. The absence of the known, of the predictable, is mind-altering, creating the felt imbalance due to shock and confusion.

Jim, who experienced the breakup of a 2½ year-long relationship with Sarah, said: "My first reaction was 'No! You don't really mean it. It's just a test to see my reactions.' However, she assured me that it was no joke. For the first couple of minutes I refused to believe it." With some losses, disbelief lasts for long periods of time. When denial and disbelief persist for weeks or months, they becomes a major problem in the healing process.

Generally, this state of imbalance may last for minutes, hours, or days depending on the circumstances surrounding the loss. Sensitivity to those around the bereaved is frequently blunted. They are grappling with an adversary that totally consumes their energies. Thus, the grief process has begun. And not infrequently, the bereaved are unable to recall at a later time many of the events which occurred during this initial confrontation.

2. ANGER AND HOSTILITY

When suddenly deprived of someone loved or something cherished, if we are thrust into a situation in which the future looks bleak, it is not unusual to feel cheated. Anger or hostility often run rampant; it is the common reaction to rejection or a loss of self-esteem in such cases. The bereaved may become obsessed with what has happened to *them;* the needs of others are not considered. They may curse the doctor or emergency room staff, turn their hostility on a family member, or even blame God for their plight. Sometimes whatever anyone tries to do for survivors is interpreted as wrong and a reason to castigate their actions. Survivors may look at someone else and think: why is she still alive while our loved one is dead, or why is my love relationship ended while my best friends are still going together? How unfair! Sometimes anger is directed at the legal system as in situations when death occurred by accident or from murder, and persons responsible for loss get off scot-free. While still confronting the after-effects of shock, survivors feel the need to lash out and inflict some of their felt pain on someone or something else. They feel cheated, betrayed, and used, all at the same time. Such hostility sometimes is perceived as "signs of approaching insanity" (Lindemann, 1944).

This is a time when friends and family have to understand that such erratic behavior is only an attempt to deal with a seemingly unmanageable situation. Sometimes anger is directed at the deceased, as if dying had been one's choice rather than one's fate (Osterweis, Solomon and Green, 1984). A colleague once told me that at age 15 his father died. His reaction was: "How could you do this to me when I need you?" Anger commonly emerges from frustration and helplessness. "I had a strong urge for revenge," said Sheila during the breakup of her love relationship. "I was very angry, wishing death on that person." The universal reaction to feelings of rejection, to a perceived loss of respect by others, is hostility and anger. When we perceive a loss as a personal affront, a lowering of the respect others owe us, hostility naturally follows (Layden, 1977). We are experiencing a wounded ego.

Relationships with friends often become strained just at the time when relationships are most needed and vital in the progression of becoming well again. Many psychiatrists believe that repressed anger based on guilt is the basis for depression. When the bereaved refuse to acknowledge anger, they complicate their ability to cope with grief. However, a supportive environment can provide the medium by which pent-up anger can be vented, thus preventing the development of additional physical stress. Most individuals have typically kept themselves in emotional check during years of rejection, or perhaps anger has accumulated from many other unresolved losses in the past. Now it must be expended as one would let go of any harmful substance. Storing anger alienates survivors from the real world just as it isolates them from support persons. And the physical aftermath of letting anger seethe within for any length of time is devastating. One pays a heavy price at the cellular level.

Anger may surface with the shock of hearing the news of the death. During the tears and disbelief which explode at the moment of hearing of the tragedy, oftentimes anger is immediately directed at the person who brought the message. When I informed one of my sons that his friend took his own life, he angrily shouted: "He wouldn't do that!" Anger is not abnormal in these situations. Our awareness that its presence is actually therapeutic helps us understand behavior which frequently causes long-term misery and conflict between survivors and friends. The frustration, feeling of abandonment, belief that what has happened is unfair, are all grounds for eruptions which under other circumstances would not occur. Denise explains her response: "When someone dies suddenly, at such a young age, you just want to hold on to someone and cry. My boyfriend helped me a lot. Also, I threw myself into my job and worked really hard to get my anger and frustration out because I felt it was so unfair." Remember, anger is an outlet for turbulent conditions. It's all right if we feel anger; it means we are coping. But we have to be careful not to allow its violence to consume us; we can use it constructively.

There is increased difficulty for those who have never learned how to deal with anger. With such persons it may be that there were unspoken family rules which limited the expression of anger during childhood; anger always had to be buried. (If it is all right for an adult to discharge anger over a loss, why not a child?) The consequences of not being allowed to express anger is highly damaging and manifested in destructive behavior, or if it is not expressed, anger may culminate in excessive alcohol use or other health-compromising effects. Anger should be seen as a powerful source of energy which can be used as a motivator to seek changes in behavior; it can be channeled to help, not hurt. How one decides to use this force will affect the progress of grief work. And if anger is directed at the self, the same guidelines apply: accept it, remember you are human, let it surface and discuss it, then give it up.

3. GUILT

Many counselors believe that, next to depression, guilt is the most common emotion associated with relationship losses. The natural response to expressed anger is the eventual feeling of guilt for having thought or acted in ways which are deeply regretted. When a survivor recalls what was said or done, or what she refrained from doing, when thoughts about others are reviewed, one comes momentarily to that point where she condemns herself for real or imagined transgressions. Some psychoanalysts believe that guilt evolves as a form of self-hate, while others view it as a signal that one has done something wrong; both views are valid.

Self-blame is a condition which surfaces in adulthood as well as child-hood when one is confronting a major loss.

Guilt also occurs even when anger has not preceded it. But each person, with the help of others, has to make a distinction between normal guilt and neurotic guilt, which is not easy to do when grieving. If we have done something unjust or something that hurts someone else, it is normal to feel guilty about it. This is a motivating force for anyone to change their behavior. One must seek pardon—*and then forget the incident.* In the *Rubaiyat of Omar Khayyam* we find:

> The moving Finger writes' and, having writ Moves on: nor all your Piety
> nor Wit, Shall lure it back to cancel half a Line, Nor all your tears wash out a
> word of it.

We can do nothing to change what has already occurred. In one sense, guilt is good for us. It is a reminder that we have created disorder, chaos or ill feelings; it signals us to restore the balance of order and good relationships in our lives. Such rational guilt helps to reestablish our values and priorities. Guilt, in this context, becomes a motive for chang-ing behavior and seeking renewal. However, the vast majority of people who suffer guilt related to major loss are not dealing with normal cause-and-effect guilt, but rather with neurotic guilt. Here, guilt blinds and diminishes their ability to overcome the lack of power to reestablish control over the effects of traumatic change.

Neurotic guilt is a source of much anguish, irritability, and complica-tion in the grief process; it makes life a living hell. But it is difficult to avoid slipping into some form of neurotic guilt which has little or no basis in fact. Consider this: Have you ever opened that last bottle of softdrink on a hot day and have it slip from your hand, or knock it over and it smashes into many pieces? Or, how about dropping one of your favorite dishes, a beer mug, or a special momento from a happy occasion? These objects cannot be put back into their original condition. No matter what we say or do, no matter how angry or sad we become, the fact remains that what has been done has been done. *We must go on despite what has happened.* Action was not purposely taken. To dwell on the "what ifs" only prolongs agony. And so it is with neurotic guilt due to major loss. What has occurred is not a result of *conscious* cause-and-effect on our part; it must not be given power to distort true cause-and-effect, to make rational what is irrational.

I felt what I believed to be real guilt when my mother died because I could not remember the last time I had told her I loved her. I had missed opportunities to be with her and talk with her before her sudden death. It became neurotic guilt when I overemphasized my lack of contact with her and dwelt on it too much; I blamed myself out of all proportion. I did not *choose* not to tell her I loved her. I had forgotten to do so, had taken her for granted (which is not unusual), and death had reminded me, had emphasized my laxness in a very guilt-ridden way. My guilt could not stand the test of reality and I was eventually able to overcome it.

It is probably impossible to have lived with and loved one dearly and not felt guilty about a part of the relationship with her after death occurs. It is not unusual to feel that we did not do enough to get her to change unhealthy habits so that she could have lived longer. We may feel guilty that we waited too long before calling the physician, that we forgot how to perform cardiopulmonary resuscitation, or perhaps we made excuses for not doing something the person had wanted us to do when she was alive and well. When neurotic guilt takes over, we must search out reasons for our feelings, often with the help of a trusted friend. Are we being unreasonable with ourselves at this time? Are we being realistic? It is unwarranted to expect so much more from ourselves than we can possibly deliver. The reassurance of a friend that we are punishing ourselves by unreasonable expectations can be helpful in relieving an unjustifiable burden.

More important is the realization that the basis for making decisions about guilt is usually built on faulty assumptions. Survivors often think and act as though they are superhuman in terms of having been able to prevent events from happening. *Yet no one has the power to be perfect in relationships;* that is not human. No one prevents certain physical events from occurring. If such perfection could be attained, we would be superhuman. *No one has the power to foretell the exact way future events will unfold.* The false assumption in neurotic guilt is that we are all-powerful, all-knowing. We need to defuse such irrational thinking because neurotic guilt destroys the self-image and damages relationships needed for recovery. To think that we have direct control over events, some supernatural foreknowledge that would have prevented what occurred, is a subtle form of arrogance. It happens with many professional people who feel they could have changed history or the progress of disease, if only. . . .

Physicians often tend to isolate themselves from dying patients because they believe they have failed. But who can save everyone? We all must be easier on ourselves when loss occurs and not assume blame out of proportion to our capacities, as physicians so frequently do. Every professional errs at some time or other. It is not uncommon for survivors of accidents, where friends have died, to feel guilty that they got out alive, as though it was somehow their fault that the other people in the accident died. Survivors do not have the power to determine life or death any more than physicians do who are convinced they should keep everyone from dying.

Guilt may last for long periods of time, even to the point of precipitating anger and creating a vicious cycle of anger-guilt-anger. Experiencing guilt is normal, whether it is neurotic or real in origin (Rando, 1984). Most helpful in coping with the effects of guilt is to get its cause out in the open, examine it, and place it in perspective. *Talk about guilt.* A clinical example is Anne, who had slept with her boyfriend, and was experiencing much guilt now that she was no longer seeing him. She came to see me and explained her dilemma. The simple act of expressing guilt was the beginning of making inroads on feelings which had been constant reminders of her past behavior. *To talk about it* was the courageous first step. Using guilt as a motivator for changing behavior is to take advantage of an emotion which prevades the grief process. Ridding ourselves of neurotic or real guilt takes time. Let us give ourselves that time to gradually let go.

We must also be aware of the guilt in anticipatory grief which may surface before a sick loved one dies. Such guilt evolves from past conflicts that we regret, or it can occur when death is expected but the dying person rallies again and again. In the latter circumstance, sometimes referred to as the Lazarus Syndrome, if family members feel that death is a blessing, a relief for the painful condition in which they see the loved one, and then the person seems to get better, they chastize themselves for hoping that death would occur soon and end the loved one's suffering. Whether the death event is continuously postponed or not, some family members may emotionally detach themselves from the dying loved one (Shneidman, 1982). These feelings must be aired quickly lest they grow and cause psychological problems.

4. Physical Reactions

Grief has been responsible for much illness, numerous cardiovascular accidents, severe nutritional deficiencies, and the abuse of drugs, particularly alcohol. How does this happen? The inability to cope with the changes that loss demands, plus getting "stuck" in the normal progression of grief, being overwhelmed by the emotional impact, extracts a damaging toll on survivors. Grief and illness are not unknown partners. Studies have linked the stress of grief to the death of an immediate survivor (Lynch, 1977; Parkes, Benjamin and Fitzgerald, 1969).

The significance of these events points up an age-old concept concerning the intricate relationship between mind and body: emotions affect physical health. Our thought processes can cause emotional and physical problems that we normally would attribute to outside agents. *For every thought or emotion there is a corresponding physical manifestation.* This is seldom more graphically illustrated than in an analysis of grief states. Bill describes his physical reactions to the loss of his fiancée, who began dating his best friend. "Physically, I felt very weak. I was having very intense headaches and absolutely no appetite. Another complication hit when I was diagnosed as having a mild strep throat. Physically, I was at the lowest point I had ever been at. I had no energy and no appetite and when I did eat it never stayed in me." It is not uncommon to come down with infections when grieving; bouts with the flu or the common cold are frequently reported. Also, the organic response to unmet *unconscious needs* is illness in a variety of forms (Jackson, 1981).

There are many physical reactions to grief which are entirely normal and to be expected. Major loss is commonly accompanied by the "big three"—digestive disturbances, fatigue, and insomnia. Other common physical reactions include weakness, headaches, changes in appetite, backaches, labored breathing, chills, skin rash, and feelings of tension in the throat and other body parts (LaGrand, 1981). One's body may feel as though it is undergoing a giant convulsion. It is not unusual to hallucinate about the deceased, to see her in a favorite chair or room, or even to hear footsteps or other noises normally associated with the person. The bereaved may "see" the deceased loved one or the estranged person in a crowd, and chase after her, only to discover it is someone else.

5. Depression and Loneliness

Everyone gets depressed. Days come when the birds no longer sing, no races are won, feelings of despair are overwhelming, exhaustion is ever present, and all lights are dimmed. Is this abnormal? Hardly. Drastic change often brings depression and thoughts that there is no future.

Depression has been called "the common cold of psychiatric illness." There are many types of depression, extending from mild to severe. Reactive depression is most common and, as the name implies, it is a state of lethargy, hopelessness, and despair that comes about as a reaction to an outside event.

Just as anxiety and guilt vary in their impact and intensity, so does depression. There are many theories concerning the causes of depression. It is said to be connected with feelings of worthlessness, distorted perceptions of the past, present and future (Cognitive Model), role transitions and disputes, genetic predisposition, interpersonal conflicts, and the classic belief that depression is anger turned in on the self. The anger-in hypothesis and the Cognitive Model of depression are often most applicable to the grief response. In particular, feelings of *hopelessness for the future* and *loneliness* contribute heavily to the depressed state. The effects of the latter are expressed by 20-year-old Karen on the death of her friend: "I found that people keeping in contact after the funeral helped. I was so numb at the time, I couldn't deal with everyone. After a few months, a loneliness sets in and then friends are really needed." There are vast numbers of lonely young people who seek the interest of others in their desire to adapt to change and overcome their depressed state; loneliness kills (Lynch, 1977; Cobb, 1976). Part of the loneliness builds on feelings that no one cares or understands, that no one shares their feelings or sense of loss. Loneliness plays a major role in the *pining* and *searching* for the loved one which Parkes (1972) reports occurs frequently. Depression is both sporadic and, at times, long-lasting.

Normal reactive depression is manageable and will subside with time. Neurotic depression is much longer-lasting and more difficult to control. For your peers coping with major loss, *depression is the most commonly reported emotional reaction,* as it is with the general population. They describe it as follows: "I started feeling like my world was falling down around me" or "I became extremely withdrawn and depressed"; "I spent more and more time in my room"; "I was totally devastated"; "I didn't want to be around anyone." There is often a feeling such as "I will never be able to recover from what has happened."

Disorganization of thought and behavior is characteristically associated with depression and loneliness. We think nobody cares as life goes on around us and the world outside seems unaffected by our loss. Most people are unaware that the loss occurred and how we are affected by it. "How impersonal," we think. Even at the hospital, many professionals appear too busy with assigned duties to show the concern we feel should be shown. We question: "How could this happen; can't they see what has occurred?" We entertain many self-centered thoughts in our loneliness when we are unable to deal with the reality of loss.

As time passes, the awareness that there may be a future, a glimmer of hope, makes inroads on the depressed state. But before this happens much suffering occurs. Nonetheless, during this period *never drink alcohol or encourage another to drink when depressed.* Alcohol and other neural depressants augment depression making matters worse. Greg expressed it this way: "At night, I often felt so depressed that the only way I could sleep would be by getting drunk. This only helped me for a few hours; once I came down from the alcohol I became even more depressed."

Sometimes exhaustion and despair, abandonment of hope and expectation, are misread as clinical depression when in fact one needs time out to recover from shock. Sanders (1985) states:

> I have found in my research that we are examining an emotion in grief that is more akin to despair than it is to depression. . . . While a depressed state exists, it appears much more in line with a need to pull back and conserve energy. This is following the initial outpouring of sympathetic nervous system arousal. Because we translate exhaustion into depression, it is misread (Personal Communication).

When such despair exists Sanders suggests that at this time "withdrawing from others needs to be encouraged, when the body is slowly recovering from the shock of death."

6. Changes in Normal Behavior

When major loss occurs, we are subjected to inevitable change complicated by having to deal with fear, the unknown, intense emotions, and heightened physical feelings. It is impossible to follow most of the normal routines and activities of daily life. The world has been turned upside down. We are not the same person we were before the loss occurred; we will be different and view the world differently from this point on. For some, the changes will be more drastic than for others. Lynn Caine (1975) in *Widow* describes her unusual behavior in a chapter entitled "Crazy Lady." She was relating to her dead husband as though he was alive. Some of your peers report overeating or throwing themselves into new relationships. Others drink heavily, "smoke lots of dope," spend money needed to pay bills, or drive long distances, stay but a few hours, then drive all the way back to their original starting point. This is to say young and old persons alike seldom think and act reasonably in the early stages of the grief process.

Sometimes panic overwhelms us "because we think of nothing but the loss" (Westberg, 1971). We are convinced that there is little that can be done to change the hopeless condition. We are powerless to work or finish an important assignment. All is lost; there is no way out.

What can be done? *Never give up hope.* For example, several years ago, around midnight, I received a call from a young woman whose husband had been killed in an automobile accident two nights before. She had questions about her daughter and what she should do and say to her. We talked, and I later visited with her at the wake. It was a very tragic situation, causing her great pain. Two years later when I saw her again she said, "You know, I thought at the time that I would never get over it." Her behavior initially was unpredictable (a characteristic not uncommon), but hope and the love for her daughter kept her going. At these times, a caring friend is indeed needed during the hours of misery when futility, desolation, and unavoidable thoughts of abandonment seem all consuming.

Anxiety and tension seem to be constant companions. The bereaved may forget appointments, fail to meet big or little obligations, take the wrong turn on a road they've driven on hundreds of times. Why? Because of their preoccupation with all the details of the loss and the inability to stop dwelling on the image of the deceased loved one (Lindemann, 1944). It appears in their imagination over and over again as thoughts of how the tragedy could have been different if only this or that had not occurred. Not infrequently the griever appears absentminded, disinterested or incapable of making decisions.

We can be sure that when changes in our lives occur as a result of a major loss, they will one day influence how we relate to friends in need. We will come to be more sensitive to others who experience what we have experienced; the lone gift of tragedy is wisdom for the future. We will grow stronger from working through our loss and feel more confident. We will reexamine our values and beliefs, strengthen them, or make changes and new commitments to ourselves and others close to us. Our relationships will take on new meaning; *life will be different.* We will have aged in a very positive way, having passed a turning point in life.

7. HOPE AND FEAR

As the days drag on, the numbness fades, and we force ourselves to go back to work or to school, hoping to find moments where activities drive thoughts of sorrow away. We are suddenly alive for a brief time, until the reality of the tragedy returns once again. The expectation that life will get better, that we might become whole again, that good will somehow evolve from the turmoil of it all, suddenly comes into view. We regain hope almost imperceptively; suddenly there is a feeling of being alive and whole again. This feeling lasts for a short time, a fleeting moment, then it disappears and grief returns. Hope for the future is sometimes corrupted by self-pity and we return to feelings of despair, only later to reach a decision to commit ourselves again to adapting to the unacceptable.

Fear competes with hope; it tends to invade every thought, creating insecurity within. Depending on the type of loss endured, one may recoil from beginning new relationships because of the fear that another loved one would die. The bereaved are filled with thoughts of not being able to make it through life without the deceased, or they may simply feel inundated by unnamed fears. Even the strongest, those who seem to have so much self-confidence, must cope with fear because anyone's separation from the significant people in life usually brings fear of the future without the security of the past. Rejoice if you have no fear; accept the fact of fear as part of your grief work should it arise. Share it; fear can be overcome. There is something reassuring about facing fear with another; together one seems to find new courage and power.

Returning to a particular place or setting may propel one into intense fear. This was suggested by Rita after the death of her mother: "At home, in the house wherein my mother taught me so much about love and life, the wounds open up again and the fear overcomes me. Nightmares and paranoia are now all too common in that big house I spent my entire life in." After the breakup of a love relationship, Kim said: "A fear I can't describe adequately is my growing horror of being rejected by anyone. I guess once you get used to somebody, you forget what life is like without them." Fear grows especially strong when we feel we cannot cope with the future: facing financial burdens, loneliness, thoughts that we will never find another person to love us or that friends have abandoned us in our darkest hour. Fear must be faced if it is to be conquered. The first step is *talking about it with others* and uncovering the irrational thinking upon which it is commonly built. Fear also causes fatigue, as it increases stress levels and depletes energy reserves. Don't be afraid to admit you are fearful: that is the beginning of dealing with fear, for one must realize that it is thoughts about fear which makes it worse (Weekes, 1978).

Because fear in some form is part of all of our lives, and because it causes us to shrink and draw inward when we narrow our perceptions of alternatives for coping, we are forced to learn as much as we can about it and how it can be overcome. *Fears are overcome as we reengage life* and choose to dwell on hope for the future.

Hope, like faith, is the intangible aspect of a loss experience that seems to spring from within. Its tiny flame gives the first indication that life can go on, that it will go on. We clutch at that single lifeline, but it somehow eludes us, only to reappear at a later time with stronger direction. Hope brings with it the confidence that grief is approaching different levels of understanding, that it is pointing to possibilities of resolution, but never forgetting an unwanted life experience. The question changes from, "Can I ever really go on?" to "Maybe I'll have some good days!" Eventually, the hours stretch into days and sometimes into weeks. Our burden becomes lighter; going on living overcomes total preoccupation with the loss, although life is never again as it was. To some degree, time has won out. It has not erased the hurt or thoughts of suffering and loneliness, but it has dulled their impact. We are living with or despite loss, as we begin to realize that our destiny at this point lies in our own hands. Or as Albert Camus put it: "In the midst of winter, I finally learned that there was in me an invincible summer."

To sum up, grief seems to be the inevitable wrong which ultimately makes a right; it is a contradiction which presents new beginnings. It gives us a chance to breathe again, to become a new person rising from the valley of sorrow as though reborn to take another direction in living. It is a perilous journey, bringing with it a pain we seldom think can be endured. And the more we attempt to circumvent it, the worse the pain becomes. It is made easier when we find security and a sense of safety (Glick, Weiss and Parkes, 1974). However, without grief we would not be human, nor could we endure the losses yet to come. Grief fills in for the dramatic change in stability and continuity of life. It is truly a *positive* process which takes place in seemingly negative conditions. We could not survive without it. Thus, grief is a contradictory process of letting go at a time when our hearts tell us to do just the opposite. Grief, then, is a question with a thousand answers. No, it has ten thousand answers. And there may be many other "stages of grief," depending on your perception of the loss: hopelessness, hate, emptiness, confusion, spiritual disintegration or feelings of nothingness. The list is endless. So keep in mind that there is no such thing as the best way to grieve any more than there is a best way to live, a best way to cope with loss, a best way to view death, or a best way to die.

PARANORMAL EXPERIENCES

I went to a concert that I *know* he would have been at if he were alive. I felt very upset and didn't think it was fair that he couldn't experience it. Then I felt his presence, and came to the conclusion that I still *could* experience things, the concert in particular. I enjoyed myself very much for the rest of the time.

Christina, a senior

Many people, young and old alike, often encounter situations in their grief work that are labeled "paranormal experiences," which by definition means "alongside or beyond the normal." They involve a variety of situations in which a survivor believes she has had contact with the deceased; these experiences are a regular part of the grief process for many people (although they are seldom considered to be a normal part of grieving). To the outsider (the person who has never had such an experience), these incidents are shrugged off as being unimportant figments of the imagination, and those who say they experienced such events are candidates for psychotherapy. Support persons who minimize these reports by grievers jeopardize the helping relationship in which they are engaged. Because of potential rejection and ridicule, many individuals refuse to share the "unusual" experience with anyone. However, through the years, such experiences have been reported by various researchers. Bowlby (1980) suggests they are an expected part of the yearning and searching phase of grieving, and indicates that they occur in many other cultures. Parkes (1972) refers to paranormal experiences as illusions which involve one's misinterpretations of sensory input during the bereavement period. He found that many widows felt the presence of their dead husbands, which was helpful to them in their early months of grieving.

A number of bereaved people report both auditory and visual hallucinations which are generally reported as useful in coping with their losses although a small number question their sanity after the experience (Rees, 1975). In my own work, your peers and other adults have reported a number of paranormal events which took place after the deaths of loved ones. For example, a young woman, whose father died suddenly, told me the following story in an open and convincing manner.

> It was the day of the funeral. After it was all over with, we, the family, had just said goodbye to our father for the last time. We had no idea he was going to die. He wasn't supposed to die. He had just turned fifty years old. I was in my bedroom, by myself, and in total numbness and shock. I opened my closet door and felt someone, or something, tap me on the shoulder. I turned around and heard my father's voice say to me. "Take care of your mother."

She looked at me in concluding her story, saying: "It was as real as if you and me were talking." Another middle-aged woman told of an embrace that she felt as she was waiting in the vestibule of the church after the services for her husband. She said it lasted for about a minute and a half and was so real and comforting. There was no doubt that it had happened and the experience helped her feel that her husband was all right. Could she have been mistaken? As she said, "It was so real." Each of us must draw our own conclusions in this regard.

Although these experiences usually occur when one is alone, there are instances when two or more people experience the feelings together. A 24-year old woman told me of an incident that happened two months after the death of her close friend, during her first year at college at a time when she had not been at an intense point in her grief work.

> A few months after my friend committed suicide I was in another friend's room and felt the presence of my deceased friend. I felt someone sit down on the bed with me and I turned around and all there was was an imprint of someone sitting there. My other friend also saw this and I knew it was Ray. It was a very warm, comforting feeling; almost like he was saying goodbye."

Notice that the experience was interpreted as being a "farewell," not a frightening confrontation. It is also significant to note that this event did not take place at the height of her grief. She told me that, at the time it occurred, she had not been thinking about her dead friend.

These are not abnormal experiences, although the bereaved may think they are abnormal for having had them. Lindstrom (1982) has classified paranormal experiences as follows:

1. *Intuitive.* These are the most frequently reported experiences, and have been found in much of the literature on grief. They are characterized by a sense of presence of the deceased, that the person is "with" the survivor.
2. *Auditory.* As shown above, this experience involves hearing the deceased talk or coming up the stairs by the sound of footsteps. Some report hearing the deceased breathing when lying in bed.
3. *Tactile.* Though less common, the feeling of touch occurs though no

one is there. It is thought by the survivors to be the deceased, God, or someone else.

4. *Olfactory.* This type of experience involves the sense of smell associated with the deceased. It could be a soap used by the deceased, perfume, or cologne. In these situations, cosmetics are not presently being used by anyone else in the immediate area.

5. *Visual.* Visual experiences can be the most alarming, as the survivor reports actually seeing the deceased in a favorite chair or standing right there before her eyes.

6. *Dreams.* Also very common are dreams about the deceased. The dreams are almost always of the person as they were when alive, sometimes wearing a favorite piece of clothing. These dreams can be very traumatic when the survivor awakens and realizes that the person is not alive.

The repetition of certain dreams about the deceased may become a persistent source of discomfort, and in my experience, they appear to occur as frequently as the intuitive event. Kathy said: "I used to have the same dream over and over about my dad. I pictured him in our trailer, dressed in his plaid coat and black hat. He said to me that everything is o.k. and that he would see me soon. I used to try to walk over to him to hug him but he would disappear." As time goes on dreams of the deceased begin to occur less frequently and eventually stop. For some people, however, a different dream of the deceased will occur but only at long-term intervals. Bowlby (1980) reports that half of all widows and widowers dream of the deceased partner being alive. Death dreams seem to be so common that it is questionable that they should even be considered as paranormal experiences. Nightmares are sometimes reported causing great fear; later they are usually replaced with more pleasant dreams of the deceased. Dreams of one's own death also occur; theorists suggest that such dreams almost always reflect the willingness of the dreamer to relinquish old roles and self-images (Faraday, 1974).

The discussion of this subconscious information can be useful to you; find a trusted friend or professional who will allow you the freedom to tell of these experiences. But beware of accepting their interpretations of the paranormal. If you keep a dream journal, which can provide helpful information, it is best to discuss its contents only with an expert on these matters. Dreams do provide us with much information about ourselves and assist the healing process, although all of the data may not be useful. This is why an expert should be consulted if one is concerned about the significance of dreams.

A Visual Experience

One of the most unusual paranormal experiences was related to me by an elderly woman whose daughter had died of cancer three months previously. She had come to see me before her daughter died, but I had not spoken to her again for many months until one day we met in the cafeteria line and she said she had something to tell me. It involved her four-year-old grandson of another daughter. She was very worried about this youngster because her daughter's marriage was coming apart and on various occasions he had been the victim of excessive discipline by the father. She had relayed these feelings to her dying daughter, as they had become very close during the illness. A couple of days before her daughter died, she had asked her to watch over the little boy when she was in heaven and to let her know that she (the dying daughter) was all right. Three months later the woman was giving her grandson a bath and left the bathroom for a few minutes. She was startled by her grandson's alarming call of "Grandma." She quickly returned to the bathroom and the little boy said, "I saw a picture of Jan and she was smiling." Jan was the daughter who had died three months previously. The boy was frightened and wanted to get out of the bathtub. He had called the apparition which he had seen a picture. Needless to say, his grandmother was equally alarmed but was convinced that through this young child her wishes had been granted. Her older daughter now has full custody of the child as the marriage has ended.

It is important to be able to share these experiences with a trusted friend as this woman did, and not be questioned about their validity. They are a legitimate part of the grief process for many people. We may have to seek a professional person willing to listen to us if we fear rejection by friends. Repetition of the paranormal can be traumatic, and the need to explore its meaning will be most helpful to recovery.

Most of the time paranormal experiences, while sometimes frightening, carry a positive message indicating that the deceased is all right. For most people, the experience is a turning point in their grief; they are motivated to go on with their lives. Neil, a 20-year-old college sophomore, told of a dream in which his girlfriend, who had died suddenly, came back to life. He talked to her in the dream, telling her she was dead and could not come back. This event was a part of his coping pattern in dealing with this major loss. It reinforced his acceptance of her death.

In rare instances, paranormal experiences can be extremely frightening, as reported by Penny. "I truly believe in paranormal experiences," she said:

> After my father died, that night I looked down the hall and his clothes were hanging off the bureau in a way that I thought I was dreaming. But I really saw him standing there. I was scared to death. Maybe my eyes were playing tricks on me because of the shock of his death.

Sam's experiences were also disturbing:

> I totaled my mother's car with three of my friends in it. We all were able to walk away from it by some miracle. But I dream about it still and sometimes pretend that one of us had been killed and what it would be like now if that had happened.

Regardless of how paranormal experiences are explained away by well-meaning friends, they have very special meaning for the bereaved. They may occur shortly after the death or years later and appear to be related to searching behavior. Pincus (1974) suggests that searching is the principal behavior associated with the death of a loved one. "As the bereaved becomes more relaxed, and tension, frustration, and pain decrease, *searching* may lead to *finding* a sense of the lost person's presence.... For me it took years before I could experience this 'tonic' of Fritz's presence, and it is a wonderful surprise that this is increasing as time goes on" (p.116–117).

By unburdening the self and learning that the phenomenon is normal, if it occurs, one is able to eliminate an unnecessary psychological strain. But do they really occur? There are two basic views: some psychiatrists tell us it is the mind's way of helping one let go of the deceased and find meaning in the death, while many others believe that some paranormal experiences are proof of another world beyond this one, that a loving God does exist. Czillinger (1979) suggests that bereaved parents should hope and look for a sign of comforting presence that the deceased child is all right. This is a positive therapeutic experience reinforcing acceptance. Be thankful if you experience the paranormal. It is all right to use it as a sign that the deceased is happy. This further implies that it is all right to talk to and pray to the deceased loved one, as some religions encourage.

Having examined the basic elements of the grief process we turn now to the topic of self-help and the importance of one's belief system, for in the final analysis, each of us must make a series of difficult decisions as we struggle to put our lives back together.

Chapter Five

HELPING OURSELVES

Two months after my father died, a close friend went through the same thing. Talking with and helping her in actuality allowed me to help myself. My father had been a coach in my hometown. After his death I became *very* active in booster clubs, fund raisers and anything else involved with sports. The sports I was participating in became all the more important to me at this point. This involvement made me feel all the closer, even as though he was there participating with me.

Lee Ann, a sophomore

The basis for helping ourselves through any of the consequences of major life change lies in the *nature of the action taken* in spite of what has occurred. Behavior in all life experiences is primarily a function of our belief systems or what we *imagine* to be true (Maltz, 1969). In this chapter I suggest that one can change her beliefs (as we all do throughout life based on new experiences and maturity) in order to cope with loss in a society which tends to disown the theme of continuous loss experiences. This is followed by a discussion of eleven specific self-help approaches in coping with the flow of life changes. A number of suggestions for combatting depression is followed by answering the question: When does grief end?

Any written description of the grief process, because of the unique personal nature of grief, usually leaves as many questions unanswered as it answers. So, too, with an analysis of coping responses. There is a certain awkwardness in trying to generalize about coping techniques applicable to everyone. At the risk of oversimplifying the resolution of loss (a process which includes social, psychological, physical, situational and spiritual factors), we now cull the possibilities for facilitating our own healing. As indicated earlier, grief is both multidimensional and individual. Add the diversity of past experience with loss, one's self-concept (a key factor in adjustment), and the range of coping techniques at one's disposal, and it is clear that no single set of guidelines for coping can evolve. But there are many suggestions that can be considered, based on psychological and empirical data, and what other young adults have experienced.

YOUR BELIEF SYSTEM

Because the grief response is in part conditioned by society, in particular one's traditions and close community ties, we have suggested the importance of beliefs in the shaping of the loss experience. Strong, impelling beliefs are the forces behind all the great technical and social advances throughout history. They are the prime movers in changing habits, the reasons why the American dream has come true for so many people. *Our beliefs will hinder or benefit our adaptation to any loss.* Should we consistently feel that the loss is unacceptable, that we cannot cope with the changes it inflicts, that choices are not available, our grief work will be arduous and unending. What we believe about ourselves, our support network, and our hopes for the future can destroy or sustain. In particular, our beliefs about support persons will heavily influence how we respond to the comfort they provide (Bowlby, 1980). *Changing beliefs about the place of loss in life is the most powerful tool each person possesses in dealing with major loss events.* This is because what we think affects how we feel. New beliefs bear new fruit, renew the spirit, and bring new life. Not infrequently, major loss alters beliefs about life, death, and the reasons for both. We can take an active role in that transition or simply be pulled along by it.

Begin by becoming aware of what you believe *now* about loss. Now that "death" has occurred, what does it signal for you and for your life? Are there alternative beliefs about your options? There always are, *if you will decide to look for the choices.* Assuming a purely adversarial approach to grief, fighting it, is not the answer. It only ushers in a more heartwrenching experience by increasing anxiety. However, recognizing the inevitable pain of loss, the time involved in adapting to it, and that we cannot accelerate the process, is a good start. One must allow grief to run its course, recognizing its power but believing that it can be managed. There is always a tendency for us not to recognize alternatives that threaten deeply held beliefs. Consequently, one is unaware to what extent the perception of loss is truly one's own or primarily a result of cultural expectations (Harman, 1981). Because of this problem, one often tends to grieve on questionable assumptions. So keep in mind that the average griever is no more real than the average friend or family member who tries to help you; both are abstractions used to give some semblance of understanding to experiences which seem to be utterly incomprehensible at the moment. Allow yourself the freedom to grieve, to alter your beliefs, to build a new understanding of the place of loss in living. Marcus Aurelius spoke as follows: "If thou art pained by any external thing, it is not this thing that disturbs thee, but thine own judgement about it. And it is in thy power to wipe out this judgement now." This does not mean we can wipe out our pain — we will always have to endure that — but we can wipe out the self-pity, the withdrawal from life, the self-punishment, and the refusal to live again. We need to consider that it is *how* we are thinking about our problem that is causing us pain.

Self-fulfilling Prophecy

The self-fulfilling prophecy can be devastating to your grief response or the lifeline to recovery. The power of suggestion is well-known. Many individuals have experienced the self-fulfilling prophecy when they act out their beliefs, whether the beliefs are true or false. The world is full of examples of people who believed they could overcome adversity of the worst sorts — and they did. Or, they allowed negative thoughts to guide their every move. We need only remind ourselves of the stories of the Jewish holocaust to be convinced of the power of belief to sustain us in our need. As suggested earlier, we all tend to behave according to expectations and what we believe about the situation. If you think you will fail, make a mistake or make a poor speech, often that is exactly what happens. This is true in many aspects of life, and it readily applies to the grief response and the assimilation of major changes in one's life. Your thoughts about life can be the basis for healing and strengthening, or they can become the facade behind which fear and immobility are forever joined.

Acknowledgment

Begin the journey of self-direction: after the initial period of impact, it starts with the first rays of acknowledging that one's loss is truly real. This recognition is not easy to give. Yet, it is the fundamental coping response, because the resolution of any loss cannot begin without it. It may take hours, weeks and in some instances months before a particular loss is fully acknowledged. But when it does happen, nurture this beginning. If we fail to, grief will become a way of life, a substitute for normal healing, change, and our ability to confront a new future. Failing to accept what has occurred only plays a cruel hoax on the self; we are living a fantasy. We sometimes hold on to grief so we will not have to face new demands and experiences without the loved one or the object of loss. We are lulled by a false sense of security.

Can one escape some of the negative consequences of a belief system which says "no" to life? Put another way, can one change her belief system about loss? Beliefs change over time as we experience new events, new challenges, and new relationships. The aging process verifies this phenomenon; our view of the world changes as our stages in life change. Looking back through the years, we find many instances in which your beliefs then were radically different from what they are now. I have already suggested that previous grief models may have influenced you in a totally negative way. It is all right to adopt multiple models which differ from childhood grief models. We are not betraying our parents or loved ones in this search to alter our perception of loss. One can change direction. How?

1. Start with the assumption that there are other choices for coping with loss, there are other approaches to dealing with a changed environment, that your perceptions and beliefs are the basis of your present condition (assuming you are "stuck" in attempts to deal with the loss). Equally important is the conviction that the power of beliefs motivate behavior either positively or negatively. For example: Do you believe that events which take place are all perfectly ordered, that they happen for a reason? Or do you believe that everything occurs randomly? Or is it a combination of both? Answers to these questions (your beliefs) will heavily influence attempts to find meaning in loss and the ultimate resolution of it. Many of our problems in dealing with loss result from "commonplace processes such as faulty learning, making incorrect inferences on the basis of inadequate or correct information, and not distinguishing adequately between imagination and reality" (Beck, 1976, pp. 19–20).

2. Change your behavior. It is essential that to change beliefs one must begin by extricating oneself from the usual activities which reinforce the present belief system. For example, if you are refusing invitations to social events or cultural activities which are reinforcing withdrawal and subsequent isolation, you must begin to change the pattern. *Desire* to change must be followed with action. This is easier said than done, unless you truly wish to progress in adapting to your losses. Major change must start from within, not with the expectation that others can do it for you. Although changing behavior may lead to a change in

beliefs, it has also been argued that changing behavior without changing beliefs will only lead to further disappointment (Combs, Avila and Purkey, 1971).

3. Repetition of the behavior is required. This is probably the biggest drawback in changing beliefs because it is time-consuming, demands consistency in application and is not easy to continue with when success is not immediate. Also, one tends to persevere in not giving up long-held beliefs. Resistance is to be expected. Here we must compel ourselves to reach out, to continue the new in order to give up the old. All of this takes time, much time and patience. It is not a short-term struggle, and most likely we will need assistance. Although the final decisions are ours and we are responsible for them, it does not mean that we must make these changes all alone. We may not be emotionally ready to do so at the time. Seeking assistance is not a reflection on our personhood.

4. Search out others whose perceptions of loss events are different from yours and are more acceptable and applicable to grief resolution. Perceptions are the meanings we give to individual experiences. As we become aware of new meanings, convinced that our negative way of perceiving loss is costly to our very existence as a person, we can begin the transformation and progress in our grief work. Ask yourself the question, "How do others work through their most devastating losses?" Teachers, counselors, hospice personnel, nurses, clergy, others associated with loss experiences have differing belief systems about how to adapt. Find out what others think. *Study the belief systems of those who love unconditionally.* Such love is characteristically liberating (Powell, 1978). Go to their meetings and ask to speak with them privately; make appointments to do so so that they will be willing to discuss this subject. You may then pick and choose to create *your way* of dealing with the inevitable, once you have become aware of the many different positive approaches to coping with the stress of loss. You will learn that others have suffered through equally destructive events and have much to offer from their experience.

Now, take account of three beliefs which were strong factors in coping with the deaths of loved ones. They were beliefs which evolved from confrontations with death and were acted upon by the three young adults who expressed them to me as the basis for their coping techniques.

1. Patrick, age 21: "I kept thinking of my friend who died and how he would be watching me and that he wouldn't want me to be upset. He would want me to just carry on and enjoy myself and that has helped me cope."
2. Chloe, age 21: "I came to the conclusion that death is not worse than living. A teacher had explained right before my loss how he had experienced clinical death when he was younger and was revived. He said he had a feeling of happiness. So I concluded that death can't be much worse than living."

3. Roland, age 20: "There were many people that shared my grief with me, and expressed their sympathy and support. I also reached inside myself and decided I've just got to move onward and upward."

Whether we agree with these beliefs or classify them as irrelevant, they were instrumental factors in the grief work of these people. One person focused on what his friend would want and the belief in an afterlife. Another decided that death was not bad. And the third decided that he had to accept his great loss and continue with his life. Three different beliefs, but each assisted the person concerned in the progression of his/her grief process. What they have in common is a *positive outlook in coping with a major life change.* You may have to examine your own beliefs about the relationship that loss has to life experiences and decide whether your assumptions about death and loss events need to be reevaluated. Do not relationship losses say something about the preciousness of relationships? Does death itself say something about the importance of love? Do survivors who make it through the most devastating losses—murders of loved ones, deaths of children, the inhumanity of concentration camps— possess different beliefs from those who succumb to such conditions? It is through the correction of erroneous beliefs that excessive, inappropriate emotional reactions can be minimized (Beck, 1976).

Imagine the unlimited potential that changing beliefs holds: we can decide *not to fear the present or future* even though we have experienced a massive life change. We can choose *not to continue with our depression.* This is not wishful thinking. Much of the great literature throughout history is replete with examples of changes in the conditions of life brought on by changes in beliefs. *Anyone can make the choice to change their view of the world.*

SELF-HELP APPROACHES

If loss is a certainty, an unavoidable part of life, it would seem prudent to attempt to develop the capacity to deal with it in ways that minimize extremes, unnecessary conflict, and long-term hardships. The recommendations which follow will help you accomplish this objective as you evaluate your perceptions of loss events and begin to deal with your major life change.

Allow others to help you.
Remember that it is normal to experience what seems abnormal.
Express your thoughts and feelings.

Do not try to avoid grief.
Reach out to others.
Rise above the bitterness and resentments.
Expect to "regress" and experience setbacks.
Maintain your physical strength.
Control your self-pity.
Nurture your faith.
Deal with immediate problems and make decisions again.

Let us examine each of the above recommendations in greater detail.

1. Allow Others to Help You

In most instances of major loss, especially death, it is impossible to cope with grief alone (Burgess, 1977). To refuse to be comforted is to choose to hold hands with sadness indefinitely, to be shackled to the past. The bond between friends, within families, and between roommates is the single most important outside resource to be tapped in coping with loss. Do not allow blind devotion to being independent, or the fear you will be considered weak, keep you from accepting the wisdom or assistance of those who are older or more experienced. Assuming these relationships with your "significant others" are authentic and strong, the presence of trusting persons will provide a base from which to test feelings, consider options, find security, and rebuild your self-esteem. The quality of these relationships will bring many willing people to your side as they learn of your experience. Utilize *their strengths* in your time of weakness. This is what friendships are for: to assist one another in times of sadness, to enjoy each other's company, and to join in celebrating the good times.

Each of us has to choose, to make decisions which affect our recovery. What else is there to do? *Begin again!* Once again begin the task of reconstruction. When hope is nowhere to be found, despair reigns supreme. The search for hope begins in many ways. One of the most helpful starting points is another human being. People are life-promoting. We must connect with someone willing to listen to us and who can *eventually share our pain.* Sharing pain widens the life space which has been constricted by loss. We are vulnerable; our defenses are gone; *interdependence* is called for. "After giving myself a few minutes to think over what I had just gone through," Vickie said, "Jan was there to listen to me as long as I needed her. She was good for me because she sought out what was factual and what was 'believed to be true.' As much as her help was tremendously needed, I also felt the need for answers to questions I had concerning cancer." Vickie was exercising a choice of dependence in time of need.

In another instance, Denise's family and friends filled her need after the death of her father:

> My family was one of the most helpful, supporting things for me during all of this. We have talked openly about his death. Our feelings have been aired and shared, and through this we have learned that we can depend on each other for the comfort we need now. My close friends here at school, as well as at home, were also very helpful. They seem to know when I need to talk and when I need to be silent. With them, I can let any true feelings surface and not be afraid of what will happen.

It is all right to let others know of your deep hurt.

You will be doing two things as you accept their caring: helping yourself at a time when you need people with whom to share your feelings, and helping your friends/family who also have a need to do something to ease your burden and *their* feelings of inadequacy at your dilemma. Much good comes from this interchange, as you learn more about your true friends, find the security which is so frequently needed early in the grief response, and enhance feelings about yourself when witnessing how others really care.

Friends not only provide physical comfort for us, but more importantly, they keep us in contact with life when withdrawal would be the easy route to follow; they provide the motivation to keep going. If you reject this help and go it alone, you reject care and love which assists in healing. It does not make you less a person when allowing others to enter your world at this time. And sometimes, what you say and do will frighten friends. They are apprehensive because they do not understand grief, but they can learn. Be patient with their reactions; they, too, are struggling—with how to deal with what they are witnessing. But accept without guilt or hesitation their offers to be there, for *you* need their presence and willingness to try to comprehend your suffering: They will need your direction.

Do not be overly concerned if someone close to you does not provide the comfort you expected. If brother or sister or best friend does not say much, it may be that they just do not know what to say or do. They, too, may be dealing with uncontrollable fears, stunned by the suddeness of it all, and afraid they will make the situation worse than it is. They may need time to prepare themselves to help you.

You will be especially fortunate if one of your friends has experienced a similar loss. There is an invisible bond between grievers, especially those who have recently experienced a similar loss or are presently working through the same loss but are at a later stage in their grief work. Such persons are more sensitive and aware of your needs during your crisis. It is not a sign of inadequacy or weakness for you to try to find a person who has been through the pain you are now confronting. As Sylvia advises: "The best way to deal with a loss is to talk to someone else who has experienced the same loss. Talking to anyone, while perhaps still valuable, is much more limiting, for I feel that no one can fully understand the shock of the loss unless they themselves have experienced it." Although Sylvia's statement is arguable, self-help groups frequently provide this unique assistance to their members.

2. Remember That It Is Normal to Experience What Seems Abnormal

One's fantasies about loss are much worse than the experience itself. The surge of emotions which accompany loss at times shock one into believing that there is "something wrong with me." We may think, "I shouldn't feel this way." We believe we are going crazy. This is not an uncommon thought, and one we must get out in the open and talk about. We do become irrational in our thinking at these times, but we are certainly not mentally ill. We are groping for handles to hold on to, emotional handles that slip from our grasp. Do not allow this to alarm you, for it is only a temporary part of personal disorganization. The fantasy is most frightening if you contain it by suppression which, unfortunately, many people have learned to do early in their lives. To show outwardly what is happening inwardly is to invite rebuke from adults or teasing from peers. These unfortunate incidents make suppression a necessity and set the stage for trying to answer all our questions by ourselves. A typical response reflecting feelings of abnormality and associated with the breakup of a love relationship, came from Joanna:

> I used to spend a lot of time crying, I was very confused at the time. Some days I had the feeling I was going crazy. I would go to class and take notes and never know what was said or done. For weeks I didn't care what went on around me. I also spent a lot of time asking God why this had to happen to me.

Remember too, that a lack of awareness of what is normal or abnormal in loss experiences plays a part in believing what one experiences is abnormal. This was the plight of Jean, who wrote: "Had I been aware that so many of the negative feelings that I had were a normal part of the death experience and subsequent healing process, I would not have been so hard on myself." After a divorce, similar feelings arise: "If I had known that it was normal to expect the anger and overpowering fear," said Jerri, "I may have been able to keep more of my feelings of self-worth." There is a need for us to uncover and explore these thoughts, to come to the realization that emotions are neither good nor bad; it's what we do with them that counts. To better "read" our emotions at the time of loss is a critical ability by which we can cope, reaching its full implementation through the knowledge that "this sense of crazyness" is to be expected during major turning points in life. Regardless of the circumstances, when emotions are allowed to continuously direct behavior (at the expense of reason and intellect) the present condition only deteriorates further.

Feelings of relief sometimes follow major loss and cause us to think that we are wicked or self-centered. However, relief flows naturally from our confrontations with loss just as it does when we have been dealing with other kinds of anxiety-producing situations. We may feel relief— that we are afraid to talk about—because we are convinced others will think less of us. When the suffering ends for our loved one, when we make the final decision of the romantic breakup or the divorce (when our anxiety is partly lessened because of the loss event), it is not inhumane to experience relief. By habit we seek reduction of anxiety; it is our natural inclination. Because anxiety release may be associated with a loss event, it is no indication that one is somehow self-centered or thinking of death or unhappiness for someone else.

3. Express Your Thoughts and Feelings

Major loss experiences initiate the intensification of many emotions and feelings. These emotions rise to heights seldom experienced; they seek outlets in unpredictable ways. While we cannot eliminate these feelings, we can direct them. Usually, we direct our emotions at friends, God, a loved one, or ourselves. One can verbally attack oneself. (It is not unusual for people to yell or scream when they are alone.) Emotions have a way of causing added physical and mental stress. There is evidence to suggest that those who do not express some of their emotions early in the grief process are subject to considerable ill health later (Gorer, 1965; Parkes, 1972). Some emotions tend to come out in a distorted way; one's repressed emotions are often acted out in drunken behavior, the destruction of property, or broken relationships. "I think everyone should know in advance," explained Diana, "that readjustment takes time and that repression does not help." This is an illustration of one young woman's response to the end of a friendship. As she looked back on her recovery, her unwillingness to discuss with others her deep-seated feelings had complicated the adjustment process.

A man dying of lung cancer told me that after being diagnosed and informed by the physician of his condition, "I had to find someone to talk to, not just anybody." He had to talk about what he was feeling at the time; it was extremely helpful in his acceptance of the condition and his willingness not to give in to despair. Stifle the urge not to share the turmoil occurring within. What these illustrations presuppose is: *the first and basic step in dealing with the emotions associated with major loss is to acknowledge them.* Do not ignore or bury them for their expression is critical in grief work (Jackson, 1977; Worden, 1982; Lindemann, 1944; Freese, 1977; Vollman, et al., 1971).

The expression of feelings does not merely provide a safety valve for the release of agonizing thoughts and explosive emotions, but often through this sharing process, we are made more aware of our own thoughts by the simple act of expressing them. By this I mean that verbalizing thoughts and feelings is a way of clarifying the accuracies or inaccuracies of our perceptions of the situation, how we feel about it, and the implications for the future, while allowing listeners to gain insight into our world. This behavior allows others the opportunity of suggesting options to consider when we are dealing with specific beliefs. Martha expressed it this way: "I have found that you never block out the death of anyone who has such a great impact on your life. Over a length of time I was able to talk to my friends about my father and found that they wanted to hear what I had to say as much as I wanted to tell them. Talking was, and is, the most helpful thing for me to do in coping with death." Through dialogue with others we come to *know* what we are feeling, to legitimatize what society has taught us should be repressed. *If we fail to do this, every loss experience in life will prove to instill new despair, new fear, and confusion due to emotional withdrawal which paralyzes our ability to cope.* We must free ourselves in order to live a human existence, not the imaginary one society envisions.

Further, it is not unusual when grieving to refuse to recognize the legitimacy of certain feelings which surface. For example, it is all right to acknowledge anger, the cause and/or expression of which may be hidden, because you feel you were deserted by the deceased or the loved one who left you. Such feelings of abandonment are very real and are psychologically acceptable and *we need to identify the accompanying emotions* for what they are. When we refuse to do so, we close one door to the resolution of grief. Because anger sometimes hides in snobbishness, hatred, intolerance, rigidity, distrust, cynicism, and jealousy, these disguises make it difficult to uncover and do something about.

Talking to significant others will bring on the physical release of crying so often needed. Talking becomes a way of physically acting out feelings, which if suppressed cause excessive physical and emotional discomfort. It can help you deal with depression, especially if you become fixated on thoughts like, "it was exactly 48 hours ago that it happened," or "it was · exactly three weeks ago today and I was so happy and then . . . " Express these thoughts aloud to someone else to break the vicious cycle of torturing yourself by replaying them over and over in your mind.

A young woman who broke up with her boyfriend literally remained in bed for two weeks. Two friends helped her immensely by convincing her that other friends had experienced a similar loss, she should let her feelings surface, and that the expression of emotions was perfectly acceptable. She cried profusely and her grief work was able to continue on from its previous delayed state. She had a right to cry and rage against rejection.

Coping with the same type of loss, Marianne was encouraged to get her anger out by use of sarcasm. She said of her roommate: "She really was great because she understood why I resented his ego, his games, and his face! It may not be right, but snide remarks help let off steam. She joined in with me in the verbal abuse department." Without expression of what happens within, it is most difficult to move forward in recovery. Often anger and tears go hand in hand. Washington Irving reminds us: "There is a sacredness in tears; they are not the mark of weakness, but, of power. They speak more eloquently than ten thousand tongues. They are messengers of overwhelming grief, of deep contrition, and of unspeakable love." Crying is a fully human response as much as it is a healthy one. Do not suppress your tears, for they discharge tension just as they are a means of communicating feelings and needs to support persons. As Shakespeare's King Henry VI said: "To weep is to make less the depth of grief." Weeping is a fundamental way of communicating hurt. It is our first line of defense. *It is all right to cry for yourself.*

Why do we tend to suppress feelings? Sometimes it is due to the fear of being rejected by others, of being labeled "abnormal" because we happen to feel the way we do. Guilt, oftentimes the neurotic guilt stemming from what we have failed to do in the past, may cause us to keep internalized what should be dealt with overtly. As Penny suggests: "Many times the emotions that accompany grief cause guilt and frustration because one feels that she should not feel hatred, anger, etc." We refuse to think anger is an acceptable response and decide to push it back inside us, especially when we feel support persons would object to our emotionality. Finally, we may suppress feelings due to the belief that they simply must never be revealed because they are "bad"; they are feelings that adults must work out by themselves in private. This is part of the cultural ethic which says that grief is private and there should be little public acknowledgment of loss (Charmaz, 1980). This assumption is sometimes fueled by one's ignorance or early learning experiences where feelings could not be openly discussed.

There are many other ways to express what is within: write about what you feel; express yourself in drawing or painting. Use your creative abilities as a way to manage emotions. Keeping a diary or a notebook can also be of great assistance. Lynn Caine (1975) called her diary her paper psychiatrist. It provided her with a wonderful means of talking on paper when she felt the urge. If you feel all bottled up, sit down and write to your diary as you would to a dear trusted friend that you know will understand. Find a means to express yourself. This may even include an imaginary conversation or writing a letter to the deceased person for the purpose of finishing unfinished business, saying the things you did not get a chance to say or would like to repeat (O'Connor, 1984). We often need a way to say goodbye, to gradually let go of the bond which death has severed.

Do not fear if you are unable to let your feelings out to just anyone. It takes time to muster the courage to talk to someone seriously for many reasons (past experiences are a big one). Sometimes sadness is so overpowering that we are unable to verbalize how badly we feel. Gradually, when the opportunity arises to speak to a friend, take full advantage of it. There is no need to apologize to anyone for your emotions.

Do not fear losing control of yourself; the fear of releasing one's emotions as well as the fear of loss of control is not unusual (Raphael, 1983). Such fears are grounded in the false belief that expression of emotion is weakness and culminates in a nervous breakdown if allowed

full expression. This latter belief is also strengthened when one does not
see her grief ending as soon as she expected, or if one has cried alone for
long periods of time. Write about your fears and any other troubling
emotions. Later, when you read what you wrote, the progress since made
will be most encouraging.

4. Do Not Try to Avoid Grief

The opposite of pleasure is pain, and each of us learns to avoid both
physical and mental pain very early in life. It is not unusual, then, for
individuals to attempt to avoid the agony and pain associated with loss
(Lindemann, 1944). *Grief cannot be circumvented, nor can change be easily
assimilated when the continuity of life has been abruptly interrupted.* Anguish
and pain are automatic when expected continuity ends. The desire to
escape this feeling is overwhelming. However, there is little choice but to
face the difficulties which change entails. Recovery cannot begin until
we have fully faced the pain which is part of *all* major life changes. Grief
is not optional, excessive anguish and pain are. The effort made to avoid
pain eventuates in added misery.

There are many traps we may fall into in this regard; we can run
away from the scene thinking that all can be forgotten. While geographical change can be helpful for some, an effective means to achieve
the elimination of pain it is not. One can deny the event has happened:
that does help for a while. Through years of clinical experience Horowitz
(1982) has observed that denial early in the grief process is a form of
coping which allows one to initially adapt to the loss, dealing with
troublesome fears in the process. Eventually, however, reality must prevail and we must consolidate our shaky position by accepting the fact
of loss.

Instead of employing denial, we may choose to avoid thinking or
talking about the loss and, in place of this, plunge into work or other
avoidance activities so that the pain will not have to be faced. This also
works for a short time, but it never erases the memory of the event and
once again emotions eventually must be confronted, even though one
hoped they had been buried. For some, the avoidance of all conscious
grieving culminates in depression (Bowlby, 1980). Grief has been postponed, but so has acceptance of the loss and, consequently, ultimate
recovery.

The use of alcohol (the number one liquid drug) poses special problems for those not aware of its effect on the emotions when a major loss is involved. Never take drugs unless they are prescribed by a physician. Especially avoid Valium©, the most abused tranquilizer, and alcohol. In combination, the synergistic effect of these drugs is especially destructive. Pain has to be experienced; it will not vanish; it will gradually subside. The indiscriminate use of chemicals to replace the reliance on one's inner resources will confirm a damaging belief: the power of a drug is stronger than one's ability to respond to adversity. On the other hand, if you were taking prescription drugs for a particular condition before the loss occurred, continue with them unless a physician tells you to do differently. *Never* combine them with alcohol or arbitrarily increase the dosage. Any attempt artificially to restructure your internal environment so that you can handle an external event, only postpones the eventual confrontation with change. Because of erratic fluctuations in mood, it is wiser to seek the companionship of a trusted friend than the distorting numbness of "escape drinking."

The avoidance of legitimate expression of sorrow and sadness can be directly or indirectly influenced by others. Social expectation often forces behavior that we are not comfortable with. Friends may convince you that you are a "strong person," a "real" man or woman who can "tough it out," who can lick this problem. This is pure image manipulation and has value only if we need to increase our fantasy life. The false image we assume is one of toughness, "stiff upper lip," a tower of strength. When this is taken too literally, one robs the self of the justifiable right to grieve according to her needs. Why live up to an image imposed on us by others? Ask yourself: what do you need now, at this moment? Give yourself the freedom to be the real you. There is nothing unseemly about being real in the face of personal tragedy. The essence of being human is to be genuine, first and foremost, with yourself.

5. Reach Out

When emotions run high, when they are intense, we are vulnerable and in need of others who will be fortresses of security simply by their presence. But there is still much that must be done in order to overcome the immobilizing effects of loss. Seeking out friends and family, fostering friendship and concern, as well as sharing our hurt and upset is our responsibility. We should seek the opinions of others about what courses of action to take before making our decisions. We must seek out those who will listen, not judge, those who are willing to allow emotions to surface, regardless of their nature and who they are targeted against, while avoiding the temptation to tell us how to respond to our loss. In sum, *we must trust others.* This may not be easy to do, especially if past experience caused us to distrust the adults in our lives. There is a certain awkwardness in having to ask for help when in pain, especially when we have asked the same person before and that person has given so much. However, trusting others is essential and will be most helpful to our progress. We must choose to be healed. Time will not do it for us; it only provides the framework for action.

In the later stages of grief, we will need to reinvest our energy in new pursuits. These pursuits could involve developing new relationships, planning a trip, seeking a new career, visiting a friend in another city, or starting a new hobby. *Be good to yourself.* Pleasure is not forbidden after major loss occurs. "What's most important in learning to live with loss is letting yourself feel. Allow yourself to feel—to experience—to live again" (O'Connor, 1984, p. xi). We are responsible for initiating changes in behavior which otherwise results in loneliness. Be willing to accept opportunities to go places and do things with others. Volunteer. These are activities which force us to think, to be around others and to focus on positive outcomes while affirming a sense of social cohesion. They will bring new hope, hope that loss can be overcome. Stay away from being all alone in your room for long periods of time. Refuse to withdraw into yourself. *Remember: if we can change our behavior, we can eventually change our feelings.*

Another helpful tactic is to utilize skills in music, recreation, or cooking. *Engage in the things you do well and enjoy doing.* Linda, a music major, did just that: "My music was my mode of expression. I became immersed in it and I grew better through it. Music held me together. I could do it well and it helped me keep a positive feeling toward myself. Playing (the piano) often changed my mood." Be creative. Try writing a song about your loss. Begin a poem which you can add to as the days and weeks pass by. Write a book, cut a record, make a video tape; these are active means of directing the course of your grief work. Invite someone to accompany you to an art show, a movie, or lunch.

Later in your grief work you will need frequent temporary relief from all the attention of well-meaning friends. *You will need time to be alone.* Although silence can be deafening, it can also be refreshing and allow time to review and plan. Tell your friends you need to be alone, if they insist on being present all the time; they will understand. Because we will need to sort out our feelings, we must assert ourselves. This can be accomplished without sounding ungrateful. Time alone is important for the work of releasing the deceased (Sanders, 1985).

A walk in the woods, sitting in silence in a church or at a favorite retreat are both comforting and often a source of renewal. Sometimes one needs to be alone right after she learns of the loss as Gina tells us: "As soon as I learned over the phone of the loss of my Grandmother, I just needed time to be alone, so I walked to the Chapel House which was empty. Yet somehow, just being there made me feel closer to God, which helped me clear up my doubts and negative feelings." Gerri put it this way: "My friends were helpful and supportive, yet there also developed a certain amount of tension. I used to like to be alone and just cry until I couldn't cry anymore. Then I would feel tired and a bit relieved. I also like to see my mother's things, her pictures, and her clothes." Being by oneself just to think sometimes occurs when one has to drive a long distance. Alex found it helpful when he had to drive 400 miles to get to the scene of an accident which claimed the life of his friend: "Being able to be alone," he said, "to try and understand my own feelings before talking to other people who were affected by the loss really helped me." If you don't want to be left alone, then let others know this, too. You decide. Take the initiative. Let someone know if you need to be held, if you wish to talk, if you need to eat with someone, or when you want to be alone to rest. *Don't assume others know what you need.* When we are grieving, being assertive is essential to our mental health, and it is our right.

Help Others

Perhaps the most rewarding of all your efforts to heal the wounds that loss inflicts is found in the decision to help others. This may seem strange that you, the one who is hurting, should be trying to help others after having dealt with your initial shock and numbness. But helping others is an essential therapeutic tool; a great many people attest to this. This is also an effective lifelong strategy, because by helping others we are really helping ourselves. ("The fact that my mother needed me to be strong, that instead of me falling apart on her, I was there for her, helped me to cope.") The very act of giving is an act of receiving love and gratitude from those to whom we have freely given. Many of your peers

report that, by helping another family member or friend through difficult times, they were strengthened in faith and hope while their grief
work was made easier ("I felt that helping my father to cope helped me to
cope"). Of course, there are some instances in which this coping technique may prove to be counterproductive. This occurs when one focuses
exclusively on the needs of others as a defense against dealing with one's
own needs (Raphael, 1983; Lazare, 1979).

Usually helping others fosters a state of mind which brings extraordinary changes into our lives. It brings us closer to friends and loved ones
who are major sources of enlightenment and happiness for us, thereby
strengthening our reattachment to the flow of life. This view of helping
others is not without precedence, of course. It has been practiced by
millions of people down through the ages. All the great religions embrace
the wisdom which this "helping Golden Rule" holds. It has been tested
as no other coping mechanism has been tested, and it has been found to
bring relief as no medicine ever has. Giving of yourself to someone you
cherish in her time of need has become a major approach in dealing with
a catastrophic illness as well as with the grief which attends it (Jampolsky,
1981).

For many people, it is not possible to help someone else while still in
the early stages of their own grief; they will have to begin weeks or
months later. However, families who have experienced close ties and
openness with emotions as a normal part of their living pattern find that
the long-term support each provides for the other is a strong source of
mutual aid in recovery. The giving of ourselves comes back in the glow
and feeling which love sparks in each act of generosity. Being other-
centered reduces feelings of estrangement and separation, while it
simultaneously diminishes self-pity and the hopelessness it so frequently
generates. If you want to perpetuate the memory of your deceased loved
one, helping others is a most effective way to do it. By using the love,
guidance, and compassion received from the deceased when alive, putting into practice all they taught us, we know that they live on through
us. Can you ever obtain—or give—a greater gift than that? It is guaranteed that if we *give more than is expected*—in our relationships, in our
work, and in serving others—we will be able to cope with *any* tragedy.
The key point to be understood here is the decision to go the extra step
habitually, to do more than enough just to get by. We will not only feel
better for our efforts, but will be simultaneously creating an invaluable
inner resource for the future. We will establish never-ending relationships.

6. Rise Above the Bitterness and Resentments

Many losses bring with them ill feelings toward various persons, places, or things. A woman whose husband died of cancer, after he had lingered in the hospital for months, said to me: "I hate this hospital." These types of reactions are secondary to the deep negative feelings that often develop toward people. A common occurrence is the anger and bitterness directed toward God. For instance, when a college friend died, Dave said: "Why, God, why? For all the lousy people in the world, why did you have to pick one of the most loving, caring, giving women that I know—and why so much pain? Why couldn't you have picked a bum?" Sometimes, if the loss involved a breakup of a love relationship or a divorce, these negative feelings are directed toward those whose relationships or marriages are still intact. This bitterness is not unusual; it often fades in a short period of time, never to resurface. With others, it lingers for months or years, and that is when one needs assistance to realize that it is prolonging recovery not helping it.

Still more common are the reactions which focus on family members who clearly spoke their thoughts at the wrong time, especially when they were under great strain. We often fail to understand all the factors which cause the behavior we thought was so callous. Grudges are sometimes formed because physicians, human as they are, were not present when we feel they should have been, or because they made errors in judgment which could have contributed to the death of a loved one. The continual and conscious nurturing of *any* resentment and bitterness toward these individuals is *most hazardous to the griever.* The seductive impact of such forces on emotional outlook tends to bring back the pain of the tragedy while it foments additional misery that need not occur. By displacing blame, you prolong and temporarily block progress towards recovery. Holding grudges further depletes energy and wastes precious time. And such feelings tend to reinforce a negative self-image and internal conflict. During grief work, more than ever, you need to begin to feel good about yourself; don't get caught in the turmoil of replaying past hurts.

Not only is there a need to forgive others—the doctor, family members, or friends—we must also forgive ourselves for questionable behavior displayed during the time of tragedy. Every griever lives close to her emotions, perhaps too close when she is thrust into situations of rapid change. You may have been totally insensitive to the feelings or needs of your parents, you may have been abrasive to someone who came to visit you at home or at the wake, or perhaps you lashed out at a close friend who just happened to use the "wrong" words when she was trying to ease your pain. If you failed to realize the strain others were under when they said the "wrong" thing, and you exploded in rage, no longer dwell on the incident, give it up. Make amends. It is time to progress in your recovery. Neil had been able to cope with the death of his father by helping his mother, sister, and grandmother, but his hostility towards others *impeded* recovery. He tells us: "Everybody said, 'only the good die young,' and in his case I feel it's true, especially when I look around and see others who don't deserve to live and yet are living." When our ego has been hurt, hostility emerges, bitterness clouds our judgment; these are not unusual occurrences. Sometimes loss unleashes years of stored up hostility (Jackson, 1977). Forgive yourself and others when displays of hostility are painfully intense. Refuse to dwell on this kind of thinking; bypass these unfortunate events and transcend the issues. Such negative thinking will complicate grief work; it will not reduce your tears, it will not hasten the reorganization of your life, and it will not change what has already happened.

Should resentment keep you locked in your state of grief? Will bitterness destroy you? Will you choose to make these negative feelings a way of life or use them as a means to an end? These questions need to be considered. The choice is not whether to grieve, but *how* to grieve. Remember: you cannot adapt or renew yourself, you cannot begin again to accept life, unless you forgive everything and everyone involved in your interpretation of the tragedy. Nobody but you can remove the bitterness about what has happened, the resentment toward someone who hurt you, or the self-pity that quickly surfaces when self-esteem crumbles in the face of loss. Rid yourself of this mental poison. You alone have the built-in capacity to rise above these dehumanizing tendencies and the physical problems and low energy levels they bring. Protest your loss but do not channel your protest into a vendetta against any one individual. Above all else, do not seek revenge; this pursuit is most destructive. As the Chinese say: "He who seeks vengeance must first dig two graves."

Never forget the very delicate relationship between your emotional condition and disease states. You can choose to continue loving yourself (which is *essential* to recovery) and others, or simply exist in your world of hate. *Love does cure disease,* just as it shortens grief work. Changing hurt, resentment, anger, and disgust into love of self has resulted in miraculous cures (Simonton, Simonton & Creighton, 1980). Negative attitude is as much a cause of disease and prolonged grief work as a loving, positive attitude can be to cure. *The unconscious does heal.* As so many cancer patients tell us, their disease caused them to look at the world differently—to love again. It would be heartening to conclude that this is easy to do (it *is* easier if you are surrounded by loving people), but trusting again, serving others, reaching out with both arms is risky when our beliefs have been shattered. The alternative is for us to wither away and refuse to look for the sunrise. That is worse than *any* major loss, for living without love is to merely exist.

7. Expect to "Regress" or Experience Setbacks

Any time one talks of recovery or healing, thoughts usually turn to a gradual change for the better. This is typically pictured to be a serially progressive rise from a deep sense of hurt to complete adjustment. The belief prevails that each day one endures her loss, life gets better. In actuality, grief is erratic; it is not a smooth continuous process of healing. It is a mistake for you to expect a beginning and end to grief sandwiched between a time-span free of setbacks. Any journey from a low point in life to regaining control and direction over events is accompanied by numerous relapses; we may take several steps forward, then regress to an earlier stage of progress. In *A Grief Observed,* C.S. Lewis mourning the death of his wife wrote:

> Grief is like a long valley, a winding valley where any bend may reveal a totally new landscape. As I've already noted, not every bend does. Sometimes a surprise is the opposite one; you are presented with exactly the same sort of country you thought you had left behind miles ago. This is when you wonder whether the valley isn't a circular trench (p. 69).

Everybody experiences this phenomena, whether fighting a disease, working through grief, kicking a drug habit, or just coping with every-day problems. We often regress to an earlier state of childlike behavior. And it is all right; it is a condition to be expected. You will be fortunate, indeed, if this does not occur.

Relapses are common in physical healing. We reinjure a body part, reopen a wound, or tear a scab. The same holds true with emotional healing. There are good days and there are bad days. We think we are coping well when suddenly something reminds us of the loss and we begin the downward spiral to despair. With a death, it could be some object formerly possessed by the deceased, a visit to a place where memories of happier days are recalled, an old letter you find, or just coming back to your old home. With the breakup of a love relationship, it is the reminders of old friends you used to go on dates with, a local bar or restaurant, an object of sentimental value, a picture or, in many instances, actually seeing the person again, especially if she is with someone new.

When these things occur, the sense of self erodes, and you feel hopelessly locked into grief. It is common to feel that it will never end; hopelessness sets in. However, this is a time when you must be careful not to lose faith in yourself. These temporary setbacks are part of the process of adapting to loss.

Defusing Neurotic Guilt

Beware of the surges of grief which are caused by the tendency to allow neurotic guilt to play out its role; it merely adds to the sense of futility. It is an experience which can get the best of us. We reinforce our willingness to blame ourselves by dubious reasoning which cannot withstand a test of truth. Yet, almost always we feel that our thinking is not only justified, it's the only right way to look at the dilemma. If we continue this cycle of deluded thinking, we will continue to have constantly depressing thoughts that paint a picture of how we might have prevented the loss event, as though we originally had the power to rewrite history. Such guilt arises from many sources: forgetfulness, the relief that the loved one has died and our vigil is finally over, behavior in our past associations, beliefs that loss is punishment, feelings of neglect, ambivalent (love-hate) feelings, any hostility toward the deceased or the person we are now separated from, early childhood conflicts, or our failure to fulfill a perceived role. A significant problem here is discerning whether guilt is real or neurotic, because this may affect how it should be managed. Regardless of the source of guilt, you can begin to deal with it. Before seeking professional counseling, there are three techniques to first employ in working through it: talk about it (ventilation), study the dynamics of guilt (rationalization), and let time play its role as the universal healer.

You may recall in our discussion of the grief process (p. 83) that guilt should not be suppressed; rather, it should be discussed freely and openly. This is our first line of defense against the dread and shame that guilt inflicts. This approach seems so simple, and yet it takes courage to carry it out. If you are unable to speak about your guilt with a friend, look for someone on campus who teaches a course that deals with bereavement or the like. Most likely this person will be a member of the Department of Psychology, Health Science, or Sociology. If the response of this individual is too academic and seems to lack compassion, turn to the Counseling Center. If you cannot talk about your guilt, write it down, find a way to test the reality of it. In any case, do not ignore it—face it. Prolonged guilt is a choice you are making based on questions without answers: *If only . . .* and *What if . . .* (O'Connor, 1984).

A second technique is to understand how guilt evolves from imperfect interpersonal relationships (Raphael, 1983). Read about guilt, study how it complicates grief, and understand its many faces. Realize you are not unique in your experience with it. One way of defusing guilt is to consider that few social relationships in our lives are free of ambiguous feelings. The degree of ambivalence is often related to the intensity of grief. Many therapists tell us that love/hate relationships not only make it harder to deal with grief, but bring us intense guilt feelings as well. We must recognize that it is not unusual to have mixed feelings toward others, especially those we love and care about. These mixed feelings are to be expected in the course of our association not only with them but with virtually every significant other in our lives. When death intervenes, it is normal to review ill-feelings toward the deceased when she was alive and to magnify our shortcomings. But accept the fact that this review and the feelings of guilt it generates are simply a part of human frailty. We all have weaknesses; to be human is *not* to be perfect. It is up to us to *change our thinking in this situation*, independently of whether our guilt is neurotic or based on fact. Why? "It is a psychological fact that if we hold on to guilt, we will attempt to handle it either by attacking ourselves (frequently expressed as symptoms of depression or physical illness), or projecting the guilt on someone else" (Jampolsky, 1985, p. 32).

Finally, time may be of assistance to you. Sometimes guilt gradually lessens as the length of time between ourselves and the loss event becomes greater. This may be due to the fact that faulty reasoning which so frequently accompanies grief later becomes more rational. During this time span you must focus your attention on the following concepts:

1. No one is perfect; *you did the best you could at the time.*
2. Knowing the deceased as you did, realize she would never want you to suffer from this guilt and would want you to go on with your life. *She would forgive you.*
3. It is impossible for one to be prepared for *every* contingency, *every*

situation in our relationships with others. Therefore, we must transcend, rise above, some problems realizing there is no answer — except that we are human.

As we regain a sense of involvement in life once again, guilt can be more easily worked through. As we regain strength, particularly ego strength, we can decide to let go of the tendency to blame ourselves that often evolves from the perfectionist attitude so many of us have assumed. We will experience enough reminders of our loss without adding those which are not legitimate. Talk the self-blame out, play it out, exercise it out, but do not constantly dwell on it. Whatever has happened is history. The bottom line on guilt, whether neurotic or real, is: *we must forgive ourselves.* Others will forgive us. God will forgive us. What more is there to do? We can always vow to make amends and improve the quality of life. Because we are most susceptible to depression when we are emotionally exhausted, that is, when we have literally become emotionally bankrupt (and guilt can do this), we must be aware that such setbacks in our grief work, if allowed to continue uncorrected, will reverse the course of mourning. By forgiving ourselves, we release fear and guilt, heal our relationships and are no longer alone and separated (Jampolsky, 1985).

Perhaps the most devastating setback possible is the crumbling of our support network (i.e., those significant others upon whom we depend most for support) after several months. Our recurring need to talk about the loss and accompanying guilt may have caused others to become uncomfortable in our presence — they may begin to avoid us. Perhaps they have grown tired of our grieving. Try to understand that this is a product of living in a society which believes that grief should be short-lived. At appropriate times you may have to turn to the clergy or other support sources as needed. The point is: do not let the avoidance of friends cause additional stress; find a new support network because guilt, like anger, immobilizes.

8. Maintain Your Physical Strength

Grief (particularly guilt, anger, and depression) drains and saps energy. Sleep is difficult to attain, especially early in the grief process. You may lose your taste for food, and refuse to eat as well; later, the reverse can happen and food becomes an emotional outlet; when anxiety rises, food is used to combat it and increase feelings of well-being. These scenarios should be of concern because eventual sickness and/or complete exhaustion due to poor health habits are real possibilities.

Anyone who has studied the implications of body-mind relationships knows that feeling bad physically further influences the way one thinks and her overall emotional state. The reverse is also true: feeling good physically can impact on thinking in positive ways. Psychosomatic medicine teaches that to let yourself deteriorate physically, especially when you are emotionally distraught, only adds to the problems of recovery. Therefore, the need for exercise, food and sleep must be planned for (as inappropriate as it may seem), especially during the later grief stages.

Make use of a college or high school's physical education facilities to run, swim or play racquetball. Take long walks with a friend. Being physically tired at the close of the day not only facilitates sleep, but exercise releases neuromuscular hypertension. "In fact physical exercise can even relax and help us withstand mental frustration" (Selye, 1974, p. 78). *Everyone needs physical outlets for pent-up emotions.* This is even more important if you are struggling with the stress and anxiety of loss. *For every thought and emotion experienced, there is a corresponding physical manifestation of that thought or emotion.* Major loss causes bodily stresses, many of which can be dissipated through physical activity of an aerobic nature or even through long walks. Many individuals report the use of exercise as a way of coping with a variety of problems. Movement is life-affirming, and anything you can do to intensify life-affirming activities can only assist your grief work.

As difficult as it may seem at this time, carefully watch your diet; avoid extremes by either under-eating or overeating. If you don't feel like eating at mealtime, try to eat a very small portion. Stay away from "junk food," and their carbohydrates and too much caffeine. You may have to temporarily eliminate all caffeine-containing products from your diet. Eat something light and easily digestible. Eat small amounts more frequently until you regain your normal eating patterns.

Because of the stress imposed by major loss events, your body will be depleted in stores of calcium, iron, and vitamins C and D. Eat a leafy green salad daily. Avoid foods rich in cholesterol. Drink at least one glass of milk or a milk substitute daily as well. Avoid complete physical breakdown which will happen, if you grow careless with personal health habits. But most important: when you lose respect for your body, when you let yourself go, your emotions are affected as well. Maintaining physical strength is another form of self-discipline which, if practiced during recovery from loss, will shorten the healing process.

Finally, a word about sleep. When insomnia persists, the National Academy of Science's Institute of Medicine suggests the following:

1. Set a definite time to go to sleep and to get up.
2. Exercise daily.
3. Do not nap during the daytime.
4. Take a warm bath and/or drink warm milk before retiring.

Warm milk contains "soporifics" (sleep-inducing chemicals). During the day, imaging will be useful in helping to conserve energy and reduce anxiety. This technique, (which is recommended by many therapists) involves finding a quiet place, relaxing in a chair or in a reclining position, and recalling a pleasant scene such as a picture, or a vacation spot—something which is very special to you. Focus your full attention on it. Examine every detail, using all of your senses: smell the seashore, see the mountains, taste the salt in the air, hear the birds, and feel the sand on your feet. These calm voyages, of but 15–20 minutes duration, will reduce tension, help change thought patterns, and renew energy. Relaxation tapes may also be used for this purpose.

However, be careful to avoid overdoing strenuous exercise. Too much exercise can use up your already depleted stores of energy. Just like a well-trained athlete, you must pace yourself in all that you do. Overextending yourself in any phase of recovery, whether in exercise or work, will only increase the tension you are trying to deal with. Moderation is called for here.

9. Control Self-pity

"Why me? Why did this have to happen now? To me? It ruins everything." These thoughts often race through our minds as we play over and over again the events of the loss and its impact on our personal life. Self-pity is a demeaning human response; and, because it occurs as a digression to accepting reality and confronting new beginnings, we need to guard against its taking over every waking hour. Avoid the trap of overindulging in self-pity, which we all tend to do; the appeal of self-pity is alluring and seductive. Recognize the normalcy of it (when one feels that a loss is clearly unfair, self-pity is an expected reaction), but especially recognize its devastating power to immobilize and keep you

from involvement with your environment by promoting feelings of helplessness about the future. The cure? Recognize the fact you are pitying
yourself, but do not allow it to become the central theme of grief. Accept
it *and move on*, because it does not take much to become a permanent
victim of this emotional atrophy.

Do not confuse the need for attention, or the urge to let others know
that you are hurting, with self-pity. Not infrequently, there is an urgency
to tell others what is happening within; this is legitimate and something
that is helpful to grief work. Karen Austin, a former student of mine,
stated this most clearly when she said:

> I do not think all the feelings of wanting others' attention should go under
> the heading of "self-pity." There is a very real need to have people know.
> So at the same time that I felt embarrassed or reluctant to tell people I had a
> brother who was killed, there was still a desire to do so. Could it be that by
> telling others we evoke a response that reaffirms others' close relationships
> with us? Would this action bring security where there had been left a mass of
> insecurity?

Relating what has happened is a part of grief work for most people.
When you feel that big hurt inside and nobody knows what it is like,
when you are insecure because of tragedy, it is essential that significant
others become aware of it. In fact, many bereaved people hope someone
will ask them so they can get it out in the open; this action reinforces
their acceptance by others, and reduces feelings of being alone. It gives
them comfort when others know about their experience; clearly, the
need to share pain is not a search for self-pity, but be aware that you
could turn it into one.

Rudolph Driekurs writes, "Pity is a negative emotion—it belittles the
individual, weakens his self-reliance and destroys his faith in life." We
can overcome self-pity by focusing our attention on others, by realizing
that this emotion is self-serving. A young student wrote me the following:
"Take it day-by-day with rational thinking and do not pity yourself or let
others give you too much pity. Pity can be an enemy, not a help.
Remember that other people also have had and will have the same kind
of problem." The last sentence tells it all: others have experienced what
has happened to you. You have not been singled out for this tragedy.
Keep in mind that self-pity is not only demeaning, it isolates, causing us
to turn energies inward instead of back onto the world. This isolation
may turn hopes for peace of mind into fears, depression, and loss of
interest in life. Self-absorption can also scare away potentially helpful

friends who believe you need special assistance. In short, it distances us from support persons by placing us in an inferior position (Parkes, 1972).

There is also a tendency to encourage our self-pity when we compare our loss to the loss incurred by a friend. It is not unusual to decide that our loss is so much worse because of certain factors that are unique to the situation. Or, we may look at others around us and think: "This isn't fair. I've done so much more for others and she just sits around doing nothing. But this had to happen to me, while she goes along untouched by tragedy." *Any such comparisons between sufferers of tragedy and those not facing it feed the fires of self-pity.* Turn the focus of your tragedy to: "All right, it's happened; where must I go from here?" It will be some time before you will be able to look at your loss this way. But we have no control over the past. We can control only what we will do with the future. This is where your focus must be. There is no other effective alternative. Senator Hubert Humphrey, dying of cancer, put it this way: "If you don't overcome self-pity, the game is over."

10. Nurture Your Faith

Having faith in something outside of the self in time of crisis has been the difference in life or death for millions of people. It is most graphically illustrated in the numerous stories of prisoners of war (both military and civilian) who lived through some of the worst conditions imaginable; it is recorded in the trials of being lost without food or water on land and sea. And always, it is a faith in something outside of the self that helps one prevail when everything seems hopeless. It may be a faith in someone else who motivates you to endure tragedy, as was the subject of Victor Frankle's: *Man's Search For Meaning.* If you believe in the goodness of others, that everything has a purpose, that there is a higher power, or that a silver lining exists somewhere, if you will cling passionately to those beliefs and *develop them,* they will help in the time-consuming matter of coping. Faith will never remove your grief; it will *always* make it bearable.

If you believe in a particular religion, turn toward it and those who hold similar beliefs. Sometimes loss will cause you to question your belief in God or whatever you value. It may eventuate in thinking: "There is no God who would allow this to happen." These are not blasphemous thoughts. They are simply human responses in the face of tragedy. If you have fallen away from earlier beliefs or teachings, renew the commitment to faith. Allow it to help you come back, to relearn. It is as easy to return to faith as it was to fall away from it, when you have a purpose in life. Reestablishing a belief system about life is often needed to accommodate major loss (Rando, 1984). Rose Kennedy, the mother of President John Kennedy and Senator Robert Kennedy, and one who experienced much personal tragedy in her life, places faith on the highest pinnacle in dealing with life's crises as she asserts: "The most important element in human life is faith." She has displayed an enduring faith in the face of so many tragic losses in her life.

Louise, at nineteen, read many books on the mystery of death when her friend suddenly died. She was also taking a religion course, *Problems in Faith*, at the time. She writes:

> My loss was a friend who suddenly died. In my reading about death, to help myself overcome my loss, I recall what one woman said at the loss of her husband. She said, "Why should I keep begging him to come back when he's already made it to eternal life. I have no right doing that." This made me realize that I had to be strong. My friend is in heaven now—I have no right to ask her to come back here. I'd also like to say that there's no other way to make it but to have faith.

Finding meaning in loss, which is so difficult to do in the face of tragedy, is a crucial turning point for most people. There is a need to find a purpose, a continuity, and some sense to what initially seems utterly senseless. This search takes time, during which faith sets in motion our final acceptance. Once the question of "Why did it happen?" is settled, the answer can lift the heaviest burden from your shoulders as the purpose for the suffering or death of your loved one is seen in a larger perspective. Faith provides more than a momentary respite from what seems to be cruel reality; it offers a permanent base for balancing the losses and gains of life and eliminating despair. It is a potent instrument for health (Byrd, 1979).

For many of us, there are no answers to the question of "Why?" We can't understand why it had to happen, but we have to decide to move beyond the "whys" and reengage life (or go down with it, the choice is narrow and defined), live on or exist in a whirlpool, decrease. I would like to offer an approach to coping with the death of a loved one that has been helpful to many children and adults of every age. Perhaps it will be a beginning for you as you find yourself in one of the darkest hours of life. It is a set of beliefs that you can think about and build upon. *It begins with the understanding that we NEVER really lose someone. Oh yes, the body is gone, that shell that enclosed truth and beauty. But what NEVER leaves, what is ours forever, is the love, compassion, the wisdom, and strength that somehow flowed to us through the person. We are the perpetual recipients of her spirit. We have grown and will continue on with the legacy that is wonderously ours to keep. And we, too, can live that legacy now, for we are so much better off for having been a part of that life. We shall always retain the lessons learned from that example.* As Alicia said at the beginning of this section: the deceased "will live on in us." You can celebrate your relationships with your deceased loved ones by the way you perpetuate the love and learning they freely gave you. While your life is defined in those you love, it must be redefined when loved ones die, for *you* will have changed, too.

Through the centuries it has been proven that, if you have faith, you can overcome any trial. You can heal the strongest emotional hurt—*if you believe you can.* The *Bible, The Tibetan Book of the Dead,* the *Koran,* and other great religious writings offer faith as a road to enduring the worst in life and obtaining its best. Prayers become powerful modes of expression. Rest assured that, if you utilize the subconscious power within, you *will* overcome fear and despair. Faith has produced miracles of every kind. Build into your belief system this incontrovertible truth: *you will get better; suffering will end.*

Faith and Fear

As previously discussed, death and loss will always occur, grief will not disappear; you will always need to cope with the traumatic changes in life. Believing that you will be able to cope with the low points that life hands out provides immeasurable power to heal. Never fail to explore it with childlike zeal. And most important of all, faith makes huge inroads on fear because it forces one to take action against one's immobilized state. Even the strongest are assailed by fears associated with loss. And faith always diminishes, even eliminates fear from their thinking. Fearfulness never stands the test of hope, confidence, and the affirmation of life.

Peace of mind begins and is governed from within. This is a powerful concept to think about and understand in its entirety. It is on this concept that millions of people have developed their abilities to overcome the most tragic experiences imaginable. They have cured themselves of cancer, depression, changed the course of their lives and enhanced physical and emotional well-being. And the power to accomplish these tasks is innate, a part of every individual's life; such self-regulation is yours on demand. The will to endure, to find peace amidst turmoil, cannot be measured; this is fully acknowledged by the medical profession whose members have witnessed victories of the spirit over disease in dimensions never thought possible. Developing this inner force takes patience, practice, and conviction. Just because we cannot see, smell, hear, taste, or touch faith, never doubt its existence. Neither can we see electricity or the wind, but we know they are there. So, too, with this inner power or spirit.

You can practice your faith by the use of quotes of the thoughts of others (such as philosophers), aphorisms, or meaningful prayers which you devise. This technique is especially helpful in dealing with fear. Many people paste them on their bathroom mirrors or place them in other conspicuous places. "I will get better," "I will adjust," "I can endure the pain" are reminders which focus on positive outcomes. If you believe in God, consider the Serenity Prayer:

> God grant me the
> *Serenity* to accept the
> things I cannot change
> *Courage* to change the
> things I can, and
> *Wisdom* to know the
> difference.

Having been used by millions of people suffering from alcoholism to having been abandoned, this prayer has provided special strength for many people undergoing the recovery process. Whatever path one chooses, faith grows within as we reach out to connect with others. No one can ill-afford to use this natural resource; it is there, waiting to be developed.

11. Deal with Immediate Problems and Make Decisions Again

Grief is not a sickness, but it causes "sick" thinking; it is sometimes mainly illogical thinking. We are confused because of sudden loss and accompanying depression. Depending on the intensity of grief, decision-making abilities are quickly impaired. When one feels threatened, perceptions are narrowed, especially if one is not secure with the self (Combs, 1962). Loss, for many, is threatening. Thus, it is tempting to allow others to take over completely, and in doing so, cut off our only immediate avenue for interaction and maintaining contact with life. Here we have two problems to confront: (1) an impairment of judgment, due to the radical change experienced, and (2) the temptation to drop out of life and refuse to enter into the decision-making process, as a defense against further assaults on the ego. The answer to both of these dilemmas lies somewhere in trusting loved ones at the outset of the tragedy, and in an awareness of the need of maintaining some degree of control over life.

You should not make major decisions, like changing schools, quitting school, or selling your car, early in the grief process. Consultation with significant others is essential here. Our capacity to make long-term commitments and assessments, or to make important changes is lessened, and it is best to wait and seek consultation in this regard. At the same time, while friends can do much to lighten our immediate burden (and we truly need such help), it can be carried too far, so that we become willing to "let them provide," while we settle back and do nothing. Friends may help us with our thinking; they are not supposed to replace it. Friends should also consult with us to find out if it is all right for them to assist in a particular way. If they forget to do this, insist on it, especially if taking over a responsibility that is clearly yours. For example, during the early shock and numbness following tragedy, if you were due to give a speech in class or show up for your part-time job, it would be appropriate for your roommate to contact those in charge and explain your absence. Then again, it might not be appropriate if you are several weeks into your grief and are allowing others to do such tasks for you. The sooner you start making decisions about your own life, the better off you will be. The temptation to use grief as an excuse for shirking duties and obligations is always present. Directing your life and assuming control over it is of paramount importance; however, leave major decisions for later on. We all must take time to reaffirm our attachment to life:

> The road to recovery from grief, therefore, is to take time to do things which will enable us to give a renewed meaning to our life. That's when our journey through grief becomes a journey of discovering ourselves, our potential and our resources in the encounter with life. That's when we become *better* people rather than *bitter* people. In grief, no one can take away our pain because no one can take away our love. That call of life is to learn to love—again (Pangrazzi, 1983, p. 4).

Finding renewed meaning, a goal, a direction, a commitment or a service to give is a major part of recovery. Without it we annihilate the human spirit. *Establish new goals:* volunteer, obtain your M.A. degree, develop a new skill. Choose to see that despite the feeling of complete devastation, life can be recreated. Or, as Nietzsche remarked: "He who has a strong enough *why* can endure almost any how."

Facing problems and making decisions about daily life provides an added bonus: it obliges one to focus energies on life situations other than loss. Many of your peers report that, by coming back to school or to work and reentering the mainstream of decision-making which campus life or having a job demands, they were assisted by significant others in adjusting, particularly with the management of emotions. Prominent in this task is the confrontation with depression.

COMBATTING DEPRESSION

I didn't find anything or anyone helpful in coping. I spent several months in deep depression, which I am beginning to beat now. No one wanted to talk about it. I still feel as though I've lost something inside me. I certainly suffered a major breakdown of my beliefs.

Olivia, 20 years old, on the death of her friend

To the general public, depression is a negative emotion which one hopes to avoid at all costs. Counselors and psychiatrists see it quite differently: depression (shown plainly as gloom, melancholy, loneliness, "the blues," etc.) is a *natural* response to be expected as a result of having spent most of our emotional resources on the confrontation with loss. Depression is a mood disturbance which cycles in an irregular pattern throughout life. Therapists refer to one type of depression as "reactive depression," that is, a reaction to events occurring in one's life space which cannot be controlled. Drug therapy is not usually employed in its treatment, and one is not believed to be genetically predisposed to it. Reactive depression ranges from very mild to severe in intensity. Symptoms are numerous: apathy, depersonalization, withdrawal, decreased energy and sexual desire, hopelessness, shame, dependency; feelings of helplessness (Rando, 1984). Everyone has bouts of reactive depression and some are better able to deal with it than others, depending on a variety of personality factors and their perceptions of preceding events. Perceptions of the self and hopes for the future strongly influence its length and depth.

This mood disturbance should not be confused with endogenous depression, sometimes referred to as psychotic depression (bipolar depressive disease or unipolar depressive disease) which is a response to unexplained, internal bodily changes. These biochemical changes, which have a genetic basis, are usually more severe in their outward manifestations and require immediate professional care and treatment.

Reactive depression, in some instances, may also require professional intervention, but generally can be dealt with by the individual, especially with the support and understanding of close friends and family. Guilt and anger often accompany depression which may be viewed as a form of protest (Lifton, 1980). Reactive depression can be successfully reversed when we recognize that we have been responsible for its abatement previously and possess the ability to break through it again. Of special importance to consider is that it is healthy, *an expected consequence of change and the "giving-up" process* (Peck, 1978). We are all living in a world of permanent change which causes depression as we refuse to accept the new conditions of existence and let go of previous aspects of our lives which were familiar and reassuring. These bouts of depression associated with the "giving-up" process can be dealt with by slowly reinvesting in life. Women seem to experience reactive depression to a greater extent than do men, which may be explained in part by women's stronger orientation and sensitivity to people (as suggested by their early social learning patterns). Married people also experience depression more than those who are single.

There are a number of possible causes for reactive depression: role conflicts, various interpersonal conflicts, role transitions, losses, and perceptions of the self as worthless. Coupled with irrational thinking about present conditions and dim prospects for the future—two factors which accompany most major loss experiences—it is readily clear why depression naturally follows so many changes throughout life.

How then, can we deal with apathy, withdrawal, and the feelings of inferiority, which seem to be prime characteristics when one is depressed? Let us first consider that, when depressed, individuals have lost all sense of being in control, of possessing the power to create and shape the direction toward which they want their lives to move; the ability to concentrate is often affected. If we are to help ourselves, we must do everything possible to restore that sense of personal control. Therefore, the depressive must be allowed to control the relationship between the helper and herself in so far as possible. She must be motivated to think of herself in positive terms. What I mean by this is that, by controlling the relationship, *she must* choose when she wants a caregiver to stay or go, to talk or listen, to help at that moment or to help later. No one else must be able to dictate or to take away the depressed person's remaining power.

The depressive must grow in self-esteem in order to feel better and break out of the state of withdrawal.

In dealing with your own depression, seek help among those who will allow you to regain control in your way, not theirs. Also, there is one factor we know to be very effective with mild depression; that is to do something physical: walk, jog, or engage in whatever you do well. The point is, do *not* remain sedentary for long periods of time. Fight feelings of uselessness and the desire to be inactive. Do what will bring a sense of success. Even a short daily walk to the park or a nearby store can be helpful in breaking the cycle of inaction.

Sometimes we are not even aware of depression unless someone close brings it to our attention. And if we are to help others, we may have to begin by giving recognition to their symptoms. "You seem depressed today" or "you seem down today" could be the beginning of a constructive approach by which we help one regain feelings of wholeness. At other times, the depression will be easily recognized by the depressed person, who will counter the attempts of others to help reach out to life once again. If you are trying to help someone who is depressed, you will need to be patient and wait for the opportunity to change the negative messages of self-esteem the depressed person is constantly sending. *But communication is essential here. It is a first step in overcoming depression.*

We can help our own depression by turning to a friend in whom we can confide. In many of life's experiences, loneliness seems to be at the heart of depression; it happens to the young and more especially with the old. All too frequently, our misguided beliefs are what send us into the depressed state, as they tend to change a difficult situation into an impossible one. An intimate conversation with a loyal friend can lead to increased choices, or it can change our interpretation of the events which led to the condition. Stan advises:

> I recovered from my depression by forcing myself to look toward the future, I realized I was ruining my life by feeling miserable all the time. A close friend also helped me by pointing out my good personal qualities and making me realize that I had a lot more going for me than I thought at the time. I realized that I could not continue to live in the past; I knew I had to push ahead. I decided that life was too short to feel sad all the time.

Talking about depression is essential. Such dialogue presents us with the opportunity to discuss anger, guilt, or feelings of inferiority which are contributing to our mood. Psychiatrists tell us that repressed anger is frequently behind depression and that we need to bring it out into the open, recognize its source, and give it up. Also, a conversation with a trusted friend will provide an opportunity to talk about physical feelings, and obtain a fresh point of view on one's problems. All this is useful because we need to find acceptance once again, to find a place in a world we are convinced has shut us out. "It is extremely important to realize that *you* are valuable to others, just as you found those who have died were valuable to you" (Burgess, 1977, p.61). Regardless of the type of loss which has generated grief, our basic value to others never diminishes, it only grows—unless *we* let it decrease because of our persistent thoughts of sadness.

We need human contact when depressed. But we need the right type, by the right person, at the right time, and it is needed consistently. This is what Olivia told us at the beginning of this section that she was unable to find. The need for consistency cannot be overstressed. Brief but regular visits, frequent phone calls, and honest discussions with a significant other makes inroads on the depressed state. *We have to search for ways to overcome the lethargy, to find satisfaction from what we do.* If we will reengage life, such an honest facing-up to the situation will draw us out of the passive, depressed state. Active interchange with the external world is incompatible with depression (Bowlby, 1961). This is accomplished by deliberately planning to engage in a new experience, such as spending time at a place not previously visited, taking a short bus ride with a friend to a nearby town for lunch or dinner, or by changing your normal routines for two or three days. Start a new project or begin a meditation program. Getting out and around is particularly helpful in bringing joy back into our lives. This reduces time alone and exaggerating minor setbacks into tragic experiences, a habit easily formed when one is depressed. Many a depressed person, sitting alone in front of the television set, has reacted in a highly intense manner after observing a sad event or witnessing a very emotional scare on the TV screen. When one is depressed, being alone is a devastating influence which tends to reinforce a sense of helplessness.

Planning ahead is a critical step, especially planning activities during weekends when time is plentiful. Go with someone you trust, don't go alone. Get away from your present surroundings. Depression will abate somewhat if we will only give it an opportunity to do so. *But we must act, we must be active.* Idleness augments depression. We have to work at it by building on small successes and accomplishments; these minor successes can change depression by causing us to start expecting increased numbers of larger successes. It may be something as simple as changing one's mood by listening to music. Here are two illustrations: Toni said: "The mood of the music I play plays a role in my emotions, so when I'm depressed, I play up-beat music rather than mellow songs." Lyle adds: "I am an average musician and when it occurred (the breakup) I began playing intensely. It made my problem seem far away while I played music." Even though planning ahead is important, thinking *too far into the future* will increase depression (for example, if one begins to fear she will not be able to face her friends at her annual summer job). So, focus on the here and now. Alcoholics Anonymous has a powerful saying that all its members live by: ONE DAY AT A TIME. This applies most especially to our recovery from a major loss. Work on getting well daily, and let the distant future take care of itself.

What about those rare instances where depression has lingered too long, where it has become worse? You have tried everything (which means you have read about depression, how to treat it, and yet your depression persists). As with any other type of problem with the body, it is wise to seek professional assistance here. Know where to seek help; you must overcome the stigma that to see a counselor or psychiatrist means one is "weak" or "insane." Go to a therapist who has had extensive experience in helping depressed people. *The means for moving out of depression are available.* There are answers to the individual problems of recovery. The information is there; the difficulty is obtaining it, finding the person, resource, or experience which will help create new perceptions of ourselves and the environment. Place yourself in the care of a skilled therapist who will help change your perception of the world as it now exists. This is a courageous move on your part, for it means you have to overcome the strong, negative stereotypes that flourish about "going to a shrink." It will mean the difference between rediscovering your abilities and importance to others and spending months in self-imposed exile.

In summary, to beat depression, search for someone in whom you can confide. Reach out and do something in which you can find success, refuse to withdraw from life, make frequent contacts with trusting friends, and never fear going for professional help. *Act, and act vigorously* to overcome withdrawal.

WHEN DOES GRIEF END?

I could have been better prepared if I had learned to believe that it would happen in time and had let that person know how I felt about him. We were never demonstrative and I feel guilty for this.

Mary Lou, a junior, on the death of a friend

The lessening of one's reaction to grief demands time, and so we ask, "Will it ever end?" For a few of us who stubbornly cling to the past, perhaps never! For some others, it will be years; for still others, months or even days. Some therapists say one year or two. Each expert seems to give a different time span by which grief is supposed to abate. But healing is in the mind of the griever who may believe any of the following about what the resolution of her grief means: (1) grief is ended when she returns to the life she led before the loss, (2) grief is over when she is able to function again and manage her life to some degree or (3) grief will never be over because she will never be the same again. Consider what these beliefs imply in terms of healing. Perhaps it is best to assume that: We are at the "end" of the healing process, when we reenter the mainstream of life with relatively few impoverishments. No, we are not yet free; no one ever forgets her major loss. In fact, we will always recall happy memories which are useful tools to relieve grief work. But there will be sad memories as well. How integral a part of one's life the person or object was says much about the depth of feelings and how long the grief will last. Lindemann (1944) refers to this as the "degree of emotional investment." The nature of relationships with the person or object, and the opportunities to *express feelings about those relationships before and after loss occurs,* affect the length of the grief response just as they did with Mary Lou. Grief possesses its own individual rhythm, which makes trying to put a timetable on it a useless endeavor.

The reason that grief work varies in length and intensity is that it is linked with a multiplicity of personal variables: sex-role conditioning, level of maturity and intelligence, mental health, and cultural, social, ethnic, and religious backgrounds. The intensely symbolic meaning of the person or object lost varies with each griever. It takes time for the bereaved to reconstruct the relationship now that the loved one's physical presence is gone. The period of reconstruction is often prolonged, depending on the nature of emotions associated with the tasks undertaken. However, once one reclaims the self from the relationship and reinvests in life again, grief begins to subside. This reclaiming—Freud called it "decathecting"—also depends on one's value system and willingness to continue to love, *for unconditional love eliminates fear of the future.* Therefore, we must be careful about setting unrealistic goals or expectations for recovery, based on how friends have dealt with similar losses.

Positive things will emerge from your grief: new strength, wisdom, and confidence in your ability to cope. And since there is no escape from this evolutionary process and the changes that come with it we must think of positive gains which evolve that help balance loss. As Koestenbaum (1976) notes:

> You do not know what it means to be human, you do not know the essence of your humanity, unless you have opened the window to your nature. And this window is opened only by suffering: pain, death and all the negative experiences of life. This is an ancient truth. . . . Suffering leads to insight, to knowledge about what it really means to *be* (p.54).

Any loss that is "major" will bring new beginnings, new fears, and challenges whether we are ready or not. An environment without our loved one will be strange and foreboding testing our resources. We won't believe we can go on; but somehow the task is managed. Suddenly the strength and courage is there to make it. Be assured, this time of victory will come for you. Dick looked back on his loss experience and said:

> The most important person or thing involved with a loss are the individuals themselves. I believe it is very important for the suffering person (now I speak from my own experience) to choose when and who they need to help them through the difficult parts of grieving. The griever should try not to be afraid to let his feelings show and be sure to be honest with yourself. Remember that you are not the only one that suffers. Everybody suffers loss and grieves. Search within yourself to find what makes you happy. No one knows what makes you happy except you. I found being honest and self-dependent along with letting time help were the most important things to recovering and learning from the experience.

You, too, will make the search within, "to find what makes you happy."

In the latter stages of grief, we emerge with different feelings and perceptions about the world, unencumbered by the shadow of past fantasies. We are somehow not the same persons who were shocked and numbed at the first news of loss. Twenty-year-old Debbie said: "Having survived through the death of a parent has been *the* single most influential experience of my life." Our sensitivity to others grows; relationships with others are strengthened. We feel good that the adjustment to change has begun. We emerge from grief as we did from our high school or college graduation—i.e., wiser but still growing. I am still growing with each loss I have endured, with each passing year. Life is that way until, in the words of Elisabeth Kubler-Ross, death itself becomes "the final stage of growth" (1975). This implies that even in the process of dying one learns about the self. Grief teaches by forcing us to know ourselves better each time it is experienced.

Jerri explains the lessening of her grief which evolved from the breakup of her love relationship.

> I had spent a great deal of time and mental energy with this person, thus isolating myself from other students. My grades had suffered immensely from this relationship due to all the time and effort I exerted towards it. My boyfriend realized what I did not, I had few acquaintances and little desire to become active academically and socially. It was for this reason that our relationship was ended. At the time I felt bitter and quite alone. I wanted life to go on as it had. Gradually, I realized my stupidity and excessive self-pity. Thus, I picked up the pieces since. I have increased my activities twicefold and my grades have more than qualified me for Dean's List.
>
> At this point I am quite thankful for the discontinuation of the relationship and to Peter. I have become a more capable and adequate person. I have written to Peter to tell him of my progress, only once, not for him—for myself. The letter was a self-report. It strengthened my ambitions and reassured me that although it was a great loss, it was a major gain in my life. The letter also served as a reinforcement to Peter, that he was correct. I know he felt the loss as much as me, but his male ego would not allow him to express this loss.

Jerri had reached a turning point in her grief; it was "ending."

Having examined the grief process and related factors in our own loss management, we turn now to applying many of these principles to assist the grief work of peers and family members.

Part III

HELPING OTHERS COPE WITH LOSS

Each of us is responsible for everything to everyone else.

FYODOR DOSTOEVSKI

A faithful friend is a sturdy shelter; he who finds one finds a treasure. A faithful friend is beyond price, no sum can balance his worth. A faithful friend is a life-saving remedy....

THE BOOK OF SIRACH

Chapter Six

MILEPOSTS TO RESOLUTION

> As for as how I overcame this whole death experience, I feel it was a matter of just getting my head back together. . . . I did this by being able to accept his death, realizing that it had happened and it could happen to anyone, that no one escapes death, not even me.
>
> Rick, age 20, on the death of his father

Each person is called upon at some point in life to provide a haven for someone in the throes of a massive life change; it is inescapable. Whether you are a young adult helping one of your peers or a sibling called upon to help a brother or sister, the materials to follow will aid in creating a support system for the bereaved as they confront their oppressive obsession with the loss event. The words *support person* and *caregiver* are used interchangeably to denote one who assists the bereaved. The content in this chapter is based on clinical impressions, available research, and the "collective wisdom" of those who have experienced major life changes.

Let us begin our understanding of the helping relationship by recognizing that one of the most damaging mistakes we can make is to create artificial classifications of people, placing them in our prearranged pigeonholes for behavior. What is the alternative? Every person we try to help is special, one of a kind, and we need to relate to her accordingly. Don't impose a specific system or philosophy on a person; that is degrading. Manipulating others to cope in your preferred way diminishes their abilities to solve their own problems of adaptation. Additionally, one must be careful of approaching the helping task in a rush, acting as the Messiah who can help everyone and make everything better. No one possesses that invincible power. In reality, our greatest contribution is to become an inexhaustible active listener, a task we will be addressing shortly. Support persons can make a difference in how one survives a major loss, for there is mounting evidence that social support systems are influential in reducing the stressors which effect the general health status of the bereaved (Osterweis, Solomon and Green, 1984; Broadhead, W. et al., 1983). Shared grief can ease the pain of loss. Nonetheless, the helping role is filled with ups and downs, successes and failures. Although we are a necessary part of someone else's readjustment after a major loss, we must understand that all healing is self-healing—it begins within each grieving person.

The significance of confidentiality. The fact that someone turns to us for assistance amounts to both an honor and a vote of confidence. In the experience of helping one who is grieving, we are entrusted with feelings, values, hopes, and emotions. The person opens herself completely and expects that we will not betray her confidence, for she is highly vulnerable at this time. However, as the helping relationship progresses, there may be times when the griever fears that we might tell another person what has been intimately confided to us. Or, when one looks back on what has been discussed, feelings of embarrassment and shame begin to surface. ("How could I have been so out of control?") When we sense this uneasiness, which appears when the griever later apologizes for actions during distress, we should seize the opportunity to emphasize that what has been exchanged with us in confidence will remain forever a very private matter. There is no need for anyone to apologize for what is normal behavior, and we respect each individual's right to grieve and relate her feelings free of the fear that others will learn about these reactions. We would expect the same reassurance if the tables were turned.

SEVEN INTENSE ADAPTING EXPERIENCES

Inasmuch as major loss to some degree represents a forfeiture of part of the self, one seeks to regain the sense of control over life and fill the void that exists. Control does *not* mean we can have everything happen the way we want it to in life. In the context of recovery from loss it means assuming responsibility for our thoughts, beliefs, and behavior. In order to accomplish this goal and to find new meaning in life, to actually begin a "new" life, one must struggle to adapt to the massive changes imposed.

In helping others to deal with their major loss experiences, particularly those experiences involving death, divorce, or the breakup of a love relationship, it is meaningful for us to conceptualize several points of positive progression through the mourning process. Using the analogy of mileposts or steps along the way to the resolution of grief will highlight significant characteristics which seem to be prominent in the grief work of most young adults. These are positive steps, although they may seem to be quite the opposite to someone experiencing them. Support persons should be fully aware of these mileposts as they establish their commitment and assist the griever in the reestablishment of a sense of personal worth and motivation to live again without the relationship that has ended or the object lost.

Adaptive experiences do not necessarily occur in the order of their presentation here; they may be encountered and recur in a variety of combinations. What must a griever do to move forward in adaptation to loss? How can someone determine if the individual is progressing or may need professional help? The mileposts will guide our understanding of the confrontation being experienced by the griever and give answers to these questions.

ONE: Accepting the Reality of the Loss

We have seen on several occasions that young people tell us of the importance of acknowledging what has happened as a prerequisite to dealing with it. Nevertheless, many individuals are unable to accept what has happened to them for long periods of time. This is not unusual, for often the full impact of the loss does not become meaningful to a survivor until days or weeks later when loneliness is maximized and the reality of being without the person or object of loss is heightened. Jody said that what helped her cope with a sudden death was "... the actual realization of the death, talking about it, but *only* when I was ready to deal with the truth." In rare instances, as Shelly tells us, there is complete denial: "I denied my uncle's death for over a year and once I finally accepted it the grief really came. Also, I had lots of guilt because it took so long for me to accept his death."

The most difficult task at the outset is the recognition that the loss is real and that it cannot be magically taken back, as we often hope that it will. We constantly think that somehow all that has happened is untrue, that it can be reversed, that it is a dream soon to end. Disbelief is to be expected, because it provides a psychic numbing which has a protective function. But to carry on as though the person is not really dead, the divorce is not real, or the breakup hasn't happened, ultimately delays any reestablishing of our lives, of picking up the pieces. When helping someone else, it is important not to reinforce beliefs or statements that refer to the loss as though it had never happened. For example, talking as though the deceased is still alive sets up a frame of reference which is both illogical and detrimental to the realization that must occur. We sometimes forget that our loved one is no longer alive; we begin thinking of her as though she will be walking through the doorway at 5 o'clock—and then it hits us between the eyes: she is gone. It is difficult to change our belief about the person not being here and to accept the truth of her mortality. The recognition and eventual resignation to the fact that previous expectations must change leads to final acceptance. This must be gently and slowly assimilated by the griever; it only comes in bits and pieces. It takes patience and tact for us to avoid inadvertantly insulting or showing disregard for those we are helping, thus shattering the trust that is so desperately needed by them during the time we are trying to help maintain contact with reality. However, with our realism as a guide, as a strong rudder, we can give them caring direction. Let us keep in mind that "protection" from pain which is a product of truth ultimately leads to increased pain.

After the early shock has subsided, some young people have little difficulty in fully recognizing what has occurred as being irreversible. There are others who may appear as having too easily accepted the situation, even to the point of having minimized their monumental loss. A too-sudden loss (or gain) can evoke this response of casual acceptance in someone. A tragedy is an occurrence through which we must move slowly. Denying behavior gives one a chance to assimilate the shock; we must not take this opportunity, this defense away from the griever. In most instances, the person will eventually give up denial without our help. When this happens, great emotion may be expressed; we must then be available to bring the comfort of our presence. Here, too, is where one questions values, where death, for example, may cause the griever to confront personal philosophical and religious positions. When we discuss these matters our task is to help clarify thoughts, not to inject our beliefs, but to help sift through the seemingly insurmountable doubts and misgivings. Our task is not to offer answers to what may be unanswerable questions; we must wait. At a later time, we will be asked, "What do you think?"

TWO: *Confronting the Emotional Pain of Separation*

The second intense experience in the grief response is that of dealing with the emotional pain which is a part of major loss. Most young adults (and some older ones) have never confronted pain of such magnitude. It is temporarily overpowering and debilitating. It reminds us that life is difficult and not always fair. Because major transitions in life never occur in a vacuum, turmoil is inevitable, depending on the inflexible expectations of the griever, her resistance to change, and previous loss experiences. Furthermore, the degree to which one's personal identity is intimately linked to the circumstances surrounding the loss is an index to the degree of emotional stress to be experienced (Charmaz, 1980). It is quite natural to resist change and to fight giving up that on which we can count. The emotional pain of separation involves the various emotions which surface at this time: guilt, depression, anger, loneliness, and despair—all accompanied by the overriding fear that one is unable to continue on alone. These emotions are painful not only to the griever but also to the caregiver who observes them surface, for being near one who is loved and in pain is deeply stressful. However, when pain is shared, it is lessened. Therefore, the caregiver must persist in quiet presence as the griever reacts to life as though she is not really a part of the world, but strangely distant from it.

Is there anything we can do to help foster acceptance of pain? Again, just being there with nonjudgmental concern is a start, especially when we would prefer to let the griever be alone at the acute reaction stage. The challenge is to continue to give the right amount of care as the griever's pain becomes our pain. However, one can do more than merely show empathy, by delicately encouraging the griever to talk about the hurt. This is often done indirectly by focusing the discussion on the object of loss and allowing the person to talk about it first. *A key goal of helping efforts is to facilitate a thorough review of the griever's relationship with the person or object of loss.* "Tell me about your Mom," "What did your Dad die from?" and "Were you able to be there when your Dad died?" are the types of questions which begin the dialogue to help one confront emotions. During this time, the griever's deep hurt will begin to surface as memories are recalled. Nagging self-blame may come pouring out; don't try to stop it. Our listening at these precarious moments will assist the griever in allowing the pain of separation to rise and be experienced. Because grief can sometimes mimic a psychotic state, it is at this point that support persons must do whatever is necessary to convey the message to the griever that *it is all right to feel what she is feeling* even if it may seem as though emotions are out of control. For example, to express anger or hate towards a particular person (even the deceased) should not be met with disapproval—at least not during this time of upheaval. Anger is often episodic and may be used to cover up feelings of betrayal or deep sorrow (Young, 1984). Allow what is troublesome to come out: don't interrupt. At a later date you may suggest alternative ways of viewing the event. If appropriate, put your arms around the person, hug her, or hold her hand. Many of the griever's emotions can only be dissipated over time, and they will cause much suffering no matter what steps the two of you take now. Eventually, each emotion can be dealt with if one is reassured that to possess it is not sinful, bad, or a sign of selfishness. This is often accomplished by our nonverbal acceptance of the outburst. Remember, emotions by themselves are neutral, they are neither good nor bad; it is what one does with the feelings, that is, how feelings are translated into behaviors which hurt or help. Initially, this knowledge has little impact on the griever, but as support persons we can bring this understanding to fruition by allowing the griever's emotions to unfold and her pain to be considered a normal response to separation. Neither we nor the griever can do anything about the cause of emotional pain, but the griever can, with our assistance, control how it is addressed. The question is not can one deal with grief, it is *how* one must deal with it.

THREE: *Confronting the Physical Pain of Separation*

Physical discomfort or physical pain is an expected part of adjustment to major loss, although the nature and persistence of the discomfort or pain varies from person to person. Physical manifestations of grief are not separate from the intense emotional reactions we expect to find, but rather an integral part of them. However, we are treating discomfort and physical pain separately from the emotions which may well engender them, in order to emphasize the importance of how the physical manifestations of grief affect emotions, just as emotions precipitate physical change. It is a delicately balanced two-way link. Although most professionals recognize this "oneness" of body and mind, there is a tendency among others to forget that the impact of how one feels physically adds significantly to one's overall emotional condition. Physical pain and discomfort are expressions of emotion at the somatic or cellular level. In some instances, they have a deleterious effect on how one progresses in her grief work, as we shall see. Special attention must be paid to physical problems (Sanders, 1982–83).

Because of biochemical individuality and differences in neurological constitutions, some individuals are more heavily affected by physical pain than others. Or, to look at it another way: when we have undergone stressful events, we vary greatly in physical strength and endurance to cope with them. The typical physical response to major loss is fatigue and exhaustion, brought on by our inability to eat and sleep normally. This is a common occurrence which can lead to more serious physical problems. It has been suggested that institutionalized customs, including friends and relatives who take over arrangements and everyday routines for the bereaved, contribute heavily to these physical reactions (Charmaz, 1980). This lessens active participation by the bereaved. However, other individuals are affected by dizziness, nausea, or excruciating migraine headaches. Extreme physical responses among grievers include the intensification of previously existing conditions such as asthma or bronchitis. Vomiting, colitis, pains in various joints of the body, and dehydration are not uncommon in people suffering tragic loss and can be controlled by therapy or medication. One griever may report feeling like "a bundle of nerves." Another may complain of pain from an old injury.

Greatly increased feelings of anxiety and fear accompanying thoughts of "being all alone" are at the basis of many physical reactions and generally are partly relieved as one begins to deal with them. When we encourage the griever to speak about them, to commence her grief work, we are helping the person to engage in a process which releases tension. This positive social interaction usually leads to a partial reduction in physical symptoms.

Although physical pain may rival intense emotional pain, it is often initially minimized as being of little importance by the griever who is unaware of its serious character. In many instances, this completes a vicious cycle, adding pain due to emotional stress to the accumulating physical problems, for it is the griever's long-term inability to recognize the physical manifestations of grief in dealing with depression that often leads to even greater suffering. ("We tend to let ourselves become physically run down.") Patiently, at the opportune time, support persons can remind grievers of how ill they will become if they refuse to make some change in their health habits or to defuse the often irrational thoughts which lie at the source of the problem. Gentle reminders to grievers must be tempered by the wisdom of knowing when to discontinue suggestions temporarily; one's listening skills can be most important here in helping the griever reestablish rational thinking.

Of equal importance to the griever is an awareness that physical depletion makes significant inroads on emotional states. Poor physical health adds to the negative way grievers think about themselves and about the change in conditions they have encountered. It culminates in an even darker picture of the future, insofar as depressive reactions have been augmented. Eventually, the griever must come to the realization that physical health can continue to deteriorate sharply in direct proportion to continued emotional trauma. In extreme situations, grievers have had to be hospitalized. *The awareness of how our physical state affects our emotional state must not be minimized, as physical attrition clearly prolongs grief work.* At various points in the grief process, enhanced physical well-being can bring renewed vigor at a critical moment and make the difference in how successfully one deals with a particularly stressful day or event. Again, when under duress, the grief-stricken are called upon to make decisions about themselves and can be helped by those whom they love and trust.

FOUR: *Re-entry: Confronting the Associated Losses*

Acknowledging that a major loss has taken place is one thing; accepting all of the changes in one's life occasioned by the loss is quite another. All too soon, we must reenter a life that has changed. This is the fourth milepost: our acceptance of all the secondary or associated losses, and the work involved in coping with multiple changes in our lives. In Part 1 we discussed the fact that most major losses invariably involve several associated losses which are additional hardships to share at that time and which become a part of the grief process. It is beneficial for support persons to recognize that these ancillary problems exist, help the griever identify them, and plan strategies to deal with them. For example, what to do with Friday or Saturday evenings, with coffee breaks, or other specific hours when the person who would normally be present and providing conversation is now absent. The loneliness, the loss of companionship, the suggestions that were given, the places which were visited together, and the joy that companionship engendered, are huge voids which need to be filled. Discussion of finances, disposition of possessions of the deceased or gifts from the ex-boyfriend, or who will do the outside work around the house, are examples of legitimate concerns that must be addressed, depending upon the individual circumstances.

This is a difficult task, best approached slowly, but the major goal is to reestablish a sense of continuity in life.

Time does not necessarily heal these wounds by itself if we do not use it wisely, or if we believe we cannot be healed. For most bereaved people, time does help the healing process, while for a minority time provides the framework for increasing sickness, holding onto the past, and refusing to allow grief to flow naturally in its progression. However, during the period of bereavement, if secondary losses can be met and dealt with, if success can be tasted, it will enhance reentry into a world which has changed for the survivor. Little successes are very important in regaining one's confidence. As loss begins to become assimilated into life, the discomfort associated with reestablishing one's identity and regimen persists. The griever's awareness that the discomfort is normal, that it is part of regaining a sense of balance and direction, is helpful, although it does not erase conflicting feelings. But acknowledging the difficulty of the journey back from tragedy is the first step in reclaiming one's sense of wholeness.

Learning to live in a changed environment is a long-term task, requiring much trial-and-error learning. Adjustments to tragedy may range from having to learn how to cook, to meet new people and start a new job or school year, to find ways to fix leaky faucets or provide for other necessities that were previously furnished. Secondary losses often force these adjustments and are the most trying times, when one has to establish new routines while the old expectations have to be allowed slowly to ebb. Sometimes secondary losses cause more problems than the death itself (Rando, 1985). It is extremely difficult to give up firmly entrenched routines. One feels that one's mind is playing tricks at times when previous patterns of living seem to intrude and bring memories which insist that loss has *not* occurred, that the present is *not* different from the past.

Obviously, this long-term adjustment frequently becomes a series of confrontations with the new and unexpected. It can be a journey of assistance for caregivers who are willing to invest their time and energy when the real work of grieving begins. Once the initial shock of having experienced a loss has subsided, when friends and acquaintances have gone back to their homes and jobs, when their attention is no longer focused only on the griever, then the real work imposed by change begins. Here is where contact with the right person at the right time can be most helpful. Support persons can determine when the griever will be alone for long periods of time and suggest visits and other engagements to intervene in this isolation. Grieving persons will benefit from an invitation, a card, a phone call, or a meeting for morning coffee. Such thoughtfulness on our part is a welcome gift when one is lonely; at such times, someone with whom one can discuss the task of living (and coping with associated losses) is essential. However, the timing sequence when all these events unfold is highly variable, and it poses a challenge to the caregiver.

Be prepared to talk about the griever's loss at this time as well as at other times, for the loss is what is occupying the person's thoughts. If we are aloof, if we focus only on the practical side, our visit may result more in hurt than in help. We should expect that the emotional responses which make us feel sad sometimes cause us to feel that perhaps the griever is not healing at all. Such behavior is not unusual, although it will make us feel very uncomfortable. When we deal with it, we accept it as part of the commitment made in helping another along the rocky path of coping with secondary losses. Be the source of strength that can occasionally be called on to help weather a temporary emotional storm. Relate to the griever in a *natural,* caring way. There is no need to attempt to try to rescue someone from a condition where rescue is impossible. Your greatest contribution is *consistently* to be open to emotional needs as you help with the worldy down-to-earth needs.

FIVE: *Reinvesting in Life*

The fifth major experience in the adaptation process is the reawakening of one's interest and the directing of energy and motivations toward living without the object of loss; it is making new emotional investments. This is preceded by behavioral changes in one's life and is the crucial step forward in emotional growth and the resolution of loss. It means relating to the loss in a different context. If the loss was of another person, through death (as is so often the case), the relationship has changed, but *will never end.* The loss of a loved one simply places the relationship on a different level in one's life; it is in the past and must be acknowledged in that context. This means that the griever will cherish the loving memories, yet reinvest in living a new life in relation to the environment and to those significant others within it. It is a *reaching out* to a different world in the future, not a lessening of our love for the deceased or the world of the past. Lindemann (1944) refers to this process as "extricating oneself from the bondage of the deceased." It may also imply extricating oneself from the bondage established to a person before the divorce or the breakup of a love relationship. It is existing with a new set of rules and without the significant people or objects of the past. This new way of dealing with the world requires encouragement, perseverance, and a willingness of the bereaved to trust life and others once again. One must continue on with life or choose to remain isolated. Healthy survivors do not sit and wait to get better. They *do* things in order to help heal themselves. They become productive; they find new mountains to climb, new sights to see, new lives to live. They wince at the sometimes painful reminders of what was, but they do not wither in the face of their new lives.

As caregivers, we cannot possibly know how great a force of stability and predictability the person or object of loss was in the griever's life. But now with that force removed, the griever undergoes a temporary confusion, sees the world as chaotic, and must reshuffle priorities. The wounded person must find a new *continuity* and *predictability.* We can assist in this search, although we cannot hope that the bereaved person will be able to let go of the past for the future early in the mourning process. Eventually, however, that is the only positive choice to make. To illustrate, I recall meeting an 83-year-old man on a flight to Los Angeles. He was going home after a two-week tour of the Canadian Rockies. During our conversation, he showed me a picture of his wife, who had died eighteen months earlier. "We had talked about it [death]," he said, "and agreed that you have to look forward, not backward. It doesn't do any good to look backward." What he had said was simple, yet profound. He was not blotting out the memory of his long and happy life with his wife—not at all. But they had both agreed that the orientation of the survivor's life must be forward, and that past events must not be dwelt upon continuously. To live exclusively in the past endangers our ability to live in the present, and living in the present is what life is about.

Finding ways to release tension and replenish energies implies an *active participation* in one's recovery. It is active involvement which breaks the bonds of retreat and immobility. We should gently recommend that the griever become involved in projects outside of her contracted world: e.g., join an organization, volunteer for small jobs, or simply get out of the house or room to feel the sun's rays. The reattachment process begins with small advances.

It will be a major breakthrough when the griever begins to *accept the various changes in life* that a major loss demands, to realize that she will never be quite the same again, and that she has to choose to look ahead and begin to reattach, to develop a new life plan; it may well be the person's most taxing decision. At the core of reinvesting in life is the nurturing of hope, the awareness that one still possesses the capacity to cope and that there is still much to learn. "Everything can be taken from a man but one thing: the last of human freedoms—to choose one's attitude in any given set of circumstances, to choose one's own way" (Frankl, 1963, p. 104). This realization is the capstone to survival. This will to survive is often found in the silent caring of those who love us, making us aware that we can still give of ourselves as well as receive from others. That exchange always makes life worth living for it bonds us together.

As a caregiver, beware of expecting the person you are helping to integrate a loss into her life, based on the experiences of others who have suffered the same type of loss. Comparing grief and recovery states of friends or relatives by assuming a similar timetable and modes of coping invites confusion and disappointment for all. Give the griever time—your time.

Another part of reinvesting in one's life is the review of options available, now that a relationship has been severed with a person or the object of loss. This is often accomplished in quiet discussions with loved ones and friends who will listen to one's ideas, concur with them, or make suggestions of their own, when asked to do so. Here the caregiver must skillfully suggest the various alternatives to be considered. There are usually many new roads one may take; it becomes a matter of discovering the options, analyzing the long-and-short-term implications, and then weighing the resources one has to commit to the journey. *There are always options* if one is open to the search for them. This is the crux of reinvesting in life—*the choice of being fully open to the new,* which is sometimes frightening. Options such as enrolling in a college, or entering an apprentice training program, starting a new business, or deciding to work full-time instead of part-time are partial answers to the panic-filled question the griever asked months before: "What am I going to do now?" Every tragic loss brings questions which can be addressed if one gradually pursues reinvestment in life. Important experiences in self-discovery take place during this turbulent period.

Reinvesting in life also implies permitting the self to enjoy life again.

It is possible to find the beginnings of happiness through social engagements such as going out with friends, attending a play, going to the beach, or shopping for clothes with a friend. All of this can be accomplished without feeling guilty that one is engaging in forbidden self-indulgence. It is all right to be happy again, to give up sorrow and/or self-pity, to let go of sadness, and embrace life again. This is the behavioral test of *intellectual acceptance*, i.e., an attempt to integrate major loss into a life which has been empty and shallow since the traumatic event occurred. These are critical decision-making times when one must choose life instead of withdrawing from it and when the choice of human interaction dominates reinvestment. In short, we are redirecting emotional energy from the person or object lost back to other viable interests in the here and now. These are not easy choices for grievers to make, because although they "know" they must live again, they do not "feel" like doing so. Overcoming that lack of inertia is a most difficult transition to make. But this achievement is one of the critical tests of our ability to live with loss, rather than in opposition to it. One *must* reinvest in life—or continue to suffer endlessly.

SIX: *Accepting Recurrences and Reminders*

Memories link us to the past. Whether memories are happy and positive or sad and depressing, they are sources of strong emotional feelings especially when specific conditions are recreated or triggered by events after a loss has occurred. Sometimes one's acceptance of what has happened is challenged by them. The bereaved temporarily grieve heavily again and again, replaying all of the tragic events. Typically, too little attention is given to the serious impact these resurgent events have on the griever. These recurrences of heavy emotionality may come frequently or sporadically, they may be of long duration or merely fleeting, and they may leave one with a sense of hopelessness or despair. They are often accompanied by panic as we are reminded of the personal changes to which we have been subjected. Our illusions of control have been shattered (Davenport, 1981). The griever tends to say: "Is all of this natural? Am I falling apart? Am I weak-willed?"

The experience is energy-draining; one feels much disillusionment. It can also be a source of renewed depression, guilt or anger. What can be done about it?

First, we must recognize that strong, loving relationships, and one's happy memories of them, are the cement which binds people closely together. Being able to remember significant experiences which precede death or any other relationship-loss is a unique characteristic of being human. While these memories are a potential source of depression and sadness, they are also a major source of happiness, security, and predictability in life. The recollection of them is bound to occur; *it is not abnormal.* Being reminded of the beauty of the past, recalling a specific event or a series of happy, carefree experiences is a gift, a part of human nature which is inescapable. Recollections always occur, and they do reopen old wounds especially in the early months after loss when one dwells on the death scene and all that led up to it. The bereaved want to live in the past. Again and again they search for the person and the love shared, hoping for a return to the way life was. A young woman who came to see me many months after the death of her lover, put it this way: "When does the wanting-him-to-return hurt stop?"

Second, one should allow the experience to unfold and avoid inhibiting it. This is part of the process of letting go or realizing fully that such events *are* a part of the *past.* This means one should not fight the inclination to weep many months later, for tears still represent a healthy emotional release and a productive method of coping. Past events will not completely disappear from one's memory, but the intensity of the pain they cause as reminders of the loss will lessen. The day will come when the griever will recall that same happy memory, that beautiful sharing experience, and it will have become a part of the person, but still strangely apart. That experience is an indicator that healing has occurred.

In order to control a number of upsetting recollections, it is wise in the early phases of the grief response to recommend that the griever avoid certain places or people which may trigger unnecessary or renewed suffering. For example, after a death, divorce, or a breakup, immediately returning to a specific place frequented by the lost person often causes great anxiety, and for some increased fear. To avoid this situation is an intelligent choice, not an inherent weakness. The same holds true when one avoids certain people who do not understand grief or are perpetual cynics. Grievers must avoid the ignorant and the cynical like the plague, for such people will only increase stress levels at this highly vulnerable time.

Third, many of these painful memories will come at times and dates that can be anticipated. A birthday, an anniversary, or a very special reunion, are occasions when one's grief will temporarily resurface. One has the option to turn to understanding friends or be alone. The griever must talk with someone in advance about how to cope with those occasions. Such preparation is essential. If you are a close friend of the griever, make contact by phone, mail, or, most importantly, a visit. Your recognition of these special days can be a great source of comfort and reassurance. But what is most important for the bereaved person to realize is the normalcy of it all. When the loss being mourned is the breakup of a love relationship or a divorce, similar memories will surface, commonly tinged with anger or feelings of rejection. Once again, these experiences must be understood in the framework of a totally human response and, as such, be expected and accepted as part of the recovery process. But painful they will be, just as they will cause one to think that grief will never subside and anguish never end. Planning to cope with renewed grief will make it bearable.

Perhaps most alarming of all of these events are those which occur when one least expects them or when one seems to be near the end of grieving. It is easy to become discouraged when six months, one year, or even eighteen months later, grief comes alive because of specific thoughts or events which occur. The clarity of thoughts about the person lost seems to inspire a reaction which both surprises and saddens, especially as the griever feels that she was doing so well in her recovery. It is important not to despair at this turn of events. As the caregiver, you must be conscious of this eventuality and try to help the griever understand that a recurrence is to be expected and that it can be handled by not overreacting to it as something more than it really is. It must be accepted as other elements of the loss have been accepted, and not viewed as an emotional battle to be re-fought. Time is on the griever's side at this point if she will only persevere.

SEVEN: *Risking Again*

Undergoing a major loss causes doubts about one's sense of reality, one's sense of security in relationships, and the beliefs which underlie both. Having experienced the bitter reality that life as it was will never be again and that the past cannot be recaptured, the person is wary and unsure of the future. Despite such insecurity, secondary losses may be well managed. One can even reinvest energy and commitment into other pursuits and thus be well on the way to the resolution of loss. But a final hurdle, which is one of the most difficult when one tries to reaffirm the belief that life is worth living, is to become willing to expose oneself to the risk of losing again. There is great fear to be overcome, a fear of the repetition of circumstances that will bring new loss and the return of unbearable pain. There is fear that one will not be able to accept a world where further losses are possible. Many feel they have a solution to prevent a repetition of previous events.

When people are recovering from major loss experiences, they become extremely cautious in placing themselves in any situation which could possibly bring a similar loss and the resulting grief process. Their hurt is still too fresh, and the stormy conflicts are still too near to allow themselves the luxury of being vulnerable in another relationship or strong commitment. While many people are eventually able to move past these feelings and love again, others are locked into their prisons of fear. Sometimes they are racked with the fear that the other parent or loved one will also die. As a consequence, they become overprotective, over-concerned, and haunted by the prospect. They choose not to venture too far away from that person, or they hope the loved one will not jeopardize the relationship in any way. The potential for another separation becomes an overpowering obsession. Or they may fear any form of rejection and live solely to prevent its happening again. This occurs all too often in the breakup of a love relationship or a divorce. And there is always the fear associated with dealing with the new or the unknown which every bereaved person must confront. This tension between being ultrasafe or conservative and taking the risk to grow seems to magnify in the days and months following our tragedies. In the extreme case, one may become cynical, refusing to believe that people can still be trusted, that happiness can be found, or that there is a God who cares.

Risk levels vary in meeting these unknowns and breaking through the cynicism. Because risk is the foundation on which personal growth and happiness are built, one cannot live without it. I am not referring here to daredevil risks, but rather the willingness to place oneself in a position where a positive outcome is not always guaranteed. Whether one's risk-taking ends in success or not, willingness to risk is itself life-affirming and can be contrasted with the effects associated with not having tried and withdrawing permanently. If one chooses not to risk again, then loss is in command and is directing life, narrowing life space, and blocking out opportunities to grow and enjoy.

Some risks are imposed by others and are often beyond our control, like having to find another job, take a required course, or go for an interview. Other risks are chosen: one decides deliberately to place oneself in a win-lose situation. But whether risk has been imposed, or has been chosen, limited, or extended, the way one chooses to perceive the situation determines whether active choice (and reorganization) or passivity governs risk-taking behavior (Siegelman, 1983). The three examples mentioned above (regarding a job, a course, or an interview) could be considered imposed or chosen risks, depending on the individual. This again highlights the importance of one's belief system in the recovery from major loss and the importance of discussing the meaning of loss with those who have experienced similar traumatic changes.

After suffering a major loss, many people seldom risk "tragedy" again and maintain an aloofness for several years, while others stay in this restrictive posture for the rest of their lives. Choosing not to risk, to do nothing, is to choose to regress. Fear of change itself becomes the great impediment to personal growth, that is, to becoming fully alive again. Thus, it is easy to understand why one becomes paralyzed by memories of the past. This can prove especially harmful to a young person, because paralysis defeats the very purpose of efforts to achieve freedom and happiness once again. When the bereaved limit human interaction, when they build walls instead of bridges, they become trapped at a point in time which does not allow them to embrace the world and to live to full capacity. Of course, reaching a point of willingness to risk again takes time and energy, and requires the recovery of self-confidence. Here is where caregivers often play key roles in helping grievers to conquer fear by encouraging the utilization of their untapped potentials. This conquering of fear occurs by helping the griever set little goals, realistic goals that can be met with little trouble. It may be something as simple as finally going to the familiar coffee shop which is filled with old friends and acquaintances, attending a cocktail party, or going off to the college camp for the weekend. The little victories will sustain and eventually help the person to embrace life with both arms. It is during these initial struggles that the blending of courage and hope blossoms. Lastly, and most important to conquering fear, is one of the world's eternal truths frequently disregarded in the struggle to recovery: unconditional love banishes fear. For both caregiver and mourner, this love, when practiced through word and work, brings strength and direction. Risk taking is limited without it. Reattachment and unity are achieved with it.

Chapter Seven

ANTAGONISTS AND IMPEDIMENTS TO SUPPORT

People have a way of always saying the wrong things to try to make you feel better.

Carole, a sophomore

I t was stated earlier that those who come in contact with the mourner, whether as a support person or acquaintance, either assist or unintentionally hinder the course of grief. Negative effects of support which arise from the social environment of the griever are felt through verbal and nonverbal communication. Before addressing specific examples of antagonists it will be helpful to understand where stock phrases and blocks to support seem to evolve. There appear to be six sources:

1. A general lack of sensitivity in interpersonal relationships. One tends to dominate the helping relationship, not allowing the mourner to be in charge.
2. Using nongeneralizeable personal experiences as facts which are applicable to all mourners. That is, a support person believes that because she experienced a similar loss and reacted in a certain manner, the newly bereaved should respond accordingly.
3. Lack of understanding of the grief process itself and the individualized nature of the expression of grief work.
4. Lack of awareness of the time that grief work often takes.
5. The inability of a support person to be around pain, coupled with the urge to say something to lessen it.
6. The inability of a support person to accept silence in the presence of the griever. Silence tends to heighten anxiety in the support person— and the urge to say something, anything, results in many clichés.

TYPES OF ANTAGONISTS

Based on the anecdotal data in the young adult study, clinical impressions, and my work with the hospice program the following classification of antagonists is presented with examples.

155

1. *Avoidance behaviors*
   Friends avoid the person in public or refuse to bring up the subject of loss in conversations.

2. *Directives*
   "You have to get control of yourself." "Be strong." "You will have to be head of the family now." "You can't ask why this happened."

3. *Forcing behavior*
   Being pressured to talk about the loss when the griever does not wish to. Being forced to view the body of the deceased. Being pressured into new relationships.

4. *Judging the mourner*
   "How good you look." "Why are you acting this way?" "You know better than that." "You have to get control of yourself."

5. *Judging grief as inappropriate*
   "Why are you crying? You knew he was going to die." "Don't take it so hard." Being told: "Be strong."

6. *Suggesting full understanding*
   "I know exactly how you feel." "I can relate to that." "I understand."

7. *Comparison of losses*
   "Think how much worse it could be." "When this happened to my brother we did . . ."

8. *Random judgements*
   "It's for the best." "She's better off now." "Wasn't it good that he died while there are still people to grieve him."

9. *God's needs*
   "It was God's will." "God must have needed him in heaven."

10. *Miscellaneous*
    "At least you have your two sisters." "At least it was sudden and not prolonged." A hug at the wrong time. "It's a beautiful day" (so what!).

What is important to consider at this point are the key variables which appear to shape the impact of these statements/behaviors on the mourner. First, the mourner's perception of death and her support network determines in what context the remarks are taken. What some mourners feel are antagonists others interpret as support statements. For example, "He is better off dead," is sometimes viewed as the "wrong" comment to make by some and a good observation by others. Additionally, how one *expects* her support system to respond can influence how one misinterprets responses of particular caregivers (Bowlby, 1980).

Second, the timing of remarks has a bearing on how they are interpreted. Sometimes the "wrong" remark is meaningful later in one's grief work.

To hear, "At least she's out of pain" may be negatively interpreted in the first few hours after death whereas a week later it could be viewed quite positively.

Third, the relationship to the mourner, blood as well as emotional, influences how statements are received. Those with deep emotional investments in the deceased may take any observation made as an affront to the memory of the deceased. On the other hand, those who completed unfinished business, were not strongly dependent on the deceased, or who had not seen her for a year or more may interpret a particular remark (such as "It's for the best.") quite supportively.

Further Discussion

In daily life there are events which unfold, causing individuals considerable aggravation or worsening specific conditions of their lives. Someone minimizes another's accomplishments, or says the wrong thing at the wrong time, or makes fun of something which is held dear. There are some people who seem to antagonize others simply by the way they look at them. This antagonism usually can be dealt with by considering human frailty and common feelings of insecurity which often prompt unhappy people to make disparaging remarks, or it can be eliminated by simply avoiding its source.

These social slights are much more difficult to overcome when one is already beset with an emotional crisis. The deeper one's grief the more sensitive one becomes to questionable assertions. At this crucial time, social support is essential to managing emotions. The *timing* of critical remarks becomes a vital factor affecting support. If something is said or suggested nonverbally that gives the griever indication that her behavior is considered by a significant other to be overdone, uncalled for, or abnormal, the result is commonly an intensification of feelings of isolation because it is usual to believe that nobody really appreciates what is happening. In this case, the caregiver may be perceived as a threat instead of a source of comfort. The griever may misunderstand the caregiver's intentions, but more important, the caregiver's immediate opinion of the situation is revealed by attitude and gestures.

In this regard, caregivers should not appear to be judgmental concerning the behavior of the griever, particularly during the early period of mourning. If the caregiver has expectations of how the griever *should* be reacting, they must be held in abeyance. Caregivers who make comments such as, "you shouldn't talk that way" or "how can you say such a thing?" show their lack of understanding or feeling about the personality of the griever, the nature of the grief response, and the inner turmoil being experienced. Although what may be said or done can be most shocking and difficult for a caregiver to accept, the emotional state of the griever must be taken into account and given high priority in understanding behavior. Young and old grievers alike often need the presence of someone not shocked by utterance of profanity and outrage. Janice explains her need this way: "I have one friend who allows me to say how I feel no matter how horrible it sounds or how sad she may feel about it." The griever needs someone who can tolerate irrational behavior. Obviously, if the griever might physically injure someone, one must intervene. Aside from such an emergency, our presence as caregivers must be truly permissive, or we will be guilty of a subtle form of manipulating the grief response of another, that is, forcing *our* agenda on *another's* bereavement response.

Other equally unacceptable phrases are, "I know how you feel" or "I understand." Even if one could possibly know how someone else might feel in a given situation, saying that "I know" more frequently conveys a sense of distrust instead of support. Think about it: when one is experiencing great pain, can another person fully understand what the grieving person is suffering? And when caregivers indicate that they know exactly what is happening inside, doesn't that make the situation worse rather than ease it? I remember a young woman who was grieving the loss of her health as she was fighting cancer. She told me how the doctor at the clinic had said to her, "I understand." Her response to me was, "How ridiculous. How could he possibly understand?" His offhand remark had destroyed his chance for a meaningful patient-doctor relationship, so critical to a patient managing her disease. Even a physician with much experience in such matters does not know how someone else feels unless she tells him, and even then words will probably be inadequate, as often happens when one is trying to express the true essence of personal feelings. Someone else's "knowing" is taken by the bereaved as an oversimplification of complex feelings or a failure to understand the resentment, depth of meaning, and hurt being experienced.

Another factor in the bereaved's receptivity to help can be observed when greetings are exchanged with the caregiver. It focuses on the griever's interpretation of the intent of the caregiver's question, "How are you?" When spoken in a casual manner it is not difficult for one in need to tell if the person asking wants to hear the usual "okay" or "all right," or if the truth is being sought. If we really want to know how someone feels, the tone of voice can convey intent and sincerity. Grieving people often assume that others are merely being polite in their inquiries, unless it is made clear to them that the greeter truly cares for the person and wishes to share in the hardships of recovery. Disinterested greetings occur not only between friends but within families and in one's associations with relatives. All too often, a grieving person would actually like to talk about what kind of a miserable day it has been for her, but is fearful of creating an uneasy situation or of taking the time of another who is not really interested.

It is also obvious that showing one's feelings and emotions is not encouraged in western society. On the contrary, such displays are typically discouraged, even prohibited. Western societies seem to be especially repressive toward the open expression of grief-related feelings, a tradition traced back to the early days of "rugged individualism" and the frontier. This repressiveness has been augmented by the recent breakdown in family structure, with the resulting decrease in meaningful interpersonal relationships and the loss of "therapeutic interventions" which family life usually provides. Generally, to reinforce the fallacy that a show of emotion is out of place weeks after the loss event occurred adds to the loneliness and isolation of the griever. Many people fail to realize that they are programming the griever to channel responses in a way that is comfortable for them, not for the person concerned. This behavior of would-be friends relegates the griever's needs to a position of secondary importance at a time when venting frustrations is of primary concern. The griever now views the presumed support system as artificial and contrived, as not authentic.

Being authentic is also essential in helping the bereaved deal with self-pity. The personalities of the griever and support persons are complex variables which make each helping relationship unique, and which either enhance the progression of grief work or complicate it. For example, there are times when self-pity is carried to extremes, where it dangerously affects the bereaved's work and interpersonal relationships. This happens over the course of many weeks or months after the loss. It may be appropriate (note: some professionals would argue it is inappropriate) to call the person's attention to such self-pity and to its behavioral effects because it is impeding recovery. It is risky to intervene even then, especially if you are the only support person. Nevertheless, pity is a distancing factor between the griever and those providing comfort (Parkes, 1972). Elimination of pity, whether it comes from within the griever or from those close by, will enhance recovery.

People in crisis who are seeking a trusting listener sometimes are victimized by a person who wants to talk about how a friend or family coped with a similar loss. Such a takeover by a would-be support person is a frustrating experience for those who need to talk about how they feel and who want someone to identify with the suffering they are enduring. For an effective support relationship to develop, the focus for the griever must be in the present and not on what happened to someone else in the past. There may be time for this kind of talk later, but much later. When one needs to talk, to convey a personal dilemma to another, the urgency of the moment surpasses everything else. If a support person is to help, stories of other tragedies and triumphs must be carefully screened; they are secondary to the present situation. The pressure within the grieving person must be allowed to come out, to be cathected. Each of us, as a support person, must be sensitive to the critical time when this need surfaces, or we will destroy the relationship we are attempting to build.

There are additional remarks, made by support persons, which achieve exactly the opposite of what was intended. I am referring here to situations in which helpers call upon God to explain away one's misfortune. Although support persons often do not have to say anything, rather than saying something pretentious to reduce the painful experience unfolding before them, tiresome clichés frequently occur. For example, one of the worst phrases invoked is, "It was God's will." Another is, "God must love you to give you such a cross to bear." These are responses which are more antagonistic than comforting, even to strong believers. The thought that God willed this tragedy strikes a discordant note in the hearts of those who feel they have given so much and do not deserve the present state of affairs. They cannot help but think: "How could a just God do this to me?" Other grievers may get angry at the thought that a God of love would bring such misery to them. Religious clichés are examples of unthinking responses which can be interpreted in many different ways at a time when one's emotions are consumed with the unreality of it all. Though well-meaning and sounding logical to the person giving support, they frequently lack true meaning at the time for the griever (although later in one's grief work she may conclude it was God's will). This is a "greeting card" approach, reflecting the potential inadequacy which haunts all support persons who fail to remember that they, like the griever, are *powerless* to change what has happened. Support persons must understand this feeling of powerlessness for all concerned and choose silent communication in preference to the path of comforting with platitudes and stock phrases.

Giving unwanted advice and trying to persuade someone to follow your prearranged agenda for resolution of grief also diminishes the sense of awareness that the griever expects a support person to possess. This lack of empathic awareness involves the danger of further lowering the griever's self-esteem by suggesting, at such a precarious moment early in the grief response, that she is not capable of decision-making. Even though this may be true, it is still inappropriate for the caregiver to intervene in a dominating manner. Most of us receive all kinds of advice during life on what we should be doing, and it often runs counter to what we believe should be done at the time.

Sometimes advice is offered by a caregiver later in the mourning process when the support person feels that the griever should be coming to the conclusion of her mourning or at least beginning to return to more usual activities. The error involved here is a misunderstanding by the caregiver that grieving takes time, much more time than is commonly believed. This is a frequent bottleneck to support. The bereaved sense that others want them to "act as they did before the loss occurred," or to "pull themselves together" and start living again. This is dramatically illustrated in many relationship losses (whether by death or divorce) where friends or relatives suggest the replacement of the old relationship with someone new. Widows and young people are especially prone to these pressure tactics which, although suggested with the best of intentions, actually invade one's grief work. The bereaved need *time* and lots of it to accept, plan, and regain their sense of self. It is all right for a caregiver to attempt to help the bereaved reenter various social circles, and for the caregiver to be consistent in doing so, but pressuring such a reentry is never justified. This same problem occurs in the breakup of a love relationship, as Claire tells us:

> Even in the breakup of a love relationship, "friends" try to set you up with a new relationship too soon, when you're not ready yet. It makes you feel so pressured and that your so-called friends are just sick of your grieving. I've experienced it myself, and you resent the friends.

This passage highlights the importance of the caregiver acknowledging that breakups have very deep personal meaning for the griever. It also points out the sensitivity and awareness which are needed in the helping relationship. Individual reactions to major loss must be respected. Repair and renewal take time, and caregivers must be especially sensitive to the special needs and the meaning of the loss to the bereaved (as expressed in Claire's statement).

A similar timeframe is involved when, months after the loss occurs, the griever senses that family do not wish to discuss the loss any more. ("Everyone just tried to 'push out' the sadness quickly and we never spoke about it.") However, grief is still there, and the bereaved person is still sensitive to the loss. As indicated earlier, refusing to talk about it (i.e., avoiding the subject), is itself a very personal affront to any grieving person, especially when it involves family or relatives. Yet, there often comes a time when people who have been good listeners for a week or two, or even a month, begin to feel that they no longer have the time or energy for the phone calls and long conversations with the bereaved. They want to get on with their own lives and feel that the bereaved should let go of the past. Therefore, they find excuses for not being able to meet for lunch, for having to shorten conversations, and generally for not being available. *This is a crushing blow for the grieving person,* one that is little understood by support persons unless it has been personally experienced. To sense abandonment when grieving is to generate new fears in the griever or to rekindle old ones.

Similar feelings arise when well-intentioned friends accuse the bereaved of being self-centered and not thinking of others. They judge that the bereaved's exclusive focus on the loss and accompanying feelings is out of order, usually because they are uncomfortable around pain and intense emotion. Preoccupation and self-centeredness are integral parts of separation and loss (Stearns, 1984). When one experiences crisis it is natural to center attention on the self initially.

On the other hand, consider what happens when the caregiver realizes that grief is a long-term process. Ben was asked to write down what specific incidents were of help in coping with the death of his mother. Here is what he mentioned: "Father Bernard sent me a Christmas card saying he had a special Mass said on Christmas for my mother. This was four months after her death and he still had thoughts for her. The other thing that helped was speaking with my father for the final time about missing my mom six weeks after she died." Here we see what remembering long after most people would have forgotten did for the griever, as well as how, even with the family, feelings are often held within for long periods of time.

Finally, many so-called support people are prone to say, "call me if you need anything." This is a well-meaning phrase but it has an overused, insincere ring. Calling on the telephone for assistance is hardly something we can expect a grieving person to do. Such a person is typically too embarrassed and involved with the new conditions of her life to be reaching out to call—unless we can somehow persuade the particular individual to do so. Even if grievers believe you mean what you say, they often cannot bear to disturb your homelife, to thrust their problems on you because of their misfortune. They are self-conscious, and do not wish to intrude on your happiness. In order to be an effective, concerned person *you must call the bereaved.* Let them know you really want to help. If they believe you truly care, and your initiative will show this, they will in turn accept your help. First, however, it is your responsibility to let them know that your concern is authentic—that it is different from other merely polite offers of help. Be specific. "Can I get the milk you need at the store?" "Can I pick up the book you need at the library?" "Would you like to meet for coffee Monday or Tuesday?" These are strong indicators that you are serious about helping, and this will put you in a much better position to strengthen the bonds of true friendship as you provide relief from the uneasy tensions which develop between grievers and their support persons.

In sum, antagonisms and impediments to support can be minimized if support persons will listen and allow "the working through" of grief, refrain from telling the bereaved how they should be feeling and accept silence in their presence. It should also be noted that avoidance behaviors appear to be the most frequent and devastating source of additional pain for grievers. This implies that we need to be *willing to discuss their loss openly long after it has occurred.*

Chapter Eight

GIVING IMMEDIATE SUPPORT

Many young adults when confronted with grieving family members or friends, ask themselves the question: "What should I do or say?" This chapter examines the immediate needs of the bereaved and identifies assistance that can be rendered. Other approaches in long-term care will be discussed in the next chapter.

> A friend said: "I'll always be here if you need to talk, cry, or just need someone to hold."

> Vivian, a junior

Vivian's friend said much in that brief sentence about what is needed in the early moments of caregiving. It applies *regardless of the nature of the loss*. Because those early moments of confrontation with loss are chaotic, one needs to sense the presence of a stabilizing force. There are some people who instinctively step in and assume a support role that is unmatched in providing care. For others, great courage must be drawn upon because, as caregivers, they have to enter into a painful experience once again. They are fighting their past fears and feelings of inadequacy. This is not an unusual phenomenon even with those who are experienced caregivers. "Will I be able to help?" "What can I say, or do?" "Will there also be others to help provide assistance?" These questions fill our thoughts. They are not the questions of cowards but of those humbled and in awe of the challenges when human frailty confronts the unknown, when one witnesses the uninhibited disintegration of a griever's world.

The one-sentence statement from Vivian's friend conveys four precise messages in giving support to the bereaved: (1) be with the person; (2) to listen; (3) to allow and encourage individual expression of emotion; and (4) to give nonverbal support when appropriate.

First, *your healing presence is essential*. This means being there as much as the griever wants you there. The bereaved must be thought of as decision-makers even though they are not capable of decision-making at the time. It is this *respect* for their sensibilities that guides your presence.

165

Your gift to the bereaved is yourself. It acknowledges that you are willing to be around their intense suffering and hurt. This is not easy, for no one likes being present in the company of one who is emotionally distraught and exhibiting seemingly irrational behavior. Not uncommonly, your very presence is a healing force of great value, a nurturing never to be underestimated. To be there, without excuses or fanfare, gives inestimable comfort to the griever. Sensing how long to stay, when the griever needs to be alone with personal thoughts, and when you must give more of yourself in time and effort are continuous challenges in the helping role. It should be noted that the griever will need time alone away from everyone, as we often forget that it takes much energy to socialize (Sanders, 1985).

Here, then, is a part of the risk involved with committing yourself: you must learn to deal with silence, with uncontrolled emotion, and with not being able to express ideas which you think would bring instant comfort. Those are inadequacies we all share, and the problem for us is learning to accept them, realizing that we do not need to have "answers" for every situation. We simply need to muster the courage to share a griever's burden through our presence.

The single most import service you can render to someone who is grieving is to *be there*, to be a companion on the perilous journey. What I mean by this is to be available to the person in need *when he or she wants you there*, not merely when it is convenient for you to be there. This factor is constantly mentioned by those who look back and recall how they coped with their loss. This presence, this "being there," is no small task in most instances. It implies a time frame which will sometimes greatly inconvenience you and demand perseverence. Often, it is accompanied by the feeling that you are contributing nothing. However, you are facilitating grief work as the bereaved person recognizes your concern. Do not underestimate the power of your healing presence. How much you give of yourself in time and caring will leave an indelible mark on the memory of the bereaved.

Second, *helping primarily means listening.* There seems to be a central theme in the management of personal crises during life. It concerns understanding one's great need to communicate to another person what is happening inside. If a parent or other loved one has died, there is so much to say about what that person has meant to one's life. If a love relationship has ended, or a divorce finalized, the anguish must be sounded out. When anger or guilt are present, they will need to be put into words, reviewed, and replayed. There will be shock and numbness to wait out and talk out. So much is happening with emotions that frightens and confuses the bereaved. Therefore, the presence of others who will take the time to listen to tormented thoughts, inconsistent explanations, and agony (even though it is unnerving at times to hear), will aid the process of becoming whole again. Thus, your commitment to listen must never be underestimated; it is of profound value. Remember: if nobody is willing to listen or to share confusion in a commitment of love, the griever is marooned within herself. She is as isolated as if cast on a remote island alone in misery. "The biggest block to personal communication is man's inability to listen intelligently, understandably, and skillfully to another person" (Avila, Combs and Purkey, 1971, p. 254).

The phenomenon of avoidance in listening occurs in so many life crises, because it is natural not to inquire about the pain of others out of fear that they will experience more pain. However, it is precisely when one is in pain that communication becomes the central basis for survival. Without it, we are soon consumed by an inability to sort out feelings from facts, reality concerns from philosophical concerns. We must tell someone else how we feel. This same communication dilemma is frequently played out in the lives of those with life-threatening illness whose families find it most difficult to encourage dialogue and be open to the flood of emotions which follow. They fail to understand that the encouragement of open expression of feelings is most helpful for maintaining a sense of direction and security. Without it, one frequently loses the will to continue to fight, multiplies the impact of depression, and becomes truly isolated. Grieving survivors are liable to suffer a very similar fate. Listening is the first need of the dying as well as the bereaved (Dobihal, 1975).

When grieving, people remember most what you choose to be, not what you choose to say. It is your posture toward one in crisis, your sensitivity to hurting, *your consistency* and willingness simply to be a part of the experience which articulates more than the most erudite phrase or profound thought spoken. This is the description of love that never has a price tag, that is not an investment in another for the hope of a return. It is given freely and without conditions.

You also cannot assume that one who is grieving knows that you truly care and wish to help. You may have to make the bereaved person aware of your willingness to be a listener by asking a question such as, "Would you like to talk?" or "Please tell me about what happened." In some instances, your observation of the present condition of the griever may be the opener. "You seem very depressed." "You are deeply troubled." "You seem angry." Describing what you see in a gentle, nonthreatening way, as a normal part of the flow of conversation or as simply a part of your awareness of grief in your midst, can begin a flow of emotion and thoughts which are of deep significance to the griever's progress towards acceptance and needed expression. You are assisting the griever in confronting the many connections and relationships to the loss which strongly surface and cling to her every thought. These connections seek expression by word and action, and it is appropriate to initiate discussion about them. Once it begins, the griever must be allowed to dominate the exchange. Your asking questions or making observations that initiate dialogue may seem dangerous or intrusive. The risk is a minor one. The ultimate result—the griever's finding a willing ear—will be more than worth any apprehension you may feel.

What if people do not want to talk about their loss? This is where your commitment is even more heavily taxed. For now you must wait for their cues, or symbolic gestures that indicate where and how they wish to progress with their crisis. You can tactfully encourage them, but never force progression. You can ask, but never demand. You can be there, but never intrude. In discerning whether one wishes to talk about loss Stearns (1984) suggests that the following open-ended question be used: "I guess this whole thing is pretty hard on you?" The lack of specificity in the question gives room for one to brush it aside or respond positively so that the support person can follow up with other questions to continue the dialogue.

You may also feel at times that somehow you must break the silence. Those silent interludes, when you have nothing to say and the griever is too overwhelmed to do anything but to stare into empty space, seem to create a flood of self-conscious feelings. It is as though the whole world is looking, expecting words of wisdom which will heal. Something must be said. Must it really? Not at all. Henri Nouwen (1974) wrote: "The friend who can be silent with us in a moment of despair or confusion, who can stay with us in an hour of grief and bereavement, who can tolerate not knowing, not curing, not healing, and face us with the reality of our powerlessness, that is the friend who cares" (p. 34). Silence speaks and says, "I'm here, I'm with you. I know my presence sends a message of comfort. Idle chatter to fill time is not necessary." We begin to learn that the usual cadence of communication does not fit this relationship. We can give support without words; we can accept the silence.

Mother Teresa once said: "We are not called to be successful; we are called to be faithful." While this was her response to a success-oriented philosophy of life, it aptly describes the mission of support one must engage in for those adapting to major loss. Our perceptions of success cannot be measured in immediate, clear terms, for managing loss is first and foremost an internal matter. The griever is aware of our presence and its personal meaning, but we cannot always see it. We are called upon to be faithful to our commitment first. Sometimes the immediate reaction of a bereaved person is to withdraw, to retire to a room or to ask to be left alone. This will test your commitment if you interpret such behavior as a rejection of your willingness to help. Janice advises: "I think the best thing is just to have friends you can depend on because even though I thought to begin with that I wanted to be alone, I found that I felt so much more secure and a bit more contented to have someone that really cared with me." The message is: accept this behavior, stay nearby, and eventually you will be needed. Let the person know that you will be there when needed.

Third, *encourage the expression of emotion.* We learn very early in life to say what we are *not* feeling, to place sadness and sorrow in an obscure compartment hidden deep within the self. The reasons are obvious: the age of anxiety has dictated that emotions are too personal, too revealing of our humanness, to be allowed to be freely and openly expressed. While there are many grievers who challenge these social norms, there are many others who need some indication that what they are feeling is all right to express. It is a natural, spontaneous response to share grief— unless one has learned not to trust and exchange intimate feelings.

Support persons encourage open expression best when they accept natural reactions as they develop. For example, the person who cries or sobs must be given the freedom to continue doing so. Never tell a grieving person not to cry. We can nonverbally reinforce such a natural response by refusing to show our uneasiness, or by refusing to act as though one can only be strong in the face of crisis (i.e., no other behavior will be permitted). When we hear a friend wail and scream, "No, no, it can't be true" or some similar reaction when told of the tragedy, we as caregivers must resist the urge to counter with, "It will be all right." Silence and human touch instead will be powerful nonverbal communicators of approval of behavior. In particular, silence, often referred to as passive listening, is a powerful resource for sending the message of acceptance to a person (Gordon, 1970). *Silence around the bereaved is equally as important as the spoken word.*

Over time, an emotion acted out is an emotion that will not cause additional psychological and physiological dysfunction that commonly follow the suppression of violent emotion. As a colleague once said: "It is better to break out than break down." Breaking out emotionally speaking is healthy and normal when a massive change has occurred. One breaks down *physically* when emotion is allowed to churn within one without finding a channel for expression. We facilitate the stress-relieving expression of the bottled-up emotion when we choose to remain *with* the griever, permitting the chain of intense emotional reactions that overwhelm the individual to be let out. The caregiver's choice to encourage this openness and to be with one who is shocked and disoriented constitutes one of the most demanding responsibilities in the caring relationship. It is also one of the most needed and rewarding.

Let the griever rage. It is perfectly all right to feel that life has dealt an unfair blow. If appropriate, let anger be vented by striking a pillow, or wringing a towel, or tearing a piece of cloth. Remember: never interrupt a griever's natural reaction to separation unless self-injury is likely. Just as there is no prescriptive way to die, there is no prescription for grieving. Give others the right to grieve as they wish, and be understanding with them concerning their pain.

Cry with the griever, when appropriate. One's natural response to the reactions of grievers may be to cry with them. This may or may not be appropriate, depending on the circumstances. Crying means many things to people. Seeing others cry often triggers our own tears. Here you may have to decide if your tears will help or hinder. If the griever is younger and sees you as the primary support person, one who can be relied on regardless of the gravity of the situation, your crying may threaten her security at a time when it is most needed. Alternatively, it may be entirely appropriate to show your emotions *with* the griever's as your *natural* response to the sad event which has taken place. It can be comforting for the two of you cry together; this is a decision you alone can make. Perhaps it is most reasonable to err on the side of showing one's honest feelings rather than holding back and appearing to be insensitive. Crying relieves stress and may be helpful to the caregiver as well as the griever.

Finally, what if the griever's emotions are not expressed? The first rule is: never force a reaction. This does not mean we encourage stoicism in the griever. Some people are too stunned with the news to react to it in any manner. They will typically experience a delayed reaction. In the case of a death, there are some who immediately think of others who were close to the deceased and rush to the aid of the latter, placing their own grief in abeyance. Days or weeks later, they will confront their feelings. It is then that they will need someone to listen to them and give support. Some individuals will never show their feelings in public or around others, and must not be forced to do so. A few other people can be encouraged to vent their feelings by way of a hug or other endearment. They will need to be given "permission" to break out. You may have to say, "It's okay to cry." There is also a small minority of grievers who will not react to their loss in what are considered conventional responses. They may curse, scream, or react with silence to the news of the event. This is *not* abnormal; it is another manifestation of one's individuality. Such people will still need support, but once again it is support given to the griever based on observation of the behavior and cues that indicate specific needs.

Let us not hastily label behavior "normal" or "abnormal." This is not a part of our job as caregivers. The range of normalcy is very wide, so wide that what is "normal" for one griever may not be "normal" for another. Furthermore, overt grief behavior is not a true indicator of just how much a particular loss is affecting a person. Love or attachment is never assessed by one's behavior alone. For example, "going to pieces" is *not* abnormal grief any more than sobbing at a prayer service or choosing not to cry in public would be. Not everyone needs to express every feeling openly, although some people seem to need peer approval to respond emotionally. Let us relate to people in terms of their needs, not as a culturally-dictated ritual of grieving. The latter is a lock-step approach, very tempting for us to take in our haste to speed the griever's recovery.

Fourth, *give the griever nonverbal support.* What is not said during our relationships with grieving people is as important (some would argue more important) as what is actually spoken. Most of us have heard the remark, "Actions speak louder than words." In all human interactions, nonverbal communication takes place much more frequently than verbal exchanges. Think of bodily gestures, facial expressions, clothes, cars, homes—all that you can see—and you will recognize how much individuals communicate with others on a nonverbal level. Our possessions tell others much about our beliefs and values as well as the environment in which we live. In facilitating one's grief work we may also add that "inaction speaks louder than words" because it is the combination of action and inaction, with the absence of specially-chosen words, that sends signals of additional strength, a lifeline, to those who have temporarily lost their sense of security. Inaction in this context means allowing grievers to be who they choose to be at the height of their confrontation with the loss—with no one manipulating their reactions.

Action means human touch which, to young and old alike, sends messages that are more meaningful than ten thousand words. Our culture has neglected the value of touch for many reasons, not the least of which is connected to its sexual overtones. However, nurses, early childhood educators, and those working with the elderly know all too well the powerful healer that human touch can be. It conveys the supreme signal that someone cares, that support is real in time of desperate need. For one who is grieving, it is often in the early moments of grief that the embrace of a friend or loved one is essential in dealing with the disbelief and feelings of insecurity which overwhelm the griever. When one is stunned or filled with panic, security must be found somehow, somewhere. Feelings of rejection, depersonalization, and fear can be effectively confronted through physical closeness. This is of very special concern when loss crushes one's self-esteem.

Everyone differs in individual need to touch and be touched, depending on previous learning experiences and perception of its meaning. Upon the death of her grandfather, Tracey needed to be alone. She did not want to make another call to her parents or to have people around her. "I had no desire to show them my sadness for two reasons," she said. "One, is that I have strong needs for privacy and I wanted to grieve without the attention it would draw. A second reason was that I felt it was selfish to demand their pity when they, too, felt a loss. . . . When my friend asked me if I wanted her there with me, I had to say that I didn't, since all I wanted was to be alone." Tracey's reaction, based on her need to be alone, must be honored. Later on her need for support may include the embrace of friends. This example of an initial reaction to loss is presented to emphasize that not every person wishes to be in close proximity to others. Your intuition must serve as a guide in this regard. However, holding one's hand or placing an arm around a shoulder is often comforting and reassuring to the bereaved. At the very least it is a tiny bridge to an awareness that one is there and willing to help. Others, like Maria, need much physical contact. "During this time," she said, "I constantly wanted to be held and hugged. Having someone else touch me seemed to help more than anything. He was just *there*." Sudden deaths commonly precipitate this need in some individuals. It is hardly a sign of weakness but more a need to regress to an earlier stage of development, that is, temporarily to withdraw to safety in the face of what is perceived as a personal threat to the self.

Giving nonverbal support calls for support persons to *enter the grief experience*. If we are truly to assist the griever, we must do something which, at first glance, seems disturbing to most of us, that is, become a part of the grief experience of our friend or loved one. It is a temporary journey which caregivers must take, but it is a most significant one. This does not mean we seek to duplicate the griever's behavior and pain; we hope simply to heighten our awareness and sensitivity to the other's loss and realize the true dimensions of her hurt. We can liken this experience to a kind of protection for one who is highly vulnerable at this time and who needs to know that someone sees that she is vulnerable and will not allow that fact to be exploited. The exploitation comes in the form of others who have ready-made solutions to someone else's dilemmas. The protection of the griever includes minimizing that individual's contacts with employers, teachers, administrators, and would-be friends until she is better able to respond to such transactions.

Not only does touch say "we care," but for many grieving people it is a welcome signal for them to vent emotions. Your touch can be the catalyst for letting go when one is struggling to maintain control of emotions. Many people fight to maintain such control, either out of fear of embarrassing themselves in front of others or because they are not sure if they should be feeling the way they do. Their feelings are new, unexpected, and frightening, and the reassuring touch dispels their need to keep such feelings in check. You will be encouraging only that which is natural for the person at that time—to show her wounds.

Intuition and Touch

I have said that in helping others we must use our intuition. To some readers, this may seem like a dangerous way to proceed, for intuition seems to be an unknown quantity that is not very reliable. I would like to emphasize that intuition is not a mysterious commodity, but rather a very important part of the way we make decisions and conduct our lives. "It is not the negation of reason, nor does it contradict reason, rather it operates in a domain inaccessible to reason. It grasps reality in its totality" (Lepp, 1968). Intuition is very much a part of our interpersonal transactions. It is a heavily-used sixth sense. Intuition arises as a very special way of sensing cues of various sorts within the environment, resulting in our "knowing" that something has occurred or should be done. It dwells primarily below the level of conscious thought. One "knows" something is right or wrong or has "just happened."

There are numerous examples of how people have "known" that an event occurred before they were told, or have sensed that a relationship is good, trusting, or floundering. Coincidence? Not really, although it is written off as such very quickly. Intuition seems to be a product of the right hemisphere of the brain which scientists say is the seat of creativity and the center for abstract reasoning. This means everyone has intuition, although it appears that it is more highly developed and used more by women. "We need right brain activity as much as we do left brain activity, for we need our intuitive flashes, our creative impulses, after subconscious digestion of left brain input" (Selye, 1979, p. 64). Too many support persons fail to pay appropriate attention to its signals, and we dismiss many of the types of insights the right hemisphere provides. Let your intuition work for you in the matter of nonverbal communication. You can use it to decide when to hold a hand or when not to, to embrace or put your arm around a person or not to. Some people may not wish to be held or touched; you must determine this in each particular situation.

In a scientifically-oriented society, such as ours, we shy away from playing hunches. Yet they can provide broader insight into the needs and feelings of others. Listen to your intuitive self *as a part* of your overall decision-making when helping others. It will say much about whether you can or cannot, should or should not relate to one who is grieving in a particular way. Obviously, this will appear to be risky business. But then, helping others is always filled with risks. Use intuition cautiously, but use it.

Chapter Nine

OTHER APPROACHES IN SUPPORT

> I really think I couldn't have made it through this tragedy without my close friends. They can read me like a book. They can always tell when I'm down and need someone to talk to. They try to give their advice and still let me know that they understand and respect my feelings and actions. One afternoon I really needed to be with them but I just couldn't talk to them. They understood that and their presence was reassuring and comforting.
>
> Margo, a senior

In the initial stages of grief support persons often must assume obligations and commitments for the bereaved, while later in recovery they must focus on assisting in the development of individual autonomy (Parkes, 1972). This is commonly a long process. The following suggestions have as their goal the task of facilitating the recovery of one's autonomy. Our helping relationship must "emerge from a compassion based on recognition of the common vulnerability of all human beings in the face of loss" (Simos, 1979, p. 177).

First, *extend your caring beyond the temporary critical period.* In caring for others, it is tempting to relax concern once emotions ventilated during the early crisis period seem to have subsided, when in fact the full impact of the loss, the reality of it all, has not yet set in. After several days it appears as though the griever is composed and resolute, ready to begin school again or to return to work. For all practical purposes, this is exactly the expectation or at least the hope of the griever's fellow students or employees. Many grieving people, attuned to the expectations of others, control their emotional reactions in order to meet the criteria imposed by others. They sense that they must be careful about further emotional displays although most want someone to listen to them, as they would rather not keep their thoughts to themselves. Other grievers experience new anxieties and stresses because they are unable to find an outlet for their mixed emotions. They feel they are stigmatized by grief and have been abandoned by nongrievers.

Sensitive caregivers must be careful lest they fall victim to the charade that society often forces grievers to play. After weeks or months of support you must be willing to *initiate* discussions of the loss, refusing to wait for the griever to search for the right time to begin a frank discussion. A caregiver's interest must involve more than a single question such as "How are you feeling?" This will only be met with the usual, "okay" while the griever hides her anger at such a question. When giving care to a dying person as well as to a grieving person, a better form of the same question is: "What kind of a day are you having?" This open-ended question allows for as broad a range of responses as the griever desires. There must also be follow-up questions which show your sincere interest, not just cursory attention. "How have you been sleeping?" "Have you visited your friends?" "Have you been eating well?" These and other questions are a part of showing legitimate concern for someone, weeks or months after a significant loss has occurred. Yes, one runs the risk of bringing back unpleasant memories to the griever, but that risk pales in significance in the face of the good that concern will do at a time when the loss has been finally accepted and becomes real. Be assured that the loss has not disappeared from the thoughts of the griever. And remember that nighttime is especially difficult for grieving persons, especially if they live alone or have been left to themselves, because of obligations of other family members or roommates. Try a telephone call, a visit, or invite the griever over to your home or living area for a few hours. While grieving people need time alone, most of them have too much time on their hands and the loneliness builds and builds. You can intervene in this spiraling isolation by breaking the pattern.

Caregivers may also play a part in helping the bereaved establish new routines. A major loss usually includes associated losses, which together with the major loss bring about changes in the griever's previous social, recreational, and housekeeping routines. Relationship losses in particular sever roots and routines which eventually must be replaced by interests and commitments not previously considered as important in life. But now that loss has changed one's relationship to the world, sooner or later the bereaved must begin to rekindle that inner spark of emotional energy so that it blossoms into new meanings, new visions of living. As caregivers, we can enhance that search for new meanings and reinvestment in life by helping the griever reestablish a sense of mastery over the changed environment. At the appropriate time, we do this by asking the person's opinion on specific issues or problems (most of us feel good when someone wants our opinion), by suggesting a new recreational pursuit, or by helping the individual to learn domestic, outdoor, mechanical, or carpentry skills. These are examples of what may be important contributions in spreading care beyond the critical period after loss. Each situation must be tempered by the interests, skills, and support network available to the griever. The energy and interest formerly reserved for the object of loss must now be channeled into other living, viable entities. In a gentle, loving way, you can assist the bereaved person in the blending of new life with the old.

Long-term care not only implies that one channels emotions into worthwhile projects, but that one augment the search for meaning in loss. The latter effort may take much time and many hours of conversations. We often hear that finding meaning in the death of a loved one can assist in the healing process. Meaning is also searched for in other relationship losses, in the losses of material goods, in temporary separations, and in losses involving a part of the self or a function. Certain questions naturally arise, such as: "Why did it happen and what does it mean?" How a particular loss fits into one's philosophical or religious belief system will vary immensely, but support persons can be aware of the fact that discussion about it will emerge in time with any person who mourns a death, a relationship, or a possession. Such discussion is of supreme importance and should never be minimized.

The search for a reasonable cause of the loss meets the griever's need to draw some sense out of tragedy and place it in a rational framework. Let us not miss the opportunity to listen, to help clarify, to encourage, and even to suggest, when appropriate, that the loss does have meaning. Caregivers should encourage the reaffirmation of the griever's philosophical and religious convictions. The meaning of a loss is seldom immediately apparent to the griever, but it begins to present possibilities for increased understanding over time. That understanding may come in the form of an increased faith, a new dedication to a specific project, a new self-awareness, a recognition of the importance of *living* each precious day, a realization that one has great potential to be developed, or as an increased sensitivity in all interpersonal relationships. For some grievers a specific loss may never have meaning, and that, too, must be recognized. Some losses will always be an enigma, a question without an answer. Sometimes one cannot begin to imagine a possible answer to the question of the meaning of the tragedy. For example, how can one explain the death of an 18 year old by suicide without apparent warning?

Acceptable answers may be years away. A significant loss may go unanswered for a lifetime.

Long-term care of grievers also implies awareness of the impact on their grief work of anniversaries, holidays, or birthdays. The anniversary of a death or some other significant loss is for many people a very important day because grief is often recycled. The first anniversary of the death takes on special meaning for mourners, sometimes causing a full reawakening of the events surrounding the loss. It may be especially intense if a death was the result of suicide. Perhaps most traumatic are anniversary dates for survivors in a multisuicide family. The importance of these days may be marked with special observances, a trip to the cemetery, a religious ceremony, or a gathering of friends. For other mourners it is a time when they may wish to be alone or with only one special person. Again, allow the individual to express the feelings she has associated with the loss. This is not an indication of pathological grief, but rather a significant turning point away from such grief for many. It is appropriate to call, to send a note, or to visit the bereaved, depending on the situation. Be willing to discuss the event, not dismiss it. We can serve the griever best by indicating our willingness to contribute to her comfort either by our presence or by leaving the individual alone with private thoughts.

Whether the loss was through death, divorce, or the breakup of a love relationship, the griever cannot expect special days to be the same as they were before the loss occurred. *Those days will be different.* To help the griever recognize this, to help her accept the fact that it is all right to start a new tradition and change the old routine, is to help her face the situation on realistic terms. You can assist the person in confronting these new realities.

There are other situations in which grief is reawakened: reaching the same age as a friend, parent, or close relative when death occurred, or experiencing another but relatively minor loss after (but near) the time the major loss occurred. This could include the "loss" of a close friend who goes into the military service, gets married, or moves away. By itself, such a loss may not result in a major grief response. But following on the heels of a death, a divorce, or a breakup, it brings to the griever a resurgence of grief. In any event, you are called upon to give care and to endure with the griever once again.

One final situation should be mentioned in which grief recycles or begins anew. It is evoked when a close friend of the recovering griever suffers a major loss (Bowlby, 1980). The nature of the close relationship between the recovering mourner and the newly bereaved can precipitate a grief response in the former. This may happen between twins in a family, or between an older adult and a younger adult. These events may prolong one's grief or initiate it anew, placing special demands on support persons.

Through all of this, as the caregiver, you must refrain from unfelt comforting behaviors even as your commitment wears on you. You must continue contact with the griever and be unstinting and unassuming in giving. An invitation, a visit, a plant, an inexpensive gift, a telephone call are all reminders that we are still thinking about the griever.

Second, *never react to anger, hostility, and distancing with similar responses.* I have already indicated that a host of emotions surface when the griever is forced to adapt to the inevitable change that is imposed when tragedy occurs. The individual's inability to assimilate immediately the change that loss demands, coupled with feelings of rejection, low self-esteem, or a deep sense of how unfair life seems to be, results in the need for the griever to lash out, to grab onto anything that will salvage some pride. What comes out in the person's groping are responses which she has sometimes thought about but has seldom acted out. But these emotions must be acted out now as the individual confronts a very personal disaster. She is outraged at what has happened. In order to hang on to an upside-down world, the individual must show a volatile side through emotional outpourings. This is a coping anger, not a personal anger.

Often rage is directed at those we love most, who are our most faithful companions—our caregivers. It may well happen that someday you will find yourself on the receiving end of such a barrage of verbal abuse. Or, the abuse may come in subtle innuendoes which seem to be perfectly timed to inflict deep hurt. The natural reaction would be to withdraw or respond in kind. After all, what did you do to warrant such abuse? You will be tempted to snap back, claim innocence, or seek retribution. It takes great courage not to take such comments personally and believe that they are not meant personally but are a product of one who feels cheated, used, and humiliated. When individuals are backed up against the wall, they are fighting for survival. Let them fight—at your expense. It will be your finest hour if you refuse the temptation to respond negatively. Here is where your love and understanding will really be put to the test.

It may also help you to understand that some people possess few coping techniques other than anger. Anger has been their primary way of dealing with change throughout their lives. Their limited coping responses maximize anger and the difficulty in working through loss. This behavior is probably the most demanding on the patience of a caregiver who is trying to be supportive. It will be helpful for you to consider that many bereaved people are inordinately sensitive to everything around them—and they react accordingly. Other grievers seem able to express only a general feeling of unexplained irritability. Anger has a basis, a reason. As difficult as it may be, you must put anger in the right perspective. *Help the bereaved person cope by being angry at you.*

Distancing may also occur. The griever hardly notices you and all that you have freely given. You are taken for granted. At times you wonder if you should leave the situation and let the griever wallow alone in self-pity. The silences between the two of you seem to stretch longer and longer, straining your patience. Persevere. At that moment, you may be the only link to reality. The bereaved individual is dazed, fighting to make sense out of a personal dilemma. React with renewed dedication. Let the individual know that you are there whenever needed. Your awareness that the griever's behavior is only one part of an overall coping pattern will strengthen your resolve to remain available. Never forget that when we feel inferior because of loss, when we believe our level of respect has decreased, hostility naturally follows.

Third, *avoid pitying the mourner.* In the previous section on managing your own grief, the issue of how pity can lengthen and intensify one's grief work was discussed. It was indicated that self-pity is often part of the typical aftermath of loss. If such self-pity is simply composed of passing thoughts, it does little damage; but if it is dwelt upon at length, the result can be an immobility and stagnation which hampers regaining self-control. It is a self-defeating exercise, though most of us engage in it in some form or other as a natural response to overwhelming grief.

Support persons need to show the griever compassion but not pity. Pity reinforces a sense of helplessness as we look down from our lofty position to indicate that one so undeserving is suffering because of a particular set of circumstances. True compassion reinforces unity and oneness with the bereaved in an attempt to lighten the burden of change. Pity says: "You are beaten." Compassion says: "I recognize this low point in your life. I will do whatever I can so you can transcend this difficult experience." Pity minimizes one's inherent strength to overcome the worst that life has to offer, instead of maximizing the effect that love and truth can blend into renewal of spirit.

Fourth, *share memories*. Memories of one who has died, or of an object lost, simply do not fade away. For those not grieving the particular loss, this readily occurs. We often encounter the erroneous belief that the griever has to get on with living and that recollections of loss only impede progress towards this goal by stirring the emotional embers into a roaring inferno. But what would happen if grievers tried to do just that? Let's follow this to a logical conclusion. When someone you love dies, you become permanently separated. This person has meant much to you and your existence for years. Your identity, in part, has been molded from this relationship. Can a part of you be immediately erased as though it never existed? Should it be? Memories are roadways to healing, not avenues to destruction. They must be used to help learn about emotions. This applies to any relationship loss. No matter the tragedy, there are always fond memories to share with a caregiver.

It would take a herculean effort and more to shut out what has been a part of growth, pain, and enjoyment. Memories can be the most important therapeutic tool in adapting to one's loss, or a painful rehearsal in self-torture. One can choose to review the happy memories with survivors or refuse to do so and imply that it is best to forget and suppress everything. Cicero said: "The life of the dead is placed in the memory of the living." There is good reason for this. Memories provide a link to the past to remind survivors who they are, the transitory nature of life, and what experiences played a part in their present conceptions of the meaning of life. Each survivor is in debt to many people for sharing their lives, providing assurances, values to sustain, examples to follow, and a love shared forever to cherish. When those who gave so much leave, it is only *natural* to want to relive those beautiful times. This is especially important during the grief process. "Remembering him," Kris said, "keeps him alive in spirit. I know he'd like that."

A major goal of helping others deal with loss is to encourage the review of events preceding and accompanying it. Once again, this means talking about the person or events, but only when the griever wants to talk. This could be a minute, an hour, a day, or several months later. Even years later, talking about a particularly memorable occasion is very important for most people. Don't change the subject when it is brought up. There will be too many others who have already done just that. Add to the memory (if you can) and recall your other pleasant memories of the person or event. Humor often enters this recall. If nothing else, a little comic relief always helps to place in perspective the sadder aspects of a memory. After the death of a close relative, Colleen wrote:

> It helps to think that as long as you can remember the experiences you shared, a person never dies. I now don't take relationships for granted. Whenever possible I visit friends and relatives, or write to them, always thinking that the more memories you share, the easier it is to let go. It alleviates the guilt, that "too late" feeling.

Sharing memories with support persons facilitates letting go.

Fifth, *expect repetitive and disorganized behavior.* In providing a trusting atmosphere in which one can speak and act without reservation, caregivers must become accustomed to hearing the griever tell and retell the same or a similar story. For many people there is a need to verbalize the events which led up to the loss. Replaying the memories over and over again can be helpful to one's acceptance of loss. Repetition is a vehicle to defuse anger and allow one's sense of guilt to be purged. Frequently, the immediate reaction to these replays is to categorize repetitive behavior as signaling a serious relapse or change in thinking patterns in the griever, indicating the need for professional assistance. One reasons that perhaps the individual is heading toward a nervous breakdown. But repetition is essential if the survivor is to master loss (Simos, 1977).

All too frequently, repetitive and disorganized behavior on the part of one who is grieving alarms or frightens those attempting to provide emotional support, especially when helpers have not seen these reactions previously. The griever may suffer memory lapses, a distorted sense of time, missed meals, being late for appointments, or mismanaging financial or other family obligations. Again, keep in mind that the individual possesses natural resources which will make possible endurance through the most difficult frustration and despair. Do not underestimate this inherent capacity. Give the griever time. She will slowly leave disorganization behind. Under these circumstances, so-called unusual behavior is to be expected when one is numbed by the turn of events. Obviously, your patience will be needed to overlook unexpected mistakes and the inconvenience they may cause you or other family or friends. People are amazingly creative and resilient; they have assets that remain largely untapped. These assets will prevail, *if you prevail,* if you refuse to become discouraged and allow what may seem to be childish or "crazy" behavior to become a deterrent.

If you look closely at your own or others' behavior not associated with a particular loss, you will note that repetition—saying and doing things over and over again—is quite normal in many daily routines. Have you ever had someone tell you about an event that has occurred, only to realize that they had told you the same story several days earlier? Here one can only "grin and bear it." We incessantly talk about the weather, or about a boyfriend or girlfriend. We play the same songs and enjoy the same music continuously. In grieving, many people need to recall various events as a reflection of the deep attachment they had to the person or object of loss. A clergyman was once asked why he said the same prayer over and over again. He replied: "Do you say, 'I love you,' only once to a loved one?" Love is expressed in many ways, by both word and work. This continues to some extent indefinitely. The replay of love during grief work is also a rehearsal for letting go of the past as one assimilates the reality of traumatic change. As caregiver, be patient and allow repetition to occur. You will be providing support to the griever in the truest sense of the word.

Sixth, *never minimize a loss based on your expectations.* After her breakup, Corrine said: "It was very helpful when someone listened to me and showed love and understanding and *didn't* try to play down the problem." One of the greatest dangers in comforting others who are working through a traumatic change in life is to minimize their losses, according to your perceptions and expectations of what they should do. It is not unreasonable for you as a caregiver to think that a relationship loss or a material loss is not really as bad as it seems. For you, it isn't all that bad, because you are not experiencing it. Observing the griever you imagine the loss experience could have been so much worse. After a period of time you may even feel that the individual is clearly overreacting and should be trying to look to the future with all the available assets and options instead of looking back on the tragedy. After all, it can be reasoned, it has been weeks or months since the loss took place. It is time to return to "normal."

With this in mind, let us examine two losses—failure in a course and the loss of a job—for the impact they had on two individuals concerned:

> My loss was basically one of self-esteem. I was surrounded by a new set of friends who were very supportive and understanding. They made me aware of alternatives I could take in my life. Two friends in particular helped me through a very suicidal phase by comforting me both physically (hugs, etc.) and emotionally through long talks, etc.
>
> Billie Jean, age 21
> failure (loss of a good grade)

Billie Jean lost 35 pounds in two months from her reaction to her sense of failure.

> I began by talking to someone in a counseling center, then broke down crying. Once I cried, it felt better. Now, one month later, new things have taken the place of my job, which I never really liked. I still feel ashamed of this failure and have not told my parents.
>
> Jayne, age 21
> loss of a job

These passages suggest that caregivers must be very sensitive in how they relate to those who are coping with nondeath losses. Attempting to understand events which preceded the loss and how the individual has dealt with loss experiences in the past are important in this regard.

Minimizing is also illustrated when support persons mistakenly think that one's familial relationship to the deceased should predict how one grieves. For example, it is commonly believed that the most difficult loss for young adults to cope with is the death of a parent. This is quite true for most. But consider the death of a grandparent, sibling, or a friend. Could the emotional relationship be sufficient to generate an equally intense reaction? I am convinced this happens and there is anecdotal evidence to support this contention. Be careful of expecting grief responses based on blood relationships. Rather, consider the quality of emotional relationships which are very difficult to assess, for they are solely in the minds of survivors. To illustrate, examine carefully Estelle's response to the death of her grandfather.

> I simply went into shock and spoke to no one for 1-2 weeks. They had to hospitalize me. There were people there, friends and family, and they tried to help, but I didn't really want to hear what they had to say at the time. I sort of went into a shell. The only person able to get into my shell was my mother. It was her father and she said to me, 'that no matter whether he is dead or alive, people will always love him and always remember all the good that he did.' This seemed to help a lot. But it was said too long after he died. I feel it should have been said sooner. It might have helped me avoid getting sick.

There are many people who might feel that Estelle's reactions were too intense, even pathological, given her relationship to the deceased. Consequently, they might suspect her grief response was abnormal, when in fact the deep relationship and respect for her grandfather generated her response. Support persons indicating that her grief was "too much," would, at the same time, be minimizing the importance of her feelings toward the deceased, causing even greater pain. There is a tendency to judge the griever's response as appropriate or inappropriate, according to stereotypes and with little factual information. Counselors and parents commonly agree that young persons "take their losses much harder." That is, their responses are much more intense than older age groups. But there is good reason for it; they are just beginning to experience the crushing *reality* of personal loss while at the same time coming to grips with a part of the self which has not yet been tested.

The impact of the *first* death experience of a close relative or friend on a person is a double tragedy, as it challenges the vision one has of the world, the sense of personal control, and highlights the fact that the deceased is no longer a living part of our universe. This may apply to other major losses as well, because such events are unfamiliar to grievers who have not dealt with them before. To label the accompanying behavior as "abnormal" oversimplifies the complex nature of interpersonal relationships while at the same time restricting the type of support offered. Teachers, friends, employers, and the general public expect the griever "to quickly get over it" because the death of a grandparent or the breakup of a romance are not unexpected, and because such events are commonplace. Grandparents are supposed to die and everyone experiences at least one breakup of a love relationship, they reason. The logic is sound, but the reality of events is radically different. Caregivers must do whatever necessary to avoid seeming to expect a specific reaction or oversimplifying one's grief work. Be open to the behavior of the griever. Provide room to react, free from restraints.

Seventh, *remember, grief is erratic, not serially progressive.* The same words or phrases mean different things to different people. When talking about grief, words like "healing," "resolving," "getting better," or "returning to normal" are frequently used. The implication usually drawn from these descriptions is that grief is a process where one begins at a low point and gradually improves to a previously-achieved emotional and physical state. The trip is all uphill; each day leads to a better and healthier state of being. Experience fails to confirm this observation, something caregivers forget when the griever reverts to primitive behavior or acts as though the loss has just occurred when it actually happened weeks or months ago. It is confusing, upsetting, and difficult to understand, when a friend or loved one grieves anew.

However, using the analogy of a wound that is healing, remember that sometimes the scab is disturbed after repair has begun, and bleeding starts anew. Grief is quite similar. The griever begins recovery and readjustment only to confront thoughts or events which reawaken deep feelings in ensuing days and weeks. The upshot is a natural reaction of repeating behavior that may be interpreted as unhealthy. As the uncertainty of the bereaved's personal world is recalled, or an object or event reminds one of a disturbing aspect of the loss, grief will be revisited.

A number of therapists report a phenomenon which has been dubbed the "Six Month Syndrome" (Rando, 1984). It involves a complete regression by the griever in the grief process after a series of events more indicative of the normal adaptation process. The individual seems to be doing well and goes back to work, returning to usual activities such as hobbies and club meetings. Then five or six months after the death of the loved one, there is a complete reversal of behavior, as if the person were back in the first week of grief. Such an event is not only disturbing to friends and family who are providing support, but it is especially devastating to the griever. Flooded with feelings of inadequacy, hopelessness, and despair, the griever once again needs the renewed availability and understanding of those who have previously provided support. At this point, there is a tendency for support persons to run out of patience; but now more than ever consistency in support is essential. We must begin to help restore balance to the bereaved person's life once again—a mixture consisting of work, relaxation, time alone, meditation, social involvement, light reading, and rest. Our efforts must become more imaginative, more sustained. It will take time and your willingness to start over with caregiving for the loved one. Here again, bereaved persons need to be assured that their behavior is not a sign that they are having a nervous breakdown or losing their sanity, but rather that they are experiencing a regression which happens quite regularly in the grief process.

Eighth, *never reinforce helplessness.* Family members and friends of one working through a difficult loss experience are usually dedicated and consistent in their caring. They seldom falter in attempts to help as they plan ahead in the interests of the bereaved. They rearrange their schedules in order to spend extra time in giving support. They include the griever in family outings, provide transportation, prepare meals, or invite the person for dinner quite regularly.

Nevertheless, there is a problem: it is easy for those giving support to do too much for too long, to insist on assuming responsibilities that should rightly be carried out by the griever after a period of time. When excessive social support dominates one's recovery, grief reactions may be prolonged and intensified (Gauthier and Marshall, 1977). A hazard exists when caregivers try to help others and forget that the bereaved must begin *slowly* to assume accountability for the problems in her life and confront them once again. How soon this must occur is another issue which depends on each individual's personal characteristics. Those who have been too dependent on the person or object of loss will need special guidance and encouragement in this regard. However, the longer care-givers assume responsibilities like providing meals, obtaining library resources for assignments, doing laundry, or buying late night snacks, the more we are liable to be reinforcing a state of helplessness. All of the extra attention given a person can become a way of life that reinforces immobility and seclusion at the expense of beginning the work of establishing relationships with a world without the object of loss. Our actions may well deprive the griever of human contact which would normally force the individual to respond and interact with others in the new world.

When support persons inadvertantly encourage helplessness in the griever, at the same time they may be encouraging that person to hang on to guilt, anger, and feelings of depression, by not encouraging her to marshal inner resources and deal with these realities. The employment of coping responses will be delayed. The griever has to begin to experi-ence the successful use of personal strengths to regain control of her world. Experiencing success is important for grieving people, just as finding tasks for loved ones to perform can be so helpful for the family of a dying person. But over time one must, in a sense, be weaned from dependency on others. It is success, the feeling that, "I might be able to make it; I can manage and be useful," which is the steppingstone for the bereaved to begin living in a changed environment. The gradual return to making decisions about life is a part of one's reattachment to the human flow which reestablishes self-esteem. Remember: you help build the identity of one recovering from major loss. This is best accomplished with a love and concern which points the bereaved toward a given heading, but one which does not necessarily force one to start in that direction. We do not tell someone, we suggest. We offer suggestions as alternatives, not cure-alls. The final answers must come from within the bereaved; support persons primarily facilitate that search.

Nevertheless, the problem remains for caregivers to begin to relin-quish their role and for the griever to assume normal responsibilities.

Because it is not easy to assess when that transition should occur, you must be guided by your awareness that any griever needs first to make contact with the *reality of caring for herself* once again before she can be expected to return to relating to a new world without the object of loss. This is a delicate job when one is trying to maintain the griever's trust and confidence, and at the same time trying to keep from reinforcing helplessness. One can always be there to help, but not take over. Early on, you must be sensitive in your support of the griever, never taking away all decision-making in your enthusiasm to help in time of need. At some point, the individual must start the long trek back to living anew. You must not delay that start, and, through that delay, make the first step even more difficult.

Ninth, *discourage the griever from making immediate major decisions.* Although caregivers must not hinder or delay the griever's assumption of daily duties by insisting on providing for all needs, neither should they stand idly by and watch as individuals make decisions under duress which could affect their entire lives. In the early days and weeks of grief one does not think with clarity and conviction. For some grievers, this confusion can go on for months, especially when depression persists. Traces of residual numbness detract from the hope that one can somehow escape from the darkness that has descended. Furthermore, the illusion that the individual will never get better, that there is too much to overcome, leaves the person less able to make critical decisions. For older adults, snap decisions to sell the house, move out of state, or immediately retire, eventually prove to be disasterous. The young adult may decide to quit school or not begin the next semester, resort to discarding or selling valuable objects which are reminders of the loss. The griever may even decide not to go on to graduate school or pursue a previously chosen career.

Discouraging quick decisions on such important topics means stepping in to supply information on long-term effects, the immediate ramifications for other family members and loved ones, and other pertinent information that should motivate reconsideration or at least delay such major decisions. Knowing just how far you can go without losing the confidence and trust of the griever is again a judgment that only you as the caregiver can make.

Tenth, *encourage the maintenance of physical health.* The stress of loss often produces physical exhaustion at some point in the process of adaptation. One of the most frequent physical reactions to major loss is a variety of problems with the digestive system. Reports of nausea, vomiting, an upset stomach, or other digestive disturbances signal the results of high tension and anxiety states. The carryover effect of this initial experience is to avoid eating anything solid for several days or longer. This can be tolerated and should be for a *short* period of time. But to continue to ignore nutritional needs through overdieting is to court additional problems. Eating small amounts should be encouraged, as loss of strength and physical deterioration add to the griever's reduced self-esteem.

Evidence is accumulating which strongly suggests that high stress situations suppress the immune system (Selye, 1979). Those who possess poorly developed coping mechanisms are probably more susceptible to these effects than others. The suppression of the immune system highlights more than ever the critical importance of eating well, attempting to reduce excess stress, and encouraging light exercise to help maintain physical well-being. Physical exercise changes brain chemistry (especially when a person is depressed), just as changes in one's thoughts can change one's physiology. Therefore, getting the griever out of the room or home in order to break the cycle of immobility will be helpful. I would recommend a *daily* twenty-minute walk. This will also help to promote sleep so desperately needed because of the insomnia which accompanies adjustment to major change. The importance of physical exercise and relaxation techniques cannot be emphasized too strongly. Breathing techniques in particular provide deep muscular relaxation, especially those found in many yoga programs. Benson's (1975) relaxation response and Jacobson's (1938) progressive relaxation techniques will also prove helpful to many individuals, and so will many of the visual imagery programs which are on the market on audio cassettes. The combination of stretching one's tense muscles and deep breathing results in reduced tension and renewed energy and feelings of control. There are many groups in cities, towns, or on college campuses which provide programs employing these techniques. They are resources which too often are not utilized in the support of bereaved persons.

As a caregiver, you can suggest some of these health reminders to the griever, but it would be much more positive if you would *participate in exercise or relaxation techniques with the bereaved,* when they are appropriate. Some people need the companionship of another person to force themselves out of newly acquired habits that lead to a disease state. This will take more time on your part, but it will prove beneficial to the physical and emotional strength of a griever who has been highly stressed by recent events, not to mention the positive effect it will have on your caring relationship.

You, too, must consider your own health and the possibility of burnout. Becoming overstressed is not simply an occupational hazard of professional caregivers; it is a reality for anyone committed to helping others. One can invest so much in another person emotionally that one begins to skip meals, sleep poorly, or fail to find enough time to relax. Caregivers are all different in their abilities to cope with the long-term crises of other people. You must be willing to seek respite and assistance with your own support goals from other family members and friends.

Eleventh, *reinforce the normalcy of grief.* There will be many occasions during the grief response when the griever will feel that what she is experiencing is abnormal. You may recall our discussions in the previous section on managing your own grief that what is a normal part of the grief process—the intense feelings, the beliefs of unfairness, the persistence of it all—often causes individuals to think that they are losing their sanity. As a support person, you will be fulfilling a major part of your role by the *attitude you convey* which accepts grief work and erratic behavior as rational, only to be expected under the circumstances.

There will be times when the griever is speaking or showing emotion, and hinting that her behavior is out of place, unnatural, or unbalanced, that her thinking is demented or unsound. You must seize the opportunity then and there to allay the individual's fears, to point out that much of what seems so abnormal is, in reality, expected behavior for one in the crises of life change. At other times, you may have to say, "I hope you don't think your feelings are abnormal or that there is something wrong with you." This reinforcement is most helpful to those who are very unsure of their behavior and how they should be responding. "I never thought I could ever feel like this" is a thought which many grievers confront. At the appropriate moment you can help reduce the impact of uncertainty on the griever. Too many young adults have to deal with the fear of losing their sanity because of their grief (Collins and Sedlacek, 1973).

The occasion may also arise where friends or family of the griever may need similar assurances that her behavior is not shameful, a sign of weakness, or indicative of serious emotional illness. They will need an occasional reminder that each individual's grief is both highly personal and varied in mode of expression. Furthermore, it is essential that they accept the preoccupation of the griever with the person or object lost as the central theme of the grief response.

In attempting to convey the concept that grief is normal, be prepared to suggest some appropriate readings. *How to Survive the Loss of a Love; Living When a Loved One Has Died;* or *When Bad Things Happen to Good People* are examples of books which can be most helpful in removing the half-truths and misconceptions surrounding the grief process.

Self-help groups. Next to a professional grief counselor, self-help groups are a most important source of support. In some instances, they can provide even more help than a trained professional and are especially effective in cases of sudden death. Note that that is a controversial statement, which many professionals might challenge. Nevertheless, thousands of people would attest to the fact that being among others who have experienced similar losses has often initiated a very strong and lasting healing for them. Members of self-help groups sharing loss experiences develop a community of closeness and understanding that transcends the most catastrophic event imaginable.

Awareness and knowledge useful in adaptation and evolving in an experiential setting leave an indelible mark of reality and truth on the griever because they are learned through the experience of active participation. When the griever is part of the evolving scene and can observe the nonverbal signs which give rich meaning to experiences, the effect is both comforting and growth-producing. Such knowledge is gained within a framework which is intensely personal. Frequently, individuals find a sense of freedom to let go of repressed emotions and an ability to identify their own vague feelings as they are clarified in descriptions of similar feelings given by other members of the group. Many grievers become motivated to change their negative behaviors and try new approaches. In addition, as group members are able to verbalize their pain while realizing that others share their sense of intensity, they begin to redefine themselves and their environment. All of this occurs in a community setting without the inhibiting influence of professionals. This does not mean that professionals ought not be available to help when needed. They may be consulted for advice, but they do not direct group sessions or play dominant roles in group process.

The verbal exchanges which often take place between group members are not only sources of understanding, they are also sources of information which reduce the manifest emotional turmoil. As one listens to how another is dealing with guilt, anger, depression, or loneliness, one can restructure present approaches to cope with loss. The self-help movement focuses on people helping each other, but most importantly, helping themselves. They are not islands in the sun; rather, they are social beings who need each other at a variety of times during life changes.

Also, by eventually taking charge of one's own adaptation to loss, one makes a major step in recovery as she finds new confidence. Of equal importance is the fact that, through sharing with others, one helps oneself. This is a significant experience, typically gained within self-help groups. Caregivers must be continuously alert to the possibilities of bringing the bereaved to groups which have common concerns. It does not necessarily have to be one of the established groups for specific losses, such as suicide, murder of a relative, or the loss of a child. It may be a group of three or more persons who have much in common concerning the particular loss they are sharing. This can happen when a friend dies, for instance. Many young people report how being around other friends or family, or sharing memories and feelings with them, has been an important method of coping. Although such groups normally come together spontaneously, others can be planned for and arranged in ways which are limited only by one's creativity. This may take place on campus or in the local community. For example, there are always a number of students whose parents have recently died and would benefit from other students who are nearing the completion of their grief work.

At other times, you may be able to bring together the person you are helping and someone else who has experienced the same type of loss. Of course, you must always confer with the bereaved about meeting someone else under those circumstances. This has proved especially fruitful in my own work. I once conducted a support group consisting of cancer patients and their families. They came together as a mutually sharing community. They helped each other by listening and searching for increased understanding and meaning about the problems each was experiencing. Who originally conceived the idea and brought these people together? A twenty-eight-year-old mother with cancer of the lymph nodes.

In helping someone cope, it may be important to ask yourself if there are resources available in the immediate community which can foster dialogue on coping, whether they involve one other person or several others. Perhaps more than any other single feature, the awareness of the griever that others have made it through the loss and that their own feelings are legitimate makes self-help groups important therapeutic agents. Members forge bonds which result in the encouragement and motivation to endure, or give hope where there was only hopelessness. Finding a person or a group with direct personal experiences with a particular type of loss provides the griever with a sense of realism and meaning that the professional counselor is usually unable to match.

EPILOGUE

OMEGA—QUESTIONS TO PONDER

As we come to a close with our examination of the topic of death and loss experiences, and as we enlarge our perspective of life in view of the certainty of death experiences, it is important that we reapply the theme of what one believes to the process of assisting others in their hour of tragedy. So much of helping others confronting the crises in their lives takes place on a nonverbal level because we communicate much more by our behavior (our gentle manner, the way in which we show respect for the bereaved, and the many messages sent by our being available) than by what is said.

Assuming you are willing to give of yourself in the caring relationship, and realizing that nonverbal behavior is a product of your thinking and beliefs about what you are doing, let us close our discussion of helping others cope with loss by examining what motivates *your* behavior. It is understanding *your* perception of the griever, his or her loss, and what you can contribute to a support network that is the basis of the quality of assistance and whether you are willing to evaluate your effectiveness. It is my hope that the following questions will stimulate you to examine how the quality of your care is deeply affected by what you believe.

BELIEFS ABOUT PEOPLE, LOSS, AND YOURSELF

Let us begin with your beliefs about bereaved people. Do you believe that the bereaved are basically people who are capable of resolving their losses? Are they good, able, and worthwhile? Are people the most precious resource on the face of the earth? Do you believe that others possess an innate source of courage and strength that is utilized in time of crisis? If you hold such beliefs, they will show in your attitude, and the bereaved will sense your positive feelings toward them. Now, what do you believe about a specific griever? If you believe the individual is basically weak, incapable of coping, and not able to manage without you, that will also show through in your manner of helping. The point here is to evaluate what you think of those undergoing crisis experiences, for

197

your thoughts, as expressed in your deeds, will clearly affect how you are perceived by them. Like the dying, people in crisis are astute readers of nonverbal behavior. They will detect your respect for them, your gentleness and sincerity, even your fears; it will be written in your manner of caring. Perhaps you will need to reevaluate your beliefs about people in general.

Secondly, what do you believe about the particular loss being grieved? Is it tragic, to be expected, to be pitied, deeply traumatic for all involved, or easily worked through? What do you believe about death? Is it evil or bad? Is death an event which gives meaning to life? Is it an aggressor to be fought? And what do you believe about your own death? What do you fear? How *you* perceive loss will also influence how you relate to the bereaved. Should you focus your attention on the loss or on the person? Should the loss itself be totally disregarded and your empathy for the griever developed as much as possible? With your knowledge of the griever, in what context will he or she best understand and interpret your help? Are you aware of what may turn the individual away from your offers of assistance? With all of these questions, your central concern must focus on *what the loss means to the bereaved* and on his or her immediate needs.

Thirdly, what do you believe about yourself and your ability to help? Are you convinced you have something to offer, or are you going through the motions because it is the thing to do? Do you believe you can make a difference in how one adapts to loss? The assumptions we make about coping are critical catalysts in the nature of support given. "Good helpers perceive themselves as freeing rather than controlling people; they view events in a broad rather than a narrow perspective, and they have altruistic purposes rather than narcissistic ones" (Combs, Avila and Purkey, 1971, pp. 15–16). What do you feel about yourself as a person? Do you believe you are basically good, responsible, and compassionate? This will affect your commitment and how you relate to survivors, as well as how you are affected by them.

All of these questions need to be addressed at various times in our quest to provide the best care for those coping with loss. I have chosen to conclude our discussion with this series of questions in order to highlight the fact that books alone cannot possibly give all the answers to questions of intense interpersonal caring. This only occurs through several processes: (1) involving yourself in discussions with others, (2) sifting through many differing viewpoints, (3) *risking yourself in a helping relationship,* and (4) being willing to consider approaches other than your own in the endless search for improved answers.

Through these processes one can learn to overcome one's fear of saying the wrong thing, of being overwhelmed by suffering, and of narrowing one's perception of the meaning of loss in the plan of life. Enrichment can rise from the ashes of loss. Anne Morrow-Lindberg (1973) put it this way: "If suffering alone taught, all the world would be wise, since everyone suffers. To suffering must be added mourning, understanding, patience, love, openness, and the willingness to remain vulnerable. All these and other factors combined, if the circumstances are right, *can* teach and *can* lead to rebirth" (p. 214).

Feel free to write to me about what works or does not work for you as you confront your own life changes and help others to confront theirs. It is through such exchange that we shall all find new paths to travel in the infinity of change, for in the final analysis we all create our own dynamisms in transcending loss.

BIBLIOGRAPHY AND READING LIST

Aldrich, E. The dying patient's grief. *Journal of the American Medical Association* 1963, 185(5):329–31.

Aries, P. *The hour of our death.* New York: Alfred A. Knopf, 1981.

Aries, P. *Western attitudes toward death from the middle ages to the present.* Baltimore: Johns Hopkins University Press, 1974.

Aries, P. Death inside out. In S. Wilcox and M. Sutton (Eds.). *Understanding death and dying.* Palo Alto, CA: Mayfield Publishing Co., 1981.

Avila, D., Combs, A. and Purkey, W. *The helping relationship sourcebook.* Boston: Allyn and Bacon, 1971.

Backer, B., Hannon, N. and Russell, N. *Death and dying: Individuals and institutions.* New York: John Wiley, 1982.

Beck, A. *Cognitive therapy and the emotional disorders.* New York: New American Library, 1976.

Becker, E. *The denial of death.* New York: Free Press, 1973.

Behnke, J. and Bok, S. (Eds.). *The dilemmas of euthanasia.* Garden City, NJ: Anchor Press, 1975.

Benson, H. *The relaxation response.* New York: William Morrow, 1975.

Bertman, S. Bearing the unbearable: From loss, the gain. *Health Values,* 1983, 7(1), 24–28.

Bowlby, J. *Attachment and loss* (vol. III). New York: Basic Books, 1980.

Bowlby, J. Processes of mourning. *International Journal of Psychoanalysis,* 1961, 42, 317–340.

Brantner, J. Positive approaches to dying. *Death Education,* 1977, 1, 293–304.

Broadhead, W., Kaplan, B., James, S., Wagner, E., Schoenback, V., Gremson, R., Heyden, S., Tibblin, G., and Gehlback, S. The epidemiologic evidence for a relationship between social support and health. *American Journal of Epidemiology,* 1983, 117:521–537.

Bruehl, R. Mourning, family dynamics, and pastoral care. In J. Bane, R. Neal and R. Reeves (Eds.). *Death and ministry.* New York: Seabury, 1975.

Burgess, J. How to adjust to the death of a parent, close relative, or friend. In C. Zastrow and D. Chang (Eds.). *The Personal Problem Solver.* Englewood Cliffs, NJ: Prentice-Hall, 1977.

Byrd, J. Spiritual help in health care. In E. Goldwag (Ed.). *Inner balance: The power of holistic healing.* Englewood Cliffs, NJ: Prentice-Hall, 1979.

Caine, L. *Widow.* New York: Bantam Books, 1975.

Caine, L. *Lifelines.* New York: Dell Publishing Co., 1977.

Cappon, D. The dying. *Psychiatric Quarterly,* 1959, 133, 466–489.

Cassem, N. Bereavement as indispensable for growth. In B. Schoenberg, et al., (Eds.). *Bereavement: Its psychosocial aspects.* New York: Columbia University Press, 1975.

Charmaz, K. *The social reality of death.* Reading, MA: Addison-Wesley, 1980.

Cobb, S. Social support as a moderator of life stress. *Psychosomatic Medicine,* 1976, 38, 300–314.

Combs, A. and A.S.C.D. 1962 Yearbook Committee. *Perceiving, behaving, becoming.* Washington: A.S.C.D., 1962.

Combs, A., Avila, D. and Purkey, W. *Helping relationships.* Boston: Allyn and Bacon, 1971.

Corr, C. Reconstructing the changing face of death. In H. Wass (Ed.) *Dying facing the facts.* New York: McGraw-Hill, 1979.

Czillinger, K. Elements of healing. *Compassionate Friends Newsletter,* 1979, 2,3.

Dobihal, E. Problems which confront the minister. In J. Bane, R. Neale and R. Reeves (Eds.). *Death and ministry.* New York: Seabury, 1975.

Douglas, J. *The social meanings of suicide.* Princeton: Princeton University Press, 1967.

Downey, A. Living, loving and losing: Implications for health and well-being. *Health Values,* 1983, 7(1), 7–14.

Dumont, R. *The American view of death: Acceptance or denial?* Morristown: General Learning Press, 1972.

Eisenstadt, J. Parental loss and genius. *American Psychologist,* 1978, 33, 211–233.

Engel, G. Grief and grieving. *American Journal of Nursing,* 1964, 9, 93–98.

Engel, G. A group dynamic approach to teaching and learning about grief. *Omega,* 1980–81, 11, 45–59.

Erikson, E. Identity and the life cycle. *Psychological Issues,* 1959, 1, 1–171.

Erikson, E. Identity and uprootedness in our time. In H. Ruitenbeek (Ed.). *Varieties of modern social theory,* New York: Dutton, 1963, pp. 55–68.

Erikson, E. *Identity: Youth and Crisis.* New York: Norton, 1968.

Faraday, A. *The dream game.* New York: Harper & Row, 1974.

Feifel, H. (Ed.). *New meanings of death.* New York: McGraw-Hill, 1977.

Feifel, H. Attitudes toward death in some normal and mentally ill populations. In H. Feifel (Ed.). *The Meaning of death.* New York: McGraw-Hill, 1959.

Feifel, H. & Branscomb, A. Who's afraid of death? *Journal of Abnormal Psychology,* 1973, 81, 282–288.

Frankl, V. *Man's search for meaning.* Boston: Beacon Press, 1962.

Freese, A. *Help for your grief.* New York: Schocken Books, 1977.

Freeman, L. *The sorrow and the fury.* Englewood Cliffs, NJ: Prentice-Hall, Inc., 1978.

Freud, S. *Reflections on war and death.* New York: Moffatt, 1918.

Freud, S. Mourning and melancholia (1919). *Collected Papers* (Vol. 4). New York: Basic Books, Inc., 1959.

Freund, J. Divorce and grief. In J. Bane, A. Kutscher and R. Neale (Eds.). *Death and ministry.* New York: Seabury, 1975.

Fulton, R. (Ed.). *Death, grief and bereavement: A bibliography, 1845-1975.* New York: Arno Press, 1977.

Fulton, R. *Death and identity.* Bowie, Maryland: Charles Press, 1976.

Fulton, R. The traditional funeral and contemporary society. In V. Pine, A. Kutscher, D. Peretz, R. Slater, R. DeBellis, R. Volk and D. Cherico (Eds.). *Acute grief and the funeral.* Springfield, Ill.: Charles C Thomas, 1976.

Fulton, R. and Fulton, J. A psychosocial aspect of terminal care: Anticipatory grief. *Omega,* 1971, 2, 91–99.

Fulton, R. and Gottesman, D. Anticipatory grief: A psychosocial concept reconsidered. *British Journal of Psychiatry,* 1980, 137, 45–54.

Gauthier, Y. and Marshall, W. Grief: A cognitive behavioral analysis. *Cognitive therapy and research,* 1:39–44, 1977.

Gibran, K. *The prophet.* New York: Alfred A. Knopf, 1966.

Glick, I., Weiss, R. and Parkes, C. *The first year of bereavement.* New York: Wiley, 1974.

Goleman, D. Special abilities of the sexes: Do they begin in the brain? *Psychology Today.* November, 1978, 48–59.

Gordon, T. *Parent effectiveness training.* New York: Peter H. Wyden, Inc., 1970.

Gorer, G. *Death, grief and mourning.* New York: Doubleday, 1965.

Graham, J. *In the company of others.* New York: Harcourt, Brace, Jovanovich, 1982.

Grollman, E. (Ed.). *Concerning death: A guide for living.* Boston: Beacon, 1974.

Hafer, W. *Coping with bereavement from death or divorce.* Englewood Cliffs, NJ: Prentice-Hall, 1981.

Hardt, D. *Death: The final frontier.* Englewood Cliffs, NJ: Prentice-Hall, 1979.

Harman, W. Science and the clarification of values: Implications of recent findings in psychological and psychic research. *Journal of Humanistic Psychology.* 1981, 21, 5–12.

Havighurst, R. *Developmental tasks and education.* New York: Longmans, Green & Co., 1952.

Headington, B. Understanding a core experience: Loss. *Personnel and Guidance Journal* 1981, 59:338–341.

Hendin, D. *Death as a fact of life.* New York: Norton, 1973.

Hill, C., Rubin, Z. and Peplau, L. Breakups before marriage: The end of 103 affairs. *Journal of Social Issues,* 1976, 32, 147–168.

Hinton, J. *Dying.* Baltimore: Penguin Books, 1967.

Hoffer, E. *The ordeal of change.* New York: Harper and Row, 1952.

Holmes, T. and Rahe, R. The social readjustment rating scale. *Journal of Psychosomatic Research,* 1967, 11, 219–225.

Horowitz, M., et al. Pathological grief and the activation of latent self-images. *American Journal of Psychiatry,* 1980, 137, 1157–1162.

Horowitz, M. Psychological processes induced by illness, injury and loss. In Millon, T., Green, C., and Meagher, R. (Eds.). *Handbook of clinical health psychology,* New York: Plenum, 1982.

Hutschnecker, A. *The will to live.* New York: Simon and Schuster, 1983.

Irion, P. *The funeral: Vestige or value.* Nashville: Abingdon, 1966.

Jackson, E. *Understanding grief.* Nashville: Abingdon, 1957.

Jackson, E. *You and your grief.* Great Neck: Channel Press, 1961.

Jackson, E. Guilt and grief, *Journal of Pastoral Counseling,* 1963, 1.

Jackson, E. *The role of faith in the process of healing.* Minneapolis, MN: Winston, Press, 1981.

Jackson, E. *The many faces of grief.* Nashville, Abingdon, 1977.

Jackson, E. You and your grief. In D. Berg and G. Daugherty (Eds.). *The individual, society and death.* Baltimore, MD: Waverley Press, 1972.

Jacobson, E. *Progressive relaxation.* Chicago: University of Chicago Press, 1938.

Jampolsky, G. *Good-Bye to guilt.* New York: Bantam, 1985.

Jampolsky, G. *Love is letting go of fear.* New York: Bantam Books, 1981.

Kalish, R. *Death, grief and caring relationships.* Belmont, CA: Wadsworth, 1985.

Kastenbaum, R. and Kastenbaum, B. Hope, survival and the caring environment. In E. Palmore and F. Jeffers (Eds.). *Prediction of Life Span.* Lexington, MA: D.C. Heath, 1971.

Kastenbaum, R. *Death, society and human experience.* St. Louis: Mosby, 1977.

Kastenbaum, R. and Aisenberg, R. *The psychology of death.* New York: Springer, 1972.

Kavanaugh, R. *Facing death.* Baltimore: Penguin, 1974.

Keleman, S. *Living your dying.* New York: Random House, 1974.

Knight, J. Spiritual psychotherapy and self-regulation. In E. Goldwag (Ed.). *Inner balance: The power of holistic healing.* Englewood Cliffs, NJ: Prentice-Hall, 1979.

Koestenbaum, P. *Is there an answer to death?* Englewood Cliffs, NJ: Prentice-Hall, 1976.

Kubler-Ross, E. (Ed.). *Death: the final stage of growth.* Englewood Cliffs, NJ: Prentice-Hall, 1975.

Kubler-Ross, E. *On death and dying.* New York: Macmillan, 1969.

Kubler-Ross, E. *Questions and answers on death and dying.* New York: Macmillan, 1974.

Kubler-Ross, E. What is it like to be dying? *American Journal of Nursing,* 1971, 71, 54–62.

LaGrand, L. Differences in male-female reactions to death. *American Funeral Director,* 1983, 106, 75–82.

LaGrand, L. Loss reactions of college students: A descriptive analysis. *Death Education,* 1981, 5, 235–247.

LaGrand, L. Communicating about death: A model for reducing anxiety. *Selected proceedings from the First National Conference of the Forum for Death Education and Counseling.* Lexington, MA: Ginn and Co., 1979.

LaGrand, L. A comparison of loss reactions of male-female college and university students. In R. Pacholski and C. Corr (Eds.). *New Directions in Death Education and Counseling.* Arlington, VA: Forum for Death Education and Counseling, 1981.

Layden, M. *Escaping the hostility trap.* Englewood Cliffs, NJ: Prentice-Hall, 1977.

Lebow, G. Facilitating adaptation in anticipatory mourning. *Social Casework,* 1976, 57(7), 458–465.

Lehman, D. and Wortman, C. the impact of sudden loss. In the *Institute for Social Research Newsletter,* The University of Michigan, Winter, 1984–85.

Leviton, D. Death education. In H. Feifel (Ed.). *New meanings of death.* New York: McGraw-Hill, 1977.

Lewis, C.S. *A grief observed*. New York: Bantam, 1976.

Lifton, R. and Olson, E. *Living and dying*. New York: Praeger, 1974.

Lifton, R. *Death in life: Survivors of Hiroshima*. New York: Random House, 1967.

Lindemann, E. Symptomatology and management of acute grief. *American Journal of Psychiatry*, 1944, 101, 141–148.

Lindstrom, B. Exploring paranormal experiences of the bereaved. In C. Corr, J. Stillion and M. Ribar (Eds.). *Creativity in Death Education and Counseling*. Lakewood, Ohio: Forum for Death Education and Counseling, 1983.

Lynch, J. *The broken heart*. New York: Basic Books, 1977.

Madow, L. *Anger*. New York: Charles Scribner & Sons, 1972.

Maltz, M. *Psychocybernetics*. New York: Pocket Books, 1969.

Mandelbaum, D. Social uses of funeral rites. In H. Feifel (Ed.). *The meaning of-death*. New York: McGraw-Hill, 1959.

Markusen, E. and Fulton, R. Childhood bereavement and behavior disorder: A critical review. *Omega*, 1971, 2, 107–117.

May, R. *Existence*. New York: Basic Books, 1958.

Mecca, A. *Alcoholism in America*. Belvedere, CA: CHRF Foundation, 1980.

Miller, J. *Toward a new psychology of women*. Boston: Beacon Press, 1976.

Minkoff, K., Bergman, E., Beck, A. and Beck, R. Hopelessness, depression and attempted suicide. *American Journal of psychiatry*, 1973, 130(4), 455–459.

Mitchell, M. *The child's attitude toward death*. New York: Schocken, 1967.

Moody, R. *Life after life*. Covington, GA: Mockingbird Books, 1975.

Moro, R. *Death, grief and widowhood*. Berkeley, CA: Parallax Press, 1979.

Morrow-Lindberg, A. *Hour of Gold, Hour of Lead*. New York: Harcourt, Brace and Jovanovich, 1973.

Mount, E. Individualism and our fears of death. *Death Education*, 1983, 7, 25–31.

Myer, J., Lindenthal, J. and Pepper, M. Life events, social integration and psychiatric symptomatology. *Journal of Health and Social Behavior*, 1961, 23, 232–256.

Neale, R. *The art of dying*. New York: Harper and Row, 1973.

Nouwen, H. *Out of solitude*. Notre Dame, IN: Ave Maria Press, 1974.

O'Connor, N. *Letting go with love: The grieving process*. Tucson, AZ: LaMariposa Press, 1984.

Olin, H. and Olin, B. Bereavement, an opportunity for emotional growth. In J. Bane, R. Neale and R. Reeves (Eds.). *Death and ministry*. New York: Seabury, 1975.

Osterweis, M., Solomon, F. and Green, M. (Eds.). *Bereavement: reactions, consequences, and care*. Washington, D.C.: National Academy Press, 1984.

Parkes, C. Determinants of outcome following bereavement. *Omega*, 1975, 6, 303–323.

Parkes, C. *Bereavement: Studies of grief in adult life*. New York: International Universities Press, 1972.

Parkes, C., Benjamin, B. and Fitzgerald, R. Broken heart: A statistical study of increased mortality among widowers. *British Medical Journal*, 1969, 1, 740–743.

Parkes, C. and Weiss, R. *Recovery from bereavement*. New York: Basic Books, 1983.

Parry, H., Cisin, J., Balter, M., Mellinger, G. and Manheimer, D. *Increased Alcohol*

Intake as a Coping Mechanism for Psychic Distress. Paper presented at the International Symposia on Alcohol and Drug Research, Toronto, 1973.

Paul, N. Use of empathy in the resolution of grief. *Perspectives in Biology and Medicine*, 1967, 10, 409–418.

Pattison, E. *The experience of dying.* Englewood Cliffs, NJ: Prentice-Hall, 1977.

Peck, M. *The road less traveled.* New York: Simon and Schuster, 1978.

Pincus, L. *Death and the family.* New York: Vintage Books, 1974.

Pine, V. Grief, bereavement and mourning. In V. Pine, A. Kutscher, D. Peretz, R. Slater, R. DeBellis, R. Volk and D. Cherico (Eds.). *Acute grief and the funeral.* Springfield, IL: Charles C Thomas, 1976.

Pollock, G. Process and affect: Mourning and grief. *International Journal of Psychoanalysis,* 59:255–276, 1978.

Powell, J. *Unconditional love.* Allen, Texas: Argus, 1978.

Powell, J. *Why am I afraid to tell you who I am?* Niles, IL: Argus, 1969.

Preston, J. Toward an anthropology of death. *Intellect,* 1977, April, 343–344.

Raether, H. and Slater, R. *The funeral: Facing death as an experience of life.* Milwaukee: National Funeral Directors Association, 1974.

Rahner, K. *On the theology of death.* New York: Herder, 1961.

Ramsey, P. *The patient as a person: Explorations in medical ethics.* New Haven: Yale University Press, 1970.

Rando, T. *Your grief is not my grief: Assessment of clinical factors determining the grief response.* Keynote address presented at the Seventh Annual Conference of the Forum for Death Education and Counseling, Philadelphia, Pennsylvania, April, 1985.

Rando, T. *Grief, dying and death.* Champaign, IL: Research Press, 1984.

Raphael, B. *The anatomy of bereavement.* New York: Basic Books, 1983.

Raphael, B. Preventive intervention with the recently bereaved. *Archives of general psychiatry,* 34:1450–1454, 1977.

Rees, W. The hallucinations of widowhood. *British Medical Journal,* 1971, 4, 37–41.

Rees, W. The bereaved and their hallucinations. In B. Schoenberg, I. Gerber, A. Wiener, A. Kutscher, D. Peretz, and A. Carr *Bereavement: Its psychosocial aspects.* New York: Columbia University Press, 1975.

Rees, W. and Lutkins, S. The mortality of bereavement. *British Medical Journal,* 1967, 4, 13–16.

Reynold, F. and Waugh, E. *Religious encounters with death: Insights from the history and anthropology of religions.* University Park: Pennsylvania State University Press, 1977.

Rogers, J. and Vachon, M. Nurses can help the bereaved. *The Canadian Nurse,* 1975, 71, 1–4.

Rosenblatt, P., Jackson, D. and Walsh, R. Coping with anger and aggression in mourning. *Omega,* 1972, 3, 271–284.

Rubenstein, C., Shaver, P. and Peplau, L. Loneliness, *Human Nature,* February, 1979, 58–65.

Ruitenbeek, H. *The interpretation of death.* New York: Aronson, 1973.

Sanders, C. Personal communication, January, 1985.

Schiff, H. *The bereaved parent.* New York: Crown, 1974.

Schoenberg, B., et al., (Eds.). *Anticipatory grief.* New York: Columbia University Press, 1974.

Schoenberg, B., et al., (Eds.). *Loss and grief: Psychological management in medical practice.* New York: Columbia University Press, 1970.

Schultz, R. *The psychology of death, dying and bereavement.* Reading, MA: Addison Wesley, 1978.

Selye, H. *Stress without distress.* New York: J.B. Lippincott, 1974.

Selye, H. Self-Regulation: The response to stress. In E. Goldwag (Ed.). *Inner balance: The power of holistic healing.* Englewood Cliffs, NJ: Prentice-Hall, 1979.

Selye, H. Stress: The basis of illness. In E. Goldwag (Ed.). *Inner balance: The power of holistic healing.* Englewood Cliffs, NJ: Prentice-Hall, 1979.

Sharapin, H. It's happening right there in your living room. Speech presented at the *Third Annual Conference of the Forum for Death Education and Counseling,* Kansas City, Missouri, November 1, 1980.

Shneidman, E. *Deaths of man.* Baltimore: Penguin, 1973.

Shneidman, E. *Voices of death.* New York: Bantam, 1982.

Siegel, B. and Siegel, B. Holistic medicine. *Connecticut Medicine,* 1981, 45, 441–442.

Siegelman, E. *Personal risk.* New York: Harper and Row, 1983.

Silverman, P. *Helping each other in widowhood.* New York: Health Sciences Publishing Corp., 1974.

Simonton, O., Simonton, S. & Creighton, J. *Getting well again.* New York: Bantam Books, Inc., 1980.

Simos, B. *A time to grieve: Loss as a universal human experience.* New York: Family Service Association of America, 1979.

Simos, B. Grief therapy to facilitate healthy restitution. *Social Casework,* 1977, 58(6), 337–344.

Simpson, M. Death education—Where is thy sting. *Death Education,* 1979, 3, 165–173.

Sinnott, E. *The bridge of life: From matter to spirit.* New York: Simon and Schuster, 1966.

Stannard, D., (Ed.). *Death in America.* Philadelphia: University of Pennsylvania Press, 1975.

Steinfeld, P. and Veatch, R., (Eds.). *Death inside out.* New York: Harper, 1975.

Stephenson, J. *Death, grief, and mourning.* New York: The Free Press, 1985.

Sudnow, D. *Passing on: The social organization of dying.* Englewood Cliffs: Prentice-Hall, 1967.

Switzer, D. *The dynamics of grief.* Nashville: Abingdon, 1970.

Tanner, I. *The gift of grief.* New York: Hawthorne Books, Inc., 1976.

Tanner, I. *Loneliness: The fear of love.* New York: Harper & Row, 1973.

Tillich, P. *The courage to be.* New Haven: Yale University Press, 1952.

Toynbee, A., et al., (Eds.). *Man's concern for death.* New York: McGraw-Hill, 1969.

Volkhart, E. and Michael, S. Bereavement and mental health. In S. Wilcox and M. Sutton (Eds.). *Understanding death and dying.* Palo Alto, CA: Mayfield Publishing, 1981.

Vollman, R., Ganzert, A., Picher, L., and Williams, W. The reactions of family systems to sudden and unexpected death. *Omega,* 1971, 2, 101–106.

Wass, H. *Dying facing the facts.* New York: McGraw-Hill Book Co., 1979.

Wass, H. and Corr, C. *Helping children cope with death.* Washington: Hemisphere Publishing Corporation, 1984.

Weeks, C. *Hope and help for your nerves.* New York: Bantam, 1978.

Weintraub, P. The brain: His and hers. *Discover,* April 1981, 15–20.

Weisman, A. *On dying and denying.* New York: Behavioral Publications, 1972.

Weisman, A. and Hackett, T. Predilection to death. *Psychosomatic Medicine,* 1961, 23, 232–256.

Weisman, A. The psychiatrist and the inexorable. In H. Feifel (Ed.). *New meanings of death.* New York: McGraw-Hill, 1977.

Weir, R. (Ed.). *Ethical issues on death and dying.* New York: Columbia University Press, 1977.

Wentzel, K. *Hospice means hope.* Boston: Charles River Books, 1981.

Wertenbaker, L. *Death of a man.* New York: Random House, 1957.

Westberg, G. *Good grief.* Philadelphia: Fortress Press, 1962.

Wilcox, S. and Sutton, M. *Understanding death and dying: An interdisciplinary approach.* Palo Alto, CA: Mayfield Pub. Co., 1981.

Williams, R. *You are extraordinary.* New York: Pyramid Books, 1971.

Williams, W., Polak, P., and Voldman, R. Crisis intervention in acute grief. *Omega,* 1972, 3, 67–70.

Worden, J. and Proctor, W. *Personal death awareness.* Englewood Cliffs, NJ: Prentice-Hall, Inc., 1976.

Young, V. *Working with the dying and grieving.* Davis, CA: International Dialogue Press, 1984.

Zeltzer, L. The adolescent with cancer. In J. Kellerman (Ed.). *Psychological aspects of childhood cancer.* Springfield, IL: Charles C Thomas, 1980.

NAME INDEX

209

U

Unconditional love, 63, 99, 133, 153
Unfinished business, 107, 157

V

Vomiting, 36, 43, 143

W

Widowed Persons Program, 13

Y

Young adults
   coping mechanisms of, 47–61
   and coping styles, 30–35
   and living with loss, 7–12
   losses of, 21
   and pets, 22
   and unresolved grief, ix–xii